AF479954

WILD INDIA

VINAY PILLAI

Published by

Hawk Press
4836/24, Ansari Road, Daryaganj
New Delhi – 110 002
Phones: 91-11-23278618, 91-11-43667199
E-mail: thehawkpress@gmail.com
www.thehawkpress.com

Copyright © 2020, *Editor*
ISBN: 978-93-88841-18-4
All rights reserved.

CONTENTS

1

Introduction

The wildlife in India comprises a mix of species of different types of organisms. Apart from a handful of the major farm animals such as cows, buffaloes, goats, poultry, pigs and sheep, India has an amazingly wide variety of animals native to the country. It is home to Bengal tigers, deer, pythons, wolves, foxes, bears, crocodiles, camels, wild dogs, monkeys, snakes, antelope species, varieties of bison and not to mention the mighty Asian elephant.

The region's rich and diverse wildlife is preserved in 89 national parks, 18 Bio reserves and 400+ wildlife sanctuaries across the country. India has some of the most biodiverse regions of the world and hosts three of the world's 34 biodiversity hotspots – or treasure-houses – that is the Western Ghats, the Eastern Himalayas and Indo- Burma. Since India is home to a number of rare and threatened animal species, wildlife management in the country is essential to preserve these species. According to one study, India along with 17 mega diverse countries is home to about 60-70 % of the world's biodiversity.

India, lying within the Indomalaya ecozone, is home to about 7.6% of all mammalian, 12.6% of avian, 6.2% of reptilian, and 6.0% of flowering plant species. Many ecoregions, such as the *shola* forests, also exhibit extremely high rates of endemism; overall, 33% of Indian plant species are endemic. India's forest cover ranges from the tropical rainforest of the Andaman Islands, Western Ghats, and Northeast India to the coniferous forest of the Himalaya. Between these extremes lie the sal-dominated moist deciduous forest of eastern India; teak-dominated dry deciduous forest of central and southern India; and the babul-dominated thorn forest of the central Deccan and western Gangetic plain. Important Indian trees include the medicinal neem, widely used in rural Indian herbal remedies. The pipal fig tree, shown on the seals of Mohenjo-daro, shaded the Gautama Buddha as he sought enlightenment.

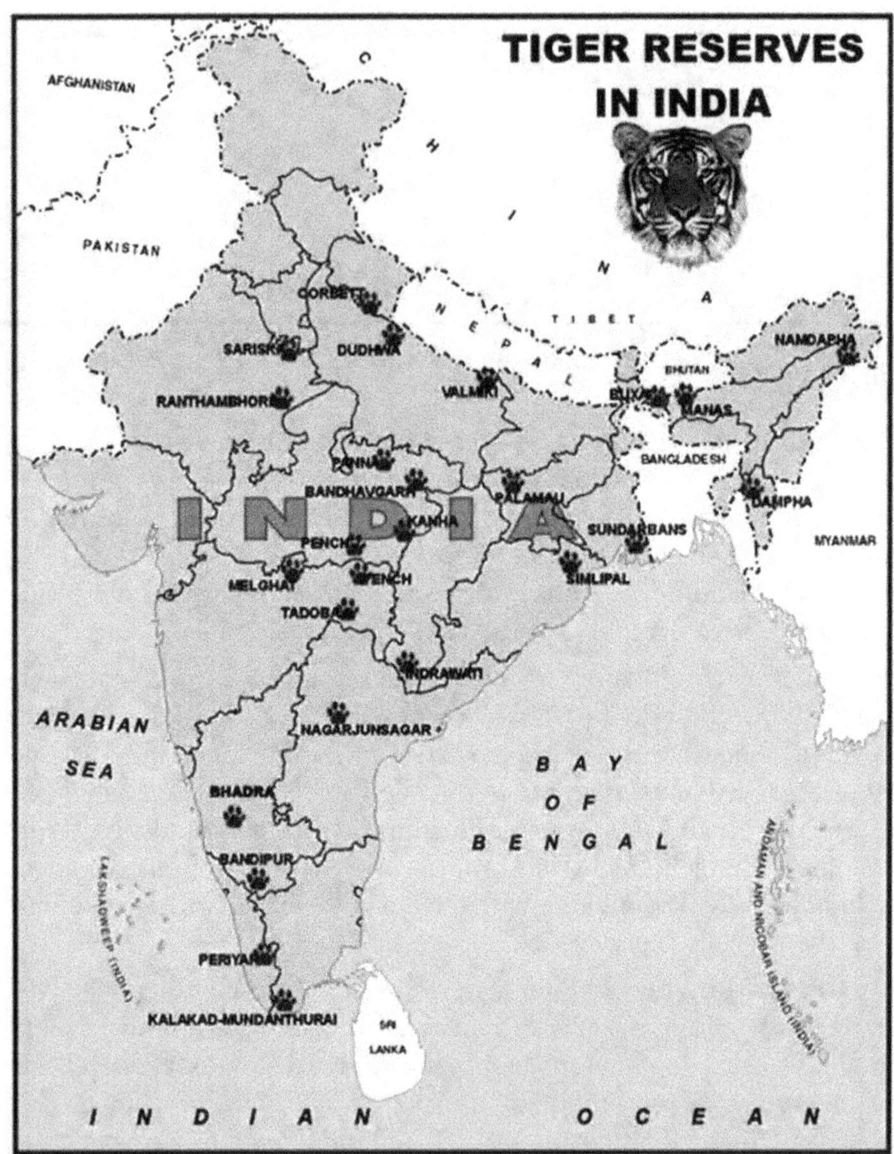

Many Indian species are descendants of taxa originating in Gondwana, to which India originally belonged. Peninsular India's subsequent movement towards, and collision with, the Laurasian landmass set off a mass exchange of species. However, volcanism and climatic change 20 million years ago caused the extinction of many endemic Indian forms. Soon thereafter, mammals entered India from Asia through two zoogeographical passes on either side of the emerging Himalaya.

As a result, among Indian species, only 12.6% of mammals and 4.5% of birds are endemic, contrasting with 45.8% of reptiles and 55.8% of amphibians. Notable endemics are the Nilgiri leaf monkey and the brown and carmine Beddome's toad of the Western Ghats. India contains 172, or 2.9%, of IUCN-designated threatened species. These include the Asian elephant, the Asiatic lion, the Bengal tiger, the Indian rhinoceros, the Mugger crocodile, and the Indian white-rumped vulture, which suffered a near-extinction from ingesting the carrion of diclofenac-treated cattle.

In recent decades, human encroachment has posed a threat to India's wildlife; in response, the system of national parks and protected areas, first established in 1935, was substantially expanded. In 1972, India enacted the Wildlife Protection Act and Project Tiger to safeguard crucial habitat; further federal protections were promulgated in the 1980s. Along with over 515 wildlife sanctuaries, India now hosts 18 biosphere reserves, 9 of which are part of the World Network of Biosphere Reserves; 26 wetlands are registered under the Ramsar Convention.

The varied and rich wildlife of India has had a profound impact on the region's popular culture. The common name for wilderness in India is Jungle, which was adopted into the English language. The word has been also made famous in *The Jungle Book* by Rudyard Kipling. India's wildlife has been the subject of numerous other tales and fables such as the *Panchatantra.*

Fauna

India is home to several well-known large mammals, including the Asian Elephant, Bengal Tiger, Asiatic Lion, Leopard, Sloth Bear and Indian Rhinoceros. Some other well-known large Indian mammals are: ungulates such as the rare Wild Asian Water buffalo, common Domestic Asian Water buffalo, Gail, Gaur, and several species of deer and antelope. Some members of the dog family, such as the Indian Wolf, Bengal Fox and Golden Jackal, and the Dhole or Wild Dogs are also widely distributed. However, the *dole,* also known as *the whistling hunter,* is the most endangered top Indian carnivore, and the Himalayan Wolf is now a critically endangered species endemic to India. It is also home to the Striped Hyena, Macaques, Langur and Mongoose species.

Conservation

The need for conservation of wildlife in India is often questioned because of the apparently incorrect priority in the face of direct poverty of the people. However, Article 48 of the Constitution of India specifies that, "The state shall endeavour to protect and improve the environment and to safeguard the forests and wildlife of the country" and Article 51-A states that "it shall be the duty of every citizen of India to protect and improve the natural environment including forests, lakes, rivers, and wildlife and to have compassion for living creatures."

Large and charismatic mammals are important for wildlife tourism in India, and several national parks and wildlife sanctuaries cater to these needs. Project Tiger, started in 1972, is a major effort to conserve the tiger and its habitats. At the turn of the 20th century, one estimate of the tiger population in India placed the figure at 40,000, yet an Indian tiger census conducted in 2008 revealed the existence of only 1,411 tigers. 2010 Tiger census revealed that there are 1700 tigers left in India.

The passing of the Forest Rights Act by the Indian government in 2008 has been the final nail in the coffin and has pushed the Indian tiger to the verge of extinction. Various pressures in the later part of the 20th century led to the progressive decline of wilderness resulting in the disturbance of viable tiger habitats.

At the International Union for the Conservation of Nature and Natural Resources (IUCN) General Assembly meeting in Delhi in 1969, serious concern was voiced about the threat to several species of wildlife and the shrinkage of wilderness in India. In 1970, a national ban on tiger hunting was imposed, and in 1972 the Wildlife Protection Act came into force.

The framework was then set up to formulate a project for tiger conservation with an ecological approach. However, there is not much optimism about this framework's ability to save the peacock, which is the national bird of India. George Schaller wrote about Tiger conservation:

"India has to decide whether it wants to keep the tiger or not. It has to decide if it is worthwhile to keep its National Symbol, its icon, representing wildlife. It has to decide if it wants to keep its natural heritage for future generations, a heritage more important than the cultural one, whether we speak of its temples, the Taj Mahal, or others, because once destroyed it cannot be replaced."

WILDLIFE MANAGEMENT

Wildlife management is the art as well as the science of changing the characteristics of, and interactions among habitats, wild animal populations and human beings so as to achieve specific human goals by means of the wildlife resources. In the context of our country, these goals may be ecological, economic or aesthetic, or their combinations. Wildlife management is not a basic science, nor is it pure technology. It draws upon several disciplines including zoology, botany, ecology and even mathematics. Despite its clear links with the natural sciences, wildlife management also employs principles of the arts. In other words, it integrates a wide range of disciplines in logical, imaginative and pragmatic ways and, therefore, can be regarded as both a science and an art, whose practice is not very different from that of medicine or law. Each is a profession requiring rigorous application of skill, knowledge and imagination.

Wildlife Conservation

India has a rich natural heritage and a long tradition of conservation. The *ashram* (hermitages) of the great sages, which were the seats of learning in ancient times, was almost always located in sylvan surroundings that symbolized the conservation ethics of the day.

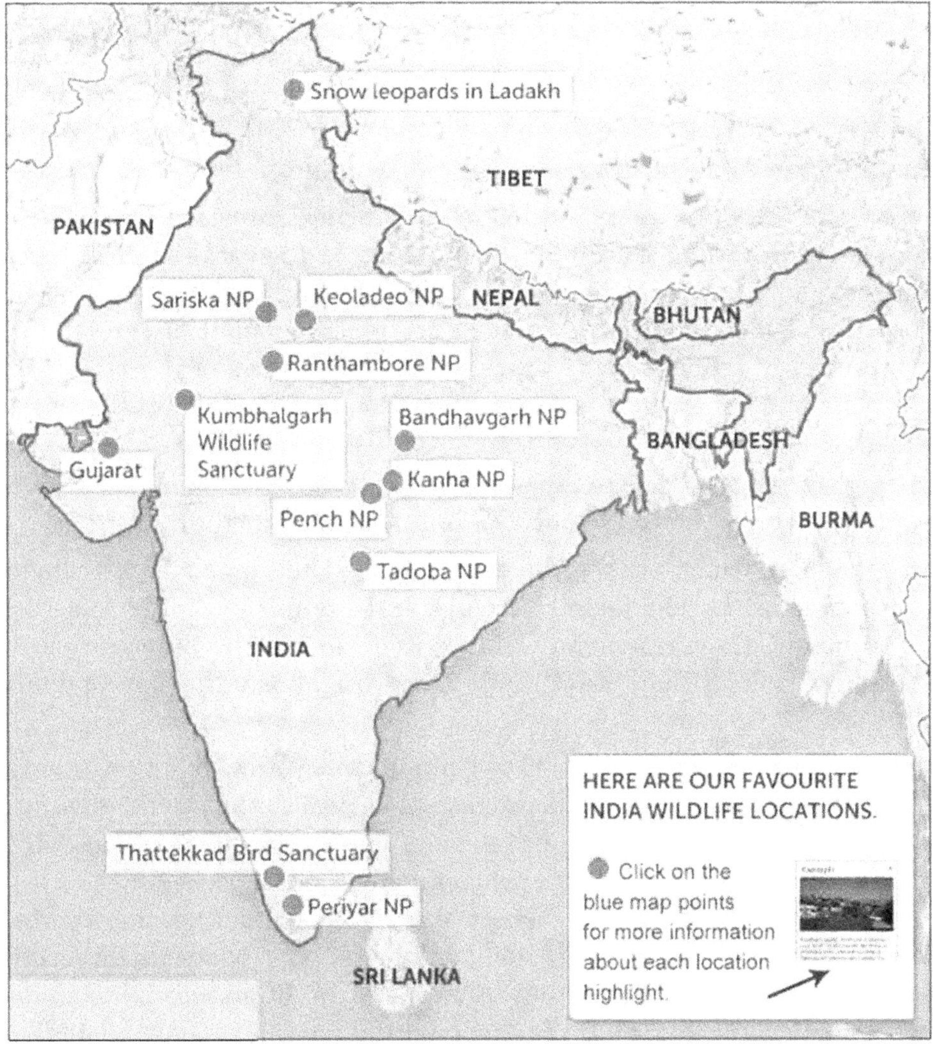

Indian mythology is replete with references to people's regard and love for wild animals. Different animals and birds were associated with different gods as their servants and vehicles. These animals and birds, therefore, were held sacred by various communities, which ensured their protection. Kautilya in his Arthashastra promulgated the first recorded game laws in the third century Be. In the year 252 Be, Emperor Ashoka passed laws for the protection of many types of animals and forests. These laws created what may well be the earliest instances of protected areas as we call them today.

Though love and respect for nature is an integral part of India's culture, the country today confronts the sad paradox of fast disappearing wildlife. A typical developing country, modern India struggles with the stiff challenge of finding solutions to development problems. But some solutions that have been worked out pose serious threats to the country's wildlife. Human population pressure, widespread industrialization, hunger for land and the crushing pressure exerted on the forests by livestock and by people's needs for firewood and small timber are the main causes of the present plight of wildlife.

The result is there for everyone to see: our prime forests and wildlife reduced to a shadow of their former self. India has already lost several species of mammals, reptiles, birds, and other life forms. As so little is known about the actual biological diversity of the country, we may not even be fully cognizant of the true extent of the loss and can only mourn the few well-known examples of the tragic extinction of wild animals and birds such as the Indian Cheetah, the Mountain Quail, or the Pink-headed Duck.

The population of the tiger which was believed to be around 40,000 by some experts only a century ago was down to only 1,827 animals by 1972!

The Asiatic lion, which adorns the country's national emblem, is today confined to a small pocket in the Gir forests of Gujarat. A number of deer species like the hangul of Kashmir, the barasingha of Madhya Pradesh, the brow-antlered deer of Manipur, and antelope like the Himalayan - all adorn the list of endangered species.

In fact, the brow-antlered deer whose number in the wild was estimated to be only 18 in 1977 has the dubious distinction of being the most endangered deer in the world. Blackbuck, the graceful antelope of the Indian plains, was found in its thousands barely 50 years ago. It is now confined to small pockets where it survives only under strict protection. The Great Indian Bustard and the White-winged Wood Duck have dwindled to precarious numbers. The beautiful Siberian Crane is a winter visitor to the Bharatpur Sanctuary in Rajasthan. Its visit to this sanctuary dwindled to just 41 birds, as reported, in the winter of 1978-79. The Gangetic gharial, the marsh mugger and the estuarine crocodile have all been hunted down to near extinction. These are only a few examples; there are many more species of wild animals and birds that are on the verge of extinction. If we are complacent towards conservation many of these beautiful creatures will be wiped out in the near future.

It was only in the early 1970s that the first actions were taken to arrest the declining trend in wildlife, and concern for nature conservation was reflected to a certain extent in the planning and development processes. Many significant initiatives in wildlife conservation have been taken since then. These include:

The enactment of the Wildlife (Protection) Act, 1972 and, subsequently, the Forest (Conservation) Act, 1980,the inclusion of wildlife conservation in the Concurrent List of the Constitution, the enlargement of the network of national parks and sanctuaries.

The launch of Project Tiger in 1973.

The Crocodile Breeding Project, 1975;

Project Elephant, early 1991;

Project Hangul, 1970;

Manipur Brow-antlered Deer Conservation Project, 1973, regulation of wildlife trade and commerce, the strengthening of education and training facilities, which culminated in the establishment of the Wildlife Institute of India; and various efforts to increase general awareness about nature conservation.

Protected Area Network

Under the Wildlife (Protection) Act, 1972 state governments are empowered to declare any area of their states as a sanctuary or a national park to protect, propagate or develop the wildlife in it or the environment of the area.

Today the network of wildlife protected areas such as national parks, sanctuaries, biosphere reserves and community reserves covers representative samples of most of the wildlife ecosystems of the country, with good geographical distribution. All these areas are endowed with remarkable ecological, floral, faunal or geomorphologic significance. At present, there are around 90 national parks and 500 sanctuaries in India.

The area under national parks and sanctuaries is around 1.561akh (.156 million) sq km. Despite this, out of the 10 identified bio-geographic zones of the country, some are still deficient in protected area coverage. An expert committee constituted by the Government of India had recommended that a minimum of 4% of the country's geographical area should be set apart as national parks or sanctuaries.

All national parks and sanctuaries, however, are not alike. Some have been created specifically to protect rare and endangered species, while some are famous for the richness and variety of their wildlife. The inestimable value of these protected areas - in safeguarding varied ecosystems and, in the process, protecting the soil from erosion, recycling wastes and preserving genetic material which is vital for sustaining agricultural crops - has been universally recognized.

Project Tiger

The famous naturalist E P Gee once opined that there were around 40,000 tigers in India in the beginning of the 20th century. Though many wildlife conservationists and naturalists disagree with him on this figure no one can deny that the population of the tiger had dwindled alarmingly by late 1960s. This perilous decline was attributed to a combination of factors including poaching, degradation of tiger habitats and loss of its prey base.

Against this backdrop, sincere efforts as well as emotional pleas were made by many people at the national and international levels. In its 10th General Assembly held at New Delhi in December 1969, the International Union for Conservation of Nature and Natural Resources (IUCN) called for a moratorium on the hunting of the Indian tiger and several other wildlife species. Taking cognizance of these recommendations, the Indian Board for Wildlife (IBWL) instructed all the states to ban the hunting of tigers for at least five years. In July 1970, tiger hunting was permanently banned throughout India.

In April 1972 a Task Force was constituted by the IBWL to study the problems relating to tiger conservation in the country and to prepare a plan to save the super predator from extinction.

An all-India tiger census was conducted in May, 1972 that estimated the total tiger population of the country at a mere 1,827. There was now no room for any doubt that the chances of the Indian tiger's survival were bleak - unless some urgent and positive conservation initiatives were taken. The same year, the Indian Wildlife (Protection) Act, 1972 was promulgated, which provided additional, legal impetus to the protection of wildlife and habitats, particularly of endangered species, in special conservation areas.

The Task Force comprising stalwarts of conservation made concerted efforts and, by November 1972, formulated a plan that was suitable for Indian conditions. This novel venture was named "Project Tiger". It was formally launched in 1973 when 9 tiger reserves were set up in the country. Today there are 28 tiger reserves which cover all the important tiger habitats of the country.

FACTOR IN DECLINING OF WILDLIFE IN THE HIMALAYA

Habitat Destruction

Rapid rate of urbanization in many parts of the Himalaya with explosion of human population has lead to deforestation and disappearances of many rare and useful species of wildlife. The tropical rain forests in the world are disappearing at an alarming rate of 50 acres per minute.

Many wild animals and bird have died and the remaining resorted to straying or incursion into the abutting geographic region in the endeavour to struggle and seek safer home ground.

The present rash and thoughtless destruction of natural resources clearly indicates our existence on earth is gravely threatened if we do not take coarse of the forest. Wisely maintained forest not only provides economic benefits to mankind but also insurances the nature against such eco-disasters as floods, droughts and landslides. Glaring examples of havoc wreaked by deforestation are known. The USA, once blessed with over 800 million acres, when colonized lost forests ruthlessly in building cities making Oklahoma, a man made desert. Fertile grass of country provided graying for thousands of cattle; farmers ploughed up to plant crops destroying thick carpet of grass roots that hold water. This followed a long period of drought with high wind that blew soils away in great sand storms. In Britain, well-wooded within the living memory the forest have dwindled to the vanishing point by relishing the precious forest wealth is "penny-wise, proud-foolish policy".

Fast increasing desertification is also a contributing factor to habitat deterioration. Loss of habitat is the main process by which species become extinct. The tropical rainforest covers only 7% of the Earth's surface area, and yet harbours more than 50% of all existing wildlife species in the world.

Agro-practices adopted by man in these isotopes are of rudimentary and in sufficient nature, wit wasteful use of land. Some aspects of improper management and commercial over-exploitation in many parts of Himalaya in Nepal are grave and proving disastrous. The Himalayan degradation and loss of habitat of wildlife can be reality be stopped by suitable and appropriate means of ecological management and conservation of the forest cover.

Indiscriminate Poaching

Hunting by man has been the second major causes contributing to the disappearance of many wildlife species. The Ranas, then ruling Nepal and their Royal guests from British India and the Shah Ruler were hunting in different sectors of Nepal and killing precious animals as a pastime. During political up heals, the protection slackened resulting in extensive poaching. Uncontrolled felling of trees, over grazing of grassland, poaching of wildlife and burning of forests-all of which have continued unabated in many parts of the Himalaya. However, some satisfaction steps have been taken at Regional/District levels of check poaching of wildlife resources.

Under the respectable camouflage of crop protection, wild animal and birds were shot everywhere even in national parks and reserves and their surrounding VDCs in Buffer zone areas. This uncontrolled massacre through unceasing poaching vanquished many magnificent and rare species and the decline of the remaining forms is still continuing.

Food, feather, fur and recreation have always enticed people raid a large number of animals and birds through indiscriminate poaching and shooting. In spite of legal protection to wildlife, poacher and unauthorized hunters seriously impairs our threatened wildlife in the Himalayan regions due to lack of attention of forest and wildlife authorities, who must take strong and penalizing steps against the abrogates of game laws. The successful protection of wildlife in the hills and high altitude areas are obviously difficult affairs. The need special laws and provision for the implementation and protection of wildlife. Some of the loopholes in the present wildlife (protection) act need amendments and inclusion are:

Hunting in group (gang) provides best means of posting a look-out to watch for wildlife authorities in hills by poachers can help easy escape at the approach of any threat.

Nominal cash fines as penalties by wildlife department can be easily paid by poachers, payment of much fine will suitably constitutes a license to the offenders by meager fines to the department.

No provision of punishing offenders by the wildlife department unless caught red handed. The standard excuse for armed poachers is self-defence against danger of wild animal.

Armed presence of civilians in forest is never questioned by wildlife staff.

Poachers had taken the precaution of skinning animals in the forest and burying of skin if no commercial value says anything at home. Thus house raids by wildlife department are circumvented.

Public opinion usually favours poachers as most hill people lack sufficient awareness of the values of wildlife preservation. The issues of eco-conservation of forest, wildlife, and other natural resources are considered as a frivolous pastime. Bhatia traders inhabiting high Himalayas reaches mainly encourage and finance commercial poaching in such inaccessible biotopes and over killed victimized wildlife eventually succumbs to extinction.

Indiscriminate Use of Pesticides

Serious human and animal health hazard have appeared with the emergence of new era of insecticide eradication campaign. Wildlife, in particular some rare birds and mammals could not escape from the hazardous effects of such insecticides.

Sprays and dusts of insecticides in open fields expose wildlife to the risk of feeding on crops treated with them bringing numerous health problems that go unnoticed causing heavy mortality in nature. Insecticides not only contaminate the environment and bring pollution but also interfere body metabolism and accumulate a poisoning activity (bio-concentration) in the body system.

DDT'! Stream, lakes, sea'! plankton '! fish (adipose tissue) '! birds '!inhibits shells gland '! thin shell '! fail to hatch '! bird population victimized.

Himalayan species of predatory bird (eagles/vultures). Long term effect of pesticides on environmental sue has been band in developed nation (USA, Canada and Scandinavian Countries).

Predation of Wildlife in Natural Environment

The impact of predators on prey varies from region to region. Of the candid predators, the red fox and Himalayan wolf are quite commons at extreme altitude and prey heavily on a variety of threatened wildlife.

The chief Himalayan predator which considerably impact the high altitude herbivore population is: Asiatic black bear, brown bear, snow leopard, wolf and red fox. Snow leopard and wolves kill bharal where as red fox and jackal is potential predator of the young.

High altitude predatory birds may kill the newborn of many threatened species of mammals and birds. Lammergeyers are known to have carried off a young goral. Likewise Giant golden eagle and lammergeyers considerably decimate the population of marmots, weasels, pheasants and other rare birds.

WILDLIFE SANCTUARIES OF INDIA

India has 515 animal sanctuaries, referred to as *Wildlife sanctuaries* (IUCN Category IV Protected Area). Among these, the 41 Tiger Reserves are governed by Project Tiger, and are of special significance in the conservation of the tiger. Some wildlife sanctuaries are specifically named *Bird Sanctuary*, e.g. Keoladeo National Park before attaining National Park status. Many National Parks were initially wildlife sanctuaries.

Wildlife sanctuaries are of national importance to conservation, usually due to some flagship faunal species, are named *National Wildlife Sanctuary*, like the tri-state National Chambal (Gharial) Wildlife Sanctuary for conserving the gharial.

Many of them being referred as a particular animal such as Jawai leopard sanctuary in Rajasthan.Many National Parks were initially wildlife sanctuaries.The conservative measures taken by the Indian Government for the conservation of Tigers was awarded by a 30% rise in the number of tigers in 2015.

List of Wildlife Sanctuaries

Wildlife Sanctuaries have been established in:

Andaman and Nicobar Islands

1. Arial Island WLS
2. Bamboo Island WLS
3. Barren Island WLS
4. Battimalv Island WLS
5. Belle Island WLS
6. Benett Island WLS
7. Bingham Island WLS
8. Blister Island WLS
9. Bluff Island WLS
10. Bondoville Island WLS
11. Brush Island WLS
12. Buchanan Island WLS
13. Chanel Island WLS
14. Cinque Islands WLS
15. Clyde Island WLS
16. Cone Island WLS
17. Curlew (B.P.) Island WLS
18. Curlew Island WLS
19. Cuthbert Bay WLS
20. Defence Island WLS
21. Dot Island WLS
22. Dottrell Island WLS
23. Duncan Island WLS
24. East Island WLS
25. East of Inglis Island WLS
26. Egg Island WLS

27. Elat Island WLS
28. Entrance Island WLS
29. Gander Island WLS
30. Girjan Island WLS
31. Galathea Bay WLS
32. Goose Island WLS
33. Hump Island WLS
34. Interview Island WLS
35. James Island WLS
36. Jungle Island WLS
37. Kwangtung Island WLS
38. Kyd Island WLS
39. Landfall Island WLS
40. Latouche Island WLS
41. Lohabarrack (Saltwater Crocodile) WLS
42. Mangrove Island WLS
43. Mask Island WLS
44. Mayo Island WLS
45. Megapode Island WLS
46. Montogemery Island WLS
47. Narcondam Island WLS
48. North Brother Island WLS
49. North Island WLS
50. North Reef Island WLS
51. Oliver Island WLS
52. Orchid Island WLS
53. Ox Island WLS
54. Oyster Island-I WLS
55. Oyster Island-II WLS
56. Paget Island WLS
57. Parkinson Island WLS
58. Passage Island WLS
59. Patric Island WLS
60. Peacock Island WLS
61. Pitman Island WLS

62. Point Island WLS
63. Potanma Islands WLS
64. Ranger Island WLS
65. Reef Island WLS
66. Roper Island WLS
67. Ross Island WLS
68. Rowe Island WLS
69. Sandy Island WLS
70. Sea Serpent Island WLS
71. Shark Island WLS
72. Shearme Island WLS
73. Sir Hugh Rose Island WLS
74. Sisters Island WLS
75. Snake Island-I WLS
76. Snake Island-II WLS
77. South Brother Island WLS
78. South Reef Island WLS
79. South Sentinel Island WLS
80. Spike Island-I WLS
81. Spike Island-II WLS
82. Stoat Island WLS
83. Surat Island WLS
84. Swamp Island WLS
85. Table (Delgarno) Island WLS
86. Table (Excelsior) Island WLS
87. Talabaicha Island WLS
88. Temple Island WLS
89. Tillongchang Island WLS
90. Tree Island WLS
91. Trilby Island WLS
92. Tuft Island WLS
93. Turtle Islands WLS
94. West Island WLS
95. Wharf Island WLS
96. White Cliff Island WLS

Andhra Pradesh

1. Coringa Wildlife Sanctuary
2. Gundla Brahmeswaram WLS
3. Kambalakonda WLS
4. Koundinya WLS
5. Kolleru WLS
6. Krishna
7. Nagarjuna Sagar-Srisailam WLS
8. Nelapattu Bird Sanctuary
9. Pulicat Lake Bird Sanctuary
10. Rollapadu WLS
11. Sri Lankamalleswara WLS
12. Sri Penusila Narasimha WLS
13. Sri Venkateswara WLS
14. Atapaka Bird WLS

Arunachal Pradesh

1. D'Ering Memorial (Lali) WLS
2. Dibang Wildlife Sanctuary
3. Eaglenest Wildlife Sanctuary
4. Itanagar WLS
5. Kamlang WLS
6. Kane WLS
7. Mehao WLS
8. Pakke Tiger Reserve
9. Sessa Orchid Sanctuary
10. Tale Valley WLS
11. Yordi-Rabe Supse WLS

Assam

1. Amchang WLS
2. Barail WLS
3. Barnadi Wildlife Sanctuary
4. Bherjan-Borajan-Padumoni WLS
5. Burachapori WLS
6. Chakrashila WLS

7. Deepor Beel WLS
8. Dihing Patkai WLS
9. East Karbi Anglong WLS
10. Garampani WLS
11. Hollongapar Gibbon WLS
12. Lawkhowa WLS
13. Marat Longri WLS
14. Nambor WLS
15. Nambor Doigrung WLS
16. Pobitora Wildlife Sanctuary
17. Pani-Dihing Bird WLS
18. Sonai Rupai WLS

Bihar

1. Barela Jheel Salim Ali Bird WLS
2. Bhimbandh WLS
3. Gautam Budha WLS
4. Kanwarjheel WLS
5. Kaimur WLS
6. Kusheshwar Asthan Bird WLS
7. Nagi Dam WLS
8. Nakti Dam WLS
9. Pant (Rajgir) WLS
10. Udaypur Wildlife Sanctuary
11. Valmiki National Park
12. Vikramshila Gangetic Dolphin WLS
13. Rajauli WLS (NEW)

Chandigarh

1. City Birds WLS
2. Sukhna Lake WLS

Chhattisgarh

1. Achanakmar WLS
2. Badalkhol WLS
3. Barnawapara WLS
4. Bhairamgarh WLS

   5. Bhoramdev WLS
   6. Sarangarh-Gomardha WLS
   7. Pamed Wild Buffalo WLS
   8. Semarsot WLS
   9. Sitanadi WLS
  10. Tamor Pingla WLS
  11. Udanti Wild Buffalo WLS

Dadra Nagar Haveli

1. Dadra and Nagar Haveli WLS

Daman and diu.

1. Fudam WLS

Delhi

1. Asola Bhati (Indira Priyadarshini) WLS

Goa

1. Bondla WLS
2. Chorao Island (Dr.Salim Ali) WLS (Bird)
3. Cotigaon WLS
4. Madei WLS
5. Bhagwan Mahavir (Mollem) WLS
6. Netravali Wildlife Sanctuary

Haryana

1. Abubshehar WLS
2. Bhindawas WLS
3. Bir Shikargarh WLS
4. Chhilchila WLS
5. Kalesar National Park
6. Khaparwas WLS
7. Morni Hills (Khol-Hi-Raitan) WLS
8. Nahar WLS
9. Sultanpur WLS (Bird)

Gujarat

1. Balaram Amji WLS

2. Barda WLS
3. Gaga Great Indian Bustard WLS
4. Gir Wildlife Sanctuary
5. Girnar WLS
6. Hingolgadh Nature Reserve WLS
7. Jambugodha WLS
8. Jessore WLS
9. Lala Great Indian Bustard WLS
10. Kachchh Desert WLS
11. Khijadiya WLS
12. Marine (Gulf of Kachchh) WLS
13. Mitiyala WLS
14. Nal Sarovar Bird WLS
15. Narayan Sarovar (Chinkara) WLS
16. Paniya WLS
17. Porbandar Lake WLS
18. Purna WLS
19. Rampara Vidi WLS
20. Ratanmahal Sloth Bear Sactuary
21. Shoolpaneswar (Dhumkhal) WLS
22. Thol Lake WLS
23. Wild Ass Wildlife Sanctuary

Himachal Pradesh

1. Bandli WLS
2. Chail WLS
3. Chandratal WLS
4. Churdhar WLS
5. Daranghati WLS
6. Dhauladhar WLS
7. Gamgul Siyabehi WLS
8. Kais WLS
9. Kalatop-Khajjiar WLS
10. Kanawar WLS
11. Khokhan WLS

12. Kibber WLS
13. Kugti WLS
14. Lippa Asrang WLS
15. Majathal WLS
16. Manali WLS
17. Nargu WLS
18. Pong Dam Lake WLS
19. Renuka WLS
20. Rupi Bhaba WLS
21. Sainj WLS
22. Sangla Valley (Rakchham Chitkul) WLS
23. Sech Tuan Nala WLS
24. Shikari Devi WLS
25. Shimla Water Catchment WLS
26. Talra WLS
27. Tirthan WLS
28. Tundah WLS

Jammu and Kashmir

1. Baltal-Thajwas WLS
2. Changthang Cold Desert WLS
3. Gulbarga WLS
4. Hirapora WLS
5. Hokersar WLS
6. Jasrota WLS
7. Karakoram (Nubra Shyok) WLS
8. Lachipora WLS
9. Limber WLS
10. Nandni WLS
11. Overa Aru WLS
12. Rajparian (Daksum) WLS
13. Ramnagar Rakha WLS
14. Surinsar Mansar WLS
15. Trikuta WLS

Jharkhand

1. Dalma WLS
2. Gautam Buddha WLS
3. Hazaribagh WLS
4. Koderma WLS
5. Lawalong WLS
6. Mahauadanr WLS
7. Palamau Tiger Reserve
8. Palkot WLS
9. Parasnath WLS
10. Topchanchi WLS
11. Udhwa Lake WLS

Karnataka

1. Adichunchunagiri WLS
2. Arabithittu WLS
3. Attiveri WLS
4. Bhadra WLS
5. Bhimgad WLS
6. Biligiri Rangaswamy Temple (B.R.T.) WLS
7. Brahmagiri WLS
8. Cauvery WLS
9. Chincholi WLS
10. Dandeli WLS
11. Daroji Bear WLS
12. Ghataprabha Bird WLS
13. Gudavi WLS
14. Gudekote Sloth Bear WLS
15. Malai Mahadeshwara WLS
16. Melkote Temple WLS
17. Mookambika WLS
18. Nugu WLS
19. Pushpagiri WLS
20. Ranebennur Black Buck WLS
21. Ranganathittu Bird WLS

22. Ramadevara Betta Vulture WLS
23. Rangayyanadurga Four-horned antelope
24. Sharavathi Valley WLS
25. Shettihalli WLS
26. Someshwara WLS
27. Talakaveri WLS
28. Jogimatti WLS
29. Thimlapura WLS
30. Yadahalli Chinkara WLS

Kerala

1. Aralam WLS
2. Chimmony WLS
3. Chinnar WLS
4. Chulannur Peafowl WLS
5. Idukki WLS
6. Kottiyoor WLS
7. Kurinjimala WLS
8. Malabar WLS
9. Mangalavanam Bird WLS
10. Neyyar WLS
11. Parambikulam WLS
12. Peechi-Vazhani WLS
13. Peppara WLS
14. Periyar WLS
15. Shendurney WLS
16. Thattekad Bird WLS
17. Wayanad WLS
18. Pathiramanal Bird WLS

Lakshadweep

1. Pitti WLS (Bird)

Madhya Pradesh

1. Bagdara WLS
2. Bori WLS
3. Gandhi Sagar WLS

4. Ghatigaon WLS
5. Karera WLS
6. Ken Gharial WLS
7. Kheoni WLS
8. Narsighgarh WLS
9. National Chambal WLS
10. Noradehi WLS
11. Orcha WLS
12. Pachmarhi WLS
13. Kuno WLS
14. Panna (Gangau) WLS
15. Panpatha WLS
16. Pench WLS
17. Phen WLS
18. Ralamandal WLS
19. Ratapani WLS
20. Sailana WLS
21. Sanjay Dubri WLS
22. Sardarpur WLS
23. Singhori WLS
24. Son Gharial WLS
25. Veerangna Durgawati WLS

Maharashtra

1. Amba Barwa WLS
2. Andhari WLS
3. Aner Dam WLS
4. Bhamragarh WLS
5. Bhimashankar Wildlife Sanctuary
6. Bor Wildlife Sanctuary
7. Bordharan Wildlife Sanctuary
8. Chaprala WLS
9. Deolgaon-Rehkuri WLS
10. Dhyanganga WLS
11. Gautala Autramghat Sanctuary
12. Ghodazari Wildlife Sanctuary

13. Great Indian Bustard Sanctuary
14. Jayakwadi Bird Sanctuary
15. Kalsubai Harishchandragad WLS
16. Karnala Bird Sanctuary
17. Karanja Sohal Blackbuck WLS
18. Katepurna WLS
19. Koyna Wildlife Sanctuary
20. Lonar WLS
21. Malvan Marine WLS
22. Mansingdeo WLS
23. Mayani Bird Sanctuary
24. Mayureshwar Wildlife Sanctuary
25. Melghat
26. Nagzira WLS
27. Naigaon Mayur WLS
28. Nandur Madhameshwar WLS
29. Narnala willife Sanctuary
30. Nawegaon WLS
31. New Bor WLS
32. New Nagzira WLS
33. Painganga WLS
34. Phansad Wildlife Sanctuary
35. Radhanagari WLS
36. Sagareshwar WLS
37. Tansa WLS
38. Thane Creek Flamingo WLS
39. Tipeshwar WLS
40. Tungareshwar Wildlife Sanctuary
41. Yawal Wildlife Sanctuary
42. Yedsi Ramlin Ghat WLS
43. Umred-Kharngla WLS
44. Wan WLS
45. Gangewadi New Great Indian Bustard WLS

Manipur

1. Khongjaingamba Ching WLS
2. Yangoupokpi-Lokchao WLS

Meghalaya

1. Baghmara Pitcher Plant WLS
2. Nongkhyllem WLS
3. Siju WLS
4. Narpuh WLS

Mizoram

1. Dampa WLS (TR)
2. Khawnglung WLS
3. Lengteng WLS
4. Ngengpui WLS
5. Pualreng WLS
6. Tawi WLS
7. Thorangtlang WLS
8. Tokalo WLS

Nagaland

1. Fakim WLS
2. Puliebadze WLS
3. Rangapahar WLS

Orissa

1. Badrama WLS
2. Baisipalli WLS
3. Balukhand Konark WLS
4. Bhitarkanika WLS
5. Chandaka Dampara WLS
6. Chilika (Nalaban) WLS
7. Debrigarh WLS
8. Gahirmatha (Marine) WLS
9. Hadgarh WLS
10. Karlapat WLS
11. Khalasuni WLS

12. Kotagarh WLS
13. Kuldiha WLS
14. Sunabeda WLS
15. Lakhari Valley WLS
16. Nandankanan WLS
17. Satkosia Gorge WLS
18. Kapilash WLS

Punjab

1. Abohar WLS
2. Bir Aishvan WLS
3. Bir Bhadson WLS
4. Bir Bunerheri WLS
5. Bir Dosanjh WLS
6. Bir Gurdialpura WLS
7. Bir Mehaswala WLS
8. Bir Motibagh WLS
9. Harike Lake WLS
10. Jhajjar Bacholi WLS
11. Kathlaur Kushlian WLS
12. Takhni-Rehampur WLS
13. Nangal WLS

Pondicherry

1. Oussudu WLS

Rajasthan

1. Bandh Baratha WLS
2. Bassi WLS
3. Bhensrodgarh WLS
4. Darrah WLS
5. Jaisamand WLS
6. Jamwa Ramgarh WLS
7. Jawahar Sagar WLS
8. Kailadevi WLS
9. Kesarbagh WLS
10. Kumbhalgarh WLS

11. Mount Abu WLS
12. Nahargarh WLS
13. National Chambal WLS
14. Phulwari Ki Nal WLS
15. Ramgarh Vishdhari WLS
16. Ramsagar WLS
17. Sajjangarh WLS
18. Sariska WLS
19. Sawaimadhopur WLS
20. Sawai Man Singh WLS
21. Shergarh WLS
22. Sitamata WLS
23. Tal Chhapper WLS
24. Todgarh Raoli WLS
25. Van Vihar WLS

TamilNadu

1. Cauvery North WLS
2. Chitrangudi Bird WLS
3. Gangaikondam Spotted Dear WLS
4. Indira Gandhi (Annamalai) WLS
5. Kalakad WLS
6. Kanjirankulam Bird WLS
7. Kanyakumari WLS
8. Karaivetti WLS
9. Karikili WLS
10. Kodaikanal WLS
11. Koonthankulam-Kadankulam WLS
12. Melaselvanoor-Keelaselvanoor WLS
13. Mudumalai WLS
14. Mundanthurai WLS
15. Nellai WLS
16. Oussudu Lake Bird Sanctuary
17. Point Calimere WLS
18. Pulicat Lake WLS

19. Satyamangalam WS
20. Srivilliputhur Grizzled Squirrel WLS
21. Udayamarthandapuram Lake WLS
22. Vaduvoor WLS
23. Vedanthangal WLS
24. Vellanadu (Blackbuck) WLS
25. Vellode WLS
26. Vettangudi WLS
27. Megamalai WLS
28. Theerthangal WLS
29. Sakkarakottai WLS

Telangana

1. Kinnersani WLS
2. Eturnagaram WLS
3. Kawal WLS
4. Lanja Madugu Siwaram WLS
5. Manjeera Crocodile WLS
6. Nagarjuna Sagar-Srisailam WLS
7. Pakhal WLS
8. Pocharam WLS
9. Pranahita WLS

Tripura

1. Gumti WLS
2. Rowa WLS
3. Sepahijala WLS
4. Trishna WLS

Uttar Pradesh

1. Bakhira WLS
2. Chandraprabha WLS
3. Dr. Bhimrao Ambedkar Bird WLS
4. Hastinapur WLS
5. Kaimur WLS
6. Katarniaghat Wildlife Sanctuary

7. Kishanpur Wildlife Sanctuary
8. Lakh Bahosi Bird WLS
9. Mahavir Swami WLS
10. National Chambal Sanctuary
11. Nawabganj WLS
12. Okhala Bird WLS
13. Parvati Aranga WLS
14. Patna WLS
15. Ranipur WLS
16. Saman Bird WLS
17. Samaspur WLS
18. Sandi Bird WLS
19. Sohagi Barwa Sanctuary
20. Sohelwa WLS
21. Sur Sarovar Sanctuary
22. Jai Prakash Narayan (Surhatal) Bird WLS
23. Turtle WLS
24. Vijai Sagar WLS
25. Pilibhit Tiger Reserve

Uttarakhand

1. Askot Musk Deer Sanctuary
2. Nandhaur Wildlife Sanctuary
3. Binsar Wildlife Sanctuary
4. Govind Pashu Vihar Wildlife Sanctuary
5. Kedarnath Wildlife Sanctuary
6. Mussoorie Wildlife Sanctuary
7. Sonanadi Wildlife Sanctuary

West Bengal

1. Ballavpur WLS
2. Bethuadahari WLS
3. Bibhuti Bhusan WLS
4. Buxa Tiger Reserve
5. Chapramari WLS
6. Chintamani Kar Bird Sanctuary

7. Haliday Island WLS
8. Jorepokhri Salamander WLS
9. Lothian Island WLS
10. Mahananda wls
11. Raiganj WLS
12. Ramnabagan WLS
13. Sajnakhali WLS
14. Senchal WLS
15. Sundarbans West Wildlife Sanctuary
16. Sundarbans East Wildlife Sanctuary.

THE GREAT HIMALAYAN NATIONAL PARK, HIMACHAL PRADESH

The Great Himalayan National Park lies among the lush coniferous forests of and the snow-capped mountain peaks Kullu, Himachal Pradesh. It is one of the high altitude national parks in India. While the location of this park is itself a stunning feature, the emerald meadows in some portions of the park makes it one of the stunning parks in India.

Snow Leopard, Himalayan Brown Bear, Blue Sheep, Musk Deer and Himalayan Thar are the commonly found animals in this park. It also houses 181 species of birds, and many more species of reptiles, annelids, amphibians and insects.

History of Great Himalayan National Park

The Great Himalayan National Park (GHNP), is one of India's national parks, is located in Kullu region in the state of Himachal Pradesh. The park was built in 1984 and is spread over an area of 1,171 km^2 at an altitude of between 1500 to 6000m. The Great Himalayan National Park is a habitat to numerous flora and more than 375 fauna species that comprises approximately 31 mammals, 181 birds, 3 reptiles, 9 amphibians, 11 annelids, 17 mollusks and 127 insects. They are protected under the strict guidelines of the Wildlife Protection Act of 1972; hence any sort of hunting is not permitted.

In June 2014, the Great Himalayan National Park was added to the UNESCO list of World Heritage Sites. The Unesco World Heritage Site Committee granted the status to the park under the criteria of "exceptional natural beauty and conservation of biological diversity".

About the park

Extent

In 1984, the Himachal Wildlife Project (HWP) surveyed the upper Beas region to help establish the boundaries of the park. An area comprising the watersheds of Jiwa, Sainj, and Tirthan rivers became the Great Himalayan National Park in 1984. Starting from an altitude of 1,700 metres above mean sea level, the highest peak within the Park approaches almost 5,800 metres. The area of the National Park at the moment is 754.4 km² and it is naturally protected on the northern, eastern and southern boundaries by permanent snow or steep ridges. To facilitate conservation a 5 km wide buffer area, extending from the westernperiphery of the Park, has been classified as the Ecodevelopment Project Area (EPA) or Ecozone.

The EPA has an area of 326.6 km² (including 61 km² of Tirthan wildlife sanctuary) with about 120 small villages, comprising 1600 households with a population of about 16,000. Since, the Indian Wildlife Protection Act 1972 does not permit any habitation in the National Park, an area of 90 km² in Sainj valley encompassing the two villages of Shakti and Marore has been classified as Sainj Wildlife Sanctuary (WLS). These two villages although technically "outside" the National Park, are physically located between two parts of GHNP. Thus the total area under the National Park administration is 1,171 km².

Natural features

Lush coniferous forests, emerald meadows strewn with exotic flora, soaring snowy peaks and pristine glaciers make for an ideal Himalayan retreat. The secluded Sainj and Tirthan valleys are home to a plethora of fauna - wild mountain goats like the bharal, goral and serow, the brown bear and predators like the leopard and the elusive snow leopard. Different varieties of pheasants - monal, khalij cheer, tragopan and other exotic Himalayan birds can be found in the region.

The Himalayas have been a source of awe and inspiration for millennia to countless individuals. They are the largest, tallest and geologically youngest mountains on our planet. In India, they are the Dehvbumi—the home of the gods. The Himalaya are also one of the most fragile mountain regions of the world and hold an enormous repository of biological diversity which is increasingly under pressure from human activities. The unique ecological aspects of the Western Himalaya led to the creation of the Great Himalayan National Park (GHNP) in the Kullu district of India's mountain state of Himachal Pradesh. These features include biodiversity, sparse human populations, inaccessibility, little tourism, and a local economy based on traditional livelihoods.

Products

GHNP is a major source of water for the rural and urban centers of the region with four major rivers of the area originating from the glaciers in the Park. It is also a source of sustenance and livelihood for the local community living close to GHNP.

In addition to lumber, the forest environment provides local people with Non-Timber Forest Produce (NTFP) such as honey, fruit nuts, bark of birch and yew, flowers and fuel wood.

Globally, as well as locally, the Great Himalayan National Park has a very high public profile. The international community regards at it as a pilot site where the community based Biodiversity Conservation approach is being tested. The local people in the Ecozone (or Buffer Zone adjacent to the park) of GHNP recognize the fact that they have overexploited the medicinal herbs and NTFPs, and their sheep and goats have overgrazed the pastures.

Biogeography

The GHNP is at the junction of world's two major faunal regions: the oriental to the south and palaearctic to the north. The temperate forest flora-fauna of GHNP represents the western most extension of the Sino-Japanese Region. The high altitude ecosystem of the Northwest Himalaya has common plant elements with the adjacent Western and Central Asiatic region. As a result of its 4,100 m elevation range the Park has a diversity of zones with their representative flora and fauna, such as alpine, glacial, temperate, and sub tropical forests.

These biogeographic elements are result of geological evolution of Himalaya which continues today from the action of plate tectonics and continental drift.

Over 100 million years ago, the Indian sub-continent broke off from the large, southern landmass, Gondwanaland and moved north. It eventually slammed into the northern land mass, Laurasia, and formed the gigantic folded mountains of the Himalaya. Due to this union of Gondwanaland and Asiatic landmasses, exchange of flora and fauna was possible and this ultimately led to the unique biogeographical features in the region.

It took twenty years from inception to inauguration for GHNP to be realized as part of the Indian National Park system. The following is a brief timeline:

1980: Preliminary Park survey of the watersheds of Tirthan, Sainj, and Jiwanal in Banjar area of Kullu district 1983: Continued Park survey, the Banjar area of Kullu district.

1984: Notification by state of Himachal Pradesh of the intention to create the Great Himalayan National Park with buffer zone.

1987: First Management Plan of the Great Himalayan National Park.

1988: Settlement Proceedings and settling of rights of local communities

1992: The Himachal Wildlife Project re-assesses wildlife abundance, livestock grazing, and herb collection and reviewed the existing management plan.

1994: The Government of HP revised the Notification of intention to include the Sainj Wildlife Sanctuary and the upper Parvati watershed.

1994-1999: Conservation of Biodiversity Project (CoB), the Wildlife Institute of India, Dehradun conducts research to assist in the management of the Park.

1999: Declaration of Award upon Completion of Settlement Proceedings. Monetary compensation for individuals who had rights of forest produce in the park area, including a package for providing alternative income generation activities to everybody living in the Ecodevelopment Project Area or Ecozone.

Final Notification of the Great Himalayan National Park. The GHNP becomes the latest and newest National Park of India.

The Conservation of Biodiversity (CoB) Project completed on 31 December 1999.

Was inscribed as World Heritage Natural Site on 23 June 2014. (Proceedings of the 38th World Heritage Committee meeting at Doha, Qatar.

Biodiversity

Fauna

The Great Himalayan National Park is home to more than 375 faunal species. So far species of 31 mammals, 181 birds, 3 reptiles, 9 amphibians, 11 annelids, 17 mollusks and 127 insects belonging to six orders have been identified and documented.

Most of the Himalayan fauna has been given protection under the high priority protection category of Schedule I of the Indian Wildlife (Protection) Act, 1972. The state government of Himachal Pradesh has banned hunting in the state for more than ten years.

A trek of 35 to 45 km in any of the Park's valleys brings one into the high altitude habitat (3,500 m and above) of animals such as blue sheep, snow leopard, Himalayan brown bear, Himalayan Tahr, and musk deer. Best sightings can be made in autumn (September–November) as animals start their seasonal migration to lower altitudes.

Flora

The GHNP also supports a great diversity of plant life thanks to its wide altitude range and relatively undisturbed habitats. From the lofty pinesand spruces and the great, spreading horse chestnuts of the lower valleys, to the dense cushions and prostrate branches of the alpine herbs and junipers, the Park presents an endless variety of vegetation.

Although some areas have been modified by grazing, this is one of the few areas of the Western Himalayas where the forests and alpine meadows can be seen in something approaching their original state. The subalpine zone is richest in species, followed by the alpine and upper temperate zones.

DANDELI WILDLIFE SANCTUARY, KARNATAKA

Dandeli Wildlife Sanctuary is the second largest wildlife sanctuary in Karnataka. Located on the banks of the Kali River, it is one of the highly visited wildlife sanctuaries in India. Black Panther, Flying Squirrel, Tiger, Elephant and Leopard can be easily spotted in this sanctuary.

Among the wide range of amphibians, Crocodiles are the major attraction of this sanctuary. It is also an ideal place for river rafting, trekking, Bird watching, Tiger and Crocodile spotting.

2

Bandipur National Park, Karnataka

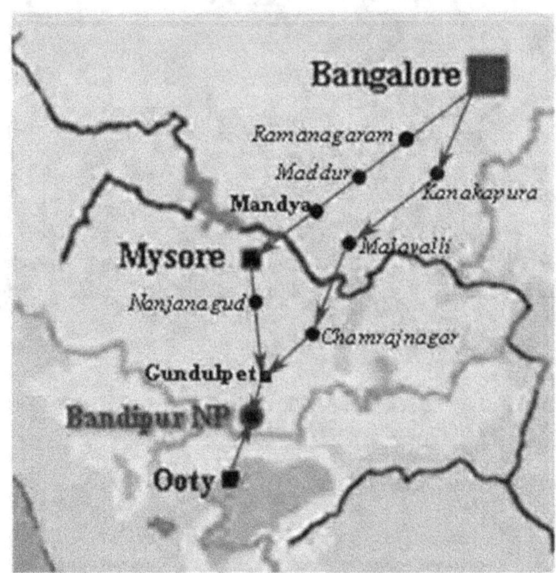

The Bandipur National Park is the most popular among all the national parks in South India. It is a natural home to Elephants and several other endangered species. Lush forest of the Deccan Plateau and the Western Ghats makes this park one of the beautiful parks in India. The park is located 80 km away from Mysore and almost 215 km away from Bangalore.

HISTORY OF BANDIPUR NATIONAL PARK

Bandipur National Park, established in 1974 as a tiger reserve under Project Tiger, is anational park located in the south Indian state of Karnataka. It was once a private hunting reserve for the Maharaja of the Kingdom of Mysore. Bandipur is known for its wildlife and has many types of biomes, but dry deciduous forest is dominant.

The park spans an area of 874 square kilometers (337 sq mi), protecting several species of India's endangered wildlife. Together with the adjoining Nagarhole National Park (643 km^2 (248 sq mi)), Mudumalai National Park (320 km^2 (120 sq mi)) and Wayanad Wildlife Sanctuary (344 km^2 (133 sq mi)), it is part of the Nilgiri Biosphere Reserve totaling 2,183 km^2 (843 sq mi) making it the largest protected area in southern India.

Bandipur is located in Gundlupet taluq of Chamarajanagar district. It is about 80 kilometers (50 mi) from the city of Mysore on the route to a major tourist destination of Ooty. As a result, Bandipur sees a lot of tourist traffic and there are a lot of wildlife fatalities caused by speeding vehicles that are reported each year. There is a ban on traffic from the hours of dusk to dawn to help bring down deaths of wildlife.

The Maharaja of the Kingdom of Mysore created a sanctuary of 90 km^2 (35 sq mi) in 1931 and named it the Venugopala Wildlife Park. The Bandipur Tiger Reserve was established under Project Tiger in 1973 by adding nearly 800 km^2 (310 sq mi) to the Venugopala Wildlife park.

GEOGRAPHY

Bandipur National Park located between 75° 12' 17" E to 76° 51' 32" E and 11° 35' 34" N to 11° 57' 02" N where the Deccan Plateau meets the Western Ghats and the altitude of the park ranges from 680 meters (2,230 ft) to 1,454 meters (4,770 ft). As a result, the park has a variety of biomes including dry deciduous forests, moist deciduous forests and shrublands.

At the Moyar gorge with Nilgiris in the background

The wide range of habitats help support a diverse range of organisms. The park is flanked by the Kabini river in the north and the Moyar river in the south. The Nugu river runs through the park. The highest point in the park is on a hill called Himavad Gopalaswamy Betta, where there is a Hindu temple at the summit. Bandipur has typical tropical climate with distinct wet and dry seasons. The dry and hot period usually begins in early March and can last till the arrival of the monsoonrains in June.

Mammals

A golden jackal family alongside the Kabini river in Bandipur National Park, Karnataka.

Birds

Changeable hawk-eagle in Bandipur reserve, Karnataka

WILDLIFE IN BANDIPUR

The Bandipur National Park is the region always accosted with tremendous counts of wildlife species including varied mammals and vulnerable kinds of species like Bonner Macaque Nilgiri Langur (adjoining areas), Dhole, Common Palm, Civet, Smooth-coated Otter, Stripe-necked Mongoose, Jungle Cat, Tiger, Wild Boar, Chital, Gaur, Grizzled Indian Squirrel, Liontail Macaque, Indian Palm, Giant Flying squirrel, Golden Jackal, Sloth Bear, Indian Grey Mongoose, Striped Hyaena, Ratel, Indian Spotted Chevrotain, Rusty-spotted Cat, Sambar, Nilgiri Tahr (adjoining areas), Indian Porcupine, Hanuman Langur, Bengal Fox, Eurasian, Otter Small Indian Civet, Ruddy, Leopard, Cat Leopard, Indian Elephant, Four-horned Antelope, Indian Muntjac, Indian Pangolin, Mongoose, Indian Hare Red, Indian Giant Squirrel with more species on the list.

Flora in Bandipur Reserve

Apart from grand varieties of wildlife in the area Bandipur National Park claims greenery all around the vicinity. The area is blooming with great varieties of timber trees including: Teak (Tectona grandis), Sandalwood (Santalum album V), Rosewood (Dalbergia latifolia), Indian Kino Tree (Pterocarpus marsupium), giant clumping bamboo (Dendrocalamus strictus), Indian-laurel (Terminalia tomentosa), clumping bamboo (Bambusa arundinacea) and Grewia tiliaefolia.

Apart from such variety, there are also several notable flowering and fruiting trees and shrubs holding the arena like: Indian Gooseberry (Emblica Officinalis), Kadam Tree (Adina Cordifolia), Crape-myrtle (Lagerstroemia Lanceolata), Axlewood

(Anogeissus latifolia), Black Myrobalan (Terminalia chebula), Schleichera Trijuga, Odina Wodiar, Flame of the Forest (Butea Monosperma), Golden Shower Tree (Cassia fistula), Black Cutch (Acacia catechu), Shorea Talura (E), Indigo Berry (Randia uliginosa), Satinwood (Chloroxylon Swietenia).

Tourist Places near Park

Wayanad - It is the most outstanding location near Bandipur area which is basically considered as the land of paddy fields and is snuggled between the western ghat mountains. Wayanad is one of the most exquisite hill stations in Kerala which is also a perfect place to find the trading of different products along with the presence of wildlife sanctuaries around the area.

Mysore - the second largest city of Karnataka, Mysore is also called the cultural capital of the state with the presence of many palaces around the city which brings the name Mysore as the city of palaces. A must watch destination for the architectural lovers. The most famous attraction of Mysore is the Mysore Palace, which is best visited during the evening, when the whole palace is lit up with sparkling lights.

Ooty - Also known as Ootacamund, the capital of Nilgiris district, Ooty is called as the Queen of the hill stations. This is the most picturesque picnic spots of the area and is preferred for the summer and weekend gateway.

Ooty has got the most blooming vegetation, lofty mountains, dense forest, sprawling grasslands and miles and miles of tea gardens.

Kabini - Quite naturally, this area is defined as the region alongside the River Kabini and is the perfect host for the Kabini Wildlife Sanctuary.

The Kabini area is promptly being mentioned as Kabini forests due to the dense lushly regions which are a mix of tropical, moist and dry deciduous types. The area of Kabini is perfectly meant for the people who love hanging around the pristine and virgin natural areas for some solicitation and freshness.

Nagarhole - the area of Kabini also highlights the regions of the Nagarhole National Park. The area of Nagarhole which means the "Snake River" in Kannada is a picture perfect tourist spot for most of the travelers. Nagarhole derives its name from the winding course of the river like a snake that flows through the forests.

Coorg - yet another fascinating hill station of the area, Coorg advances for the natural splendors and the exotic scenic environment. The area is best recognized as the "Scotland of India" as Coorg defines itself through the majestic beauty and cool ambience of the hill station at an altitude in the range of 3500 ft above sea level.

Bangalore - the main IT hub of India, Bangalore is the prettiest city of India which is embarked with many sobriquets like Garden City, Silicon Valley of India,

Pub City and so on. The city is best known for its salubrious climate and is bestowed with tall tree lined streets & several parks adding to its greenery to rightly being called as the 'Garden City'.

Thekkady - lying at the district of Idukki district, Thekkady one of the most popular destinations of India, located 160 miles from Trivandrum. It is the most unique and abundantly rich with flora, fauna with a wide range of birds. The presence of a man-made lake in the area also attracts tremendous attentions along with other attractions like trekking, wildlife train, bamboo rafting, border hiking and rock climbing.

Chennai - the capital of Tamil Nadu, Chennai brings tremendous coastal attractions to the tourist for a never-ending mystical charm South India. Chennai is best known for long expansion of sandy beaches, parks, sculptures and historic landmarks, charismatic monuments, temples, mosques and churches.

How to Reach

By Air : The nearest airport is at Bangalore which is 220 km from Bandipur.

By Rail : Mysore is nearest railhead, at a distance of 80-kms.

By Road : 220 km from Bangalore; 80 km from Mysore and 80 kms from Ooty.

Hotels in Bandipur National Park

At Bandipur National Park, different types of accommodative options are available to bring the wildlife experience more blessed and nurtured with exotic luxury services under the laps of natural beauty. The available hotels and resorts in the vicinity are being designed so as to match your necessities and preferences.

BIOLOGY AND ECOLOGY

Bandipur National Park helps protect several species of India's endangered wildlife and also provides refuge to other threatened and vulnerable species of flora and fauna.

Flora

Bandipur supports a wide range of timber trees including: Teak (*Tectona grandis*), Rosewood (*Dalbergia latifolia*), Sandalwood (*Santalum album* V), Indian-laurel (*Terminalia tomentosa*), Indian Kino Tree (*Pterocarpus marsupium*), giant clumping bamboo(*Dendrocalamus strictus*), clumping bamboo (*Bambusa arundinacea*) and *Grewia tiliaefolia*. There are also several notable flowering and fruiting trees and shrubs including: Kadam tree (*Adina cordifolia*), Indian gooseberry (*Emblica officinalis*), Crape-myrtle (*Lagerstroemia lanceolata*), axlewood (*Anogeissus latifolia*), Black Myrobalan (*Terminalia chebula*), *Schleichera trijuga*, *Odina wodiar*, Flame of the Forest (*Butea monosperma*), Golden Shower Tree (*Cassia fistula*), satinwood (*Chloroxylon swietenia*), Black Cutch (*Acacia catechu*), *Shorea talura* (E), indigoberry (*Randia uliginosa*).

Fauna

Bandipur supports a good population of endangered and vulnerable species like Indian elephants, gaurs, tigers, sloth bears, muggers, Indian rock pythons, four-horned antelopes and dholes.

Mammals

The commonly seen mammals along the public access roads in the park include chital, gray langurs, Indian giant squirrels and elephants. A list of medium to large-sized mammals in the park is given in the following census table published in 1997:

Species	1991	1993	1995	1997
Tiger	58	66	74	75
Leopard	51	81	86	88
Indian Elephant	1107	2214	2214	3471
Gaur	1097	1373	1373	2427
Dhole	148	181	181	N/A
Chital	3333	5858	5858	8204
Sambar	706	1196	1196	2386
Sloth bear	51	66	66	N/A
Four-horned antelope	14	N/A	N/A	N/A
Gray Langur	1468	1751	1751	1851
Wild boar	148	181	181	N/A
Muntjac	72	131	131	N/A

Birds

Peafowl are among the most commonly seen birds in Bandipur along with grey junglefowl, crows and drongos. Bandipur is home to over 200 species of birds including honey buzzards, red-headed vultures, Indian vultures, flowerpeckers, hoopoes, Indian rollers, brown fish owls, crested serpent eagles and changeable hawk-eagles.

Other fauna

Reptile species include Spectacled cobra, Indian rock python, vipers, rat snake, muggers, monitor lizards, Indian chameleon, Indian pond terrapin, agamids and flying lizards.

Butterflies include Common Rose, Crimson Rose, Common Jay, Tailed, Lime Butterfly, Malabar Raven, Common Mormon, Red Helen, Blue Mormon, Southern Birdwing, Common Wanderer, Mottled Emigrant, Common Grass Yellow, Spotless Grass Yellow, One spot Grass Yellow, Nilgiri Clouded Yellow, Common Jezebel, Psyche, Common Gull.,

Caper White or Pioneer, Small Orange Tip or Lesser Orange Tip, White Orange Tip, Large Salmon Arab, Common Evening Brown, Great Evening Brown, Common Palmfly, Common Bushbrown, Glad Eye Bushbrowm, Red Disk Bushbrown, Red Eye Bushbrown, Lepcha Bushbrown, Nigger, Common Threering, Common Fourring, Common Fivering, Tawny Coster, Rustic, Common Leopard, Indian Fritillary, Common Sailer, Colour Sergeant, Chestnutstreaked Sailer, Grey Count, Red Baron or Baronet, Angled Castor, Common Castor Aridane merione, Yellow Pansy, Lemon Pansy, Peacock Pansy, Chocolate Pansy, Orange Pansy, Blue Pansy, Grey Pansy, Blue Admiral, Glassy Blue Tiger, Blue Tiger, Dark Blue Tiger, Plain Tiger, Striped Tiger/ Common Tiger, Danaid Eggfly, Great Eggfly, Common Crow, Brown King Crow, Common Pierrot, Angled Pierrot, Banded Blue Pierrot, Striped Pierrot, Dark Pierrot, Red Pierrot, Lime Blue, Zebra Blue, Gram Blue, Common Cerulean, Tiny Grass Blue, Dark Grass Blue, Indian Cupid, Large Four-Line Blue, Common Silverline, Plum Judy, Plain Scupid, Pea Blue, Metallic Cerulean, Chestnut Bob, Dark Palm Dart, Brown owl

Ant species include Anenictus sp1, Anoplolepis longipes, Camponotus parius, Crematogaster biroi, Crematogaster sp 1*, Crematogaster sp 2*, Diacamma rugosum, Lepisiota capensis, Leptogenys chinesis, Leptogenys coonorensis, Leptogenys diminuta, Lophomyrmex quadripinosus, Meranoplus bicolor, Monomorium indicum, Myrmicaria striata, Myrmicaria brunnea, Oligomyrmex wroughtonii, Pachycondyla sp1*, Paratrechina sp1*, Pheidole sharpi, Pheidole sp1*, Pheidole sp2*, Pheidologeton diverus, Polyrhachis exercita, Solenopsis geminate, Tetraponera rufonigra, Tetraponera sp1* (* New species yet to be identified.)

Dung beetles include Catharsius granulatus *, Copris indicus *, Oniticellus cinctus*, Onitis singhalensis *, Onthophagus beesoni*, Onthophagus ensifer *, Onthophagus rana *, Onthophagus sp.107* #, Onthophagus tarandus*, Picnopanaleus rotundus, Caccobius diminutives, Caccobius ultor, Copris furciceps, Copris sp.1#, Heliocopris dominus, Pseudonthophagus sp.2#, Sisyphus neglectus, Caccobius inermis, Caccobius meridionalis.,

Caccobius torticornis, Caccobius sp.1#, Copris sodalist, Onthophagus socialis, Onthophagus sp.301#, Onitis phelemon, Onthophagus furcillifer, Caccobius gallinus,

Onthophagus rufulgens, Onthophagus sp.302#, Copris repertus, Pseudonthophagus sp.1#, Copris davisoni, Onitis falcatus, Onthophagus turbatus, Copris imitans, Onthophagus quadridentatus, Caccobius vulcanus, Liatongus affinis, Oniticellus spinipes, Sisyphus longipus, Onthophagus dama (* extremely rare (Represented by a single specimen in the collection), # New species yet to be identified.

Conflicts and threats

For farmers in the 200 villages along the Bandipur forest periphery, the National Park is a vast pasture for grazing cattle and for collection of firewood and other forest produce. The reserve holds nearly 150,000 cattle. The Nugu wildlife sanctuary and Himavad Gopalaswamy range located in the north-west of the park are the most used by cattle.

There are fears of possible transmission of diseases from cattle to wildlife. In 1968, large numbers of gaur were killed in an outbreak ofrinderpest. Lantana bush introduced by British in the 19th century in tea gardens has spread rapidly at the cost of other valuable herbs and saplings.

This bush is thorny, attracts mosquitoes, is not eaten by any herbivores and rapid spread has caused other species of fauna to vanish which is staple food for wild life. Rapid spread of Parthenium (*Parthenium hysterophorus*) has severely damaged bio-diversity and typical landscapes of this beautiful jungle is making way for this invasive weed.

Elephants which traditionally migrate from dry to moist zones now increasingly come into contact with human habitations and farms are often damaged. Sugarcane crops are particularly attractive to them. The National Highway (NH-67) &(NH-212) passes through Bandipur national park.

This road has been a major concern as speeding vehicles have killed many wild animals in spite of frequent warnings to travelers from the forest department officials and restriction on movement of vehicles in some stretches between 9 P.M to 6 A.M. This has raised fears of extinction of habitat of wild animals exclusively found in this national park..

3

Bandhavgarh National Park, Madhya Pradesh

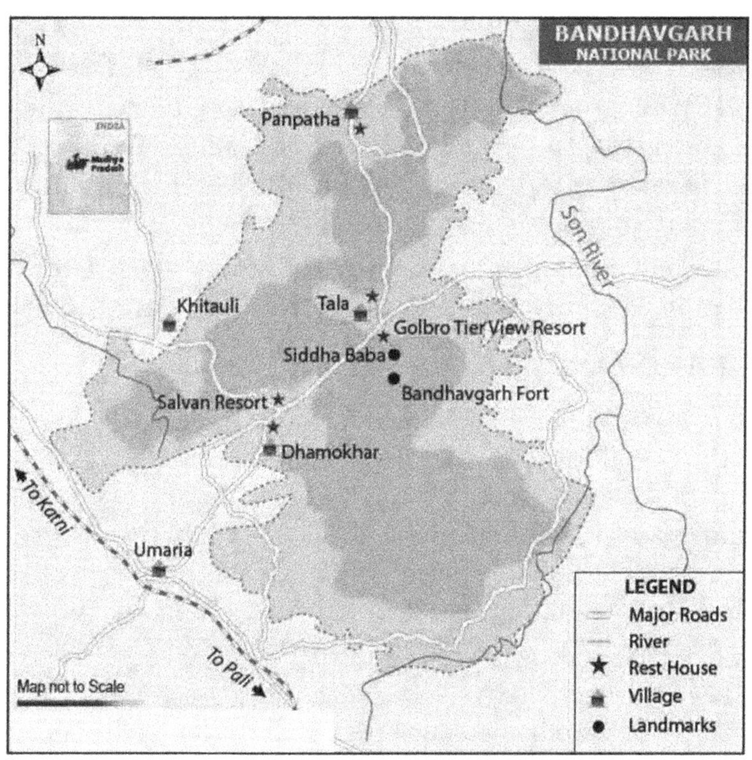

Making a magnificent trip to Bandhavgarh will definitely take you to the lush greenery of the forested regions that are incredibly the natural abode of the variant of wild species. Catching the amazing glimpses of these majestic creatures are simply incredible and with safari opportunities in Bandhavgarh you can have it all in a complete organized way. With elephant and jeep safari you can have a closer look to all these majestic creatures including the royal tigers and making a safe and visible glare to these species will complete your jungle safari in a true sense.

The Bandhavgarh National Park is another enticing name in the list of national parks of India. Located in the Umaria district of Madhya Pradesh, it is one of the largest national parks of Madhya Pradesh. Declared as a national park in 1968, this park has a noteworthy number of Tigers in India.

This park also has a significant number of Leopards and Deer. Among all the attractions of Bandhavgarh National Park, White Tigers are the most spectacular.

HISTORY OF BANDHAVGARH NATIONAL PARK

Bandhavgarh National Park is one of the popular national parks in India located in the Umaria district of Madhya Pradesh. Bandhavgarh was declared a national park in 1968, with an area of 105 km². The buffer is spread over the forest divisions of Umaria and Katni and totals 437 km². The park derives its name from the most prominent hillock of the area, which is said to be given by Hindu Lord Rama to his brother Lakshmana to keep a watch on Lanka (Ceylon). Hence the name *Bandhavgarh*.

This park has a large biodiversity. The density of the tiger population at Bandhavgarh is one of the highest known in India. The park has a large breeding population of leopards, and various species of deer. Maharaja Martand Singh of Rewa captured the first white tiger in this region in 1951. This white tiger, *Mohan*, is now stuffed and on display in the palace of the Maharajas ofRewa. Historically villagers and their cattle have been a threat to the tiger. Rising mining activities around the park are putting the tigers at risk.

Statue of Shesh-Saiya at Bandhavgarh National Park

Bandhavgarh National Park is a park with a rich historical past. Prior to becoming a national park, the forests around Bandhavgarh had long been maintained as a *Shikargah*, or game preserve, of the Maharajas and their guests.

In 1947, Rewa state was merged with Madhya Pradesh; Bandhavgarh came under the regulations of Madhya Pradesh. The Maharaja of Rewa still retained the hunting rights. No special conservation measures were taken until 1968, when the areas were constituted as a national park. Since then, numerous steps have been taken to retain Bandhavgarh National Park as an unspoilt natural habitat.

Project Tiger was constituted in 1972, and then the Wildlife Protection Act of 1972 came into force. It was realized that protection of just the 105 km^2 of prime Bandhavgarh habitat was enough, so in 1982, three more ranges were reduced, namely Khitauli, Magdhi, and Kallawah were reduced to Tala range (the original Bandhavgarh National Park) to extend the area of Bandhavgarh to 448 km^2. As Project tiger decreased its activities and area of influence, Bandhavgarh was taken into its folds in 1993, and a core area of 694 km^2 was established including the previously named ranges and the Panpatha Sanctuary along with a buffer area of 437 km^2 which was declared as the Bandhavgarh Tiger Reserve.

History

The state of Rewa owes its origins to the foundation of a state dating to 1234 by Vyaghra Dev, a descendant of the Vaghelas of Gujarat. He married the daughter of the Raja of Pirhawan and conquered the territory between Kalpi and Chandalgarh. Karan Dev, son of Vyaghra Dev married the daughter of the Raja of Ratanpur, bringing Bandhogarh (now known as Bandhavgarh) into the family as her dowry. The legendary fortress of Bandhogarh fell into Mughal hands in 1597, almost by accident. At the death of H.H. Maharaja Virbhadra Rao in 1593, his minor son succeeded as H.H. Maharaja Vikramaditya. When he was sent to Delhi for his own safety, the emperor took advantage of his absence to send one of his loyal nobles as temporary governor. Once he had taken control of the fort, the Maharaja's nobles and officials were expelled and the fort annexed by the Mughals. On his return to his remaining domains, H.H. Maharaja Vikramaditya was forced to establish a new capital at Rewa, whence the state took its name.

The history of the region can be traced back to the 1st century. There are 39 caves in the Bandhavgarh fort and in the surrounding hillocks up to a radius of about 5 km. The oldest cave dates from the 1st century. Several caves carry inscriptions in Brahmi script. Some caves have embossed figures such as tigers, pigs, elephants, and horsemen. Badi gufa, the largest cave, has a broad entrance, nine small rooms and several pillars. It has been dated back to the 10th century. The cave appears to be primitive, lacking the elaborate statues and carvings seen in the caves of the Buddhist period. Its purpose remains a mystery.

No records are available to show when Bandhavgarh Fort was constructed. However, it is thought to be some 2000 years old, and there are references to it in the ancient books, the "Narad-Panch Ratra" and the "Shiva Purana". it is also believed that Lord Rama visited Bandhavgarh and gave this fort to his younger brother Laxmana (bandhu) resulting in the name- Bandhavgarh. Various dynasties have ruled the fort; including the Mauryans from the 3rd century BC, Vakataka rulers from the 3rd to the 5th century the Sengars from the 5th century and the Kalachuris from the 10th century. In the 13th century, the Baghels took over, ruling from Bandhavgarh until 1617, when Maharaja Vikramaditya Singh moved his capital to Rewa. The last inhabitants deserted the fort in 1935.

Bandhagarh National Park is a park with a rich historical past. Prior to becoming a national park, the forests around Bandhavgarh had long been maintained as a *Shikargah*, or game preserve, of the Maharajas and their guests.

In 1947 Rewa State was merged with Madhya Pradesh; Bandhavgarh came under the regulations of Madhya Pradesh. The Maharaja of Rewa still retained the hunting rights. No special conservation measures were taken until 1968, when the areas were constituted as a national park. Since then, numerous steps have been taken to retain Bandhavgarh National Park as an unspoilt natural habitat.

Project Tiger was constituted in 1972 and then the Wildlife Protection Act of 1972 came into force.

It was realized that protection of just the 105 km^2 of prime Bandhavgarh habitat was not enough, so in 1982, three more ranges, namely Khitauli, Magdhi, and Kallawah were added to Tala range (the original Bandhavgarh National Park) to extend the area of Bandhavgarh to 448 km^2.

As Project tiger extended its activities and area of influence, Bandhavgarh was taken into its folds in 1993, and a core area of 694 km² was established including the previously named ranges and the Panpatha Sanctuary along with a buffer area of 437 km² which was declared as the Bandhavgarh Tiger Reserve.

Bengal tigers

Bandhavgarh has one of the highest density of Bengal tigers known in the world, and is home to some famous named individual tigers.

Charger, an animal so named because of his habit of charging at elephants and tourists (whom he nonetheless did not harm), was the first healthy male known to be living in Bandhavgarh since the 1990s.

A female known as Sita, who once appeared on the cover of *National Geographic* and is considered the most photographed tiger in the world was also to be found in Bandhavgarh for many years. Almost all the tigers of Bandhavgarh today are descendants of Sita and Charger. Their daughter Mohini, son Langru and B2 also maintained their tradition for frequent sighting and moving close to tourist jeeps.

Mohini, became prominent following Sita's death. She mated with Mahaman Tiger. She later died of her wounds from the vehicle accident.

Charger died in 2000 and his body was buried at Charger Point where he was kept in a closed region at his old age. Between 2003 and 2006, many of his descendants met with a series of unfortunate ends. B1 was electrocuted and B3 was killed by poachers. Sita was killed by poachers. Mohini died of serious wounds to her body. After the death of Charger, the fully grown B2 survived as the dominant male in the forest between 2004 and 2007. He also became the strongest tiger in the world. Mating with a female in the Siddhababa region of Bandhavgarh, he became a father of three cubs. One of them was a male. He was named Bamera. He was first sighted in 2008 and is now Bandhavgarh's dominant male. In November 2011, B2 died. Postmortem studies suggest that he died anatural death. But many other professional people, who know more than the officials, say that he was injured by the villagers of the village in the buffer area.

Now, the most prominent tiger in Tala zone of Bandhavgarh National Park is Bamera. However, off late he has been challenged on several occasions by a new male. Blue Eyes and Mukunda are the dominant males of Magdhi and Khitauli zone respectively. The females who are seen more frequently are Rajbehra, Mirchaini, Banbehi, Mahaman, Sukhi Pattiya and Damdama. There are a quite a few cubs also who are either in sub-adult stage or have entered the adulthood and are separate now.

Structure

The four main zones of the national park are Tala, Magdhi, Khitauli, and Panpatta. Tala is the richest zone in terms of biodiversity, mainly tigers. Together, these four ranges comprise the 'Core' of the Bandhavgarh Tiger Reserve constituting a total area of 694 km². The buffer zone is spread over the forest divisions of Umaria and Katni and totals another 437 km². The legal status as a national park dates back to 1968, but was limited only to the present Tala range for a considerable length of time. In 1993 the present scheme of things was put in place.

According to biogeographic classification, the area lies in Zone 6A- Deccan Peninsula, Central Highlands. The classification of Champion & Seth lists the area under Northern India Moist Deciduous Forests. The vegetation is chiefly of Sal forest in the valleys and on the lower slopes, gradually changing to mixed deciduous forest on the hills and in the hotter drier areas of the park in the south and west.

The wide valleys along the streams carry long linear grasslands flanked by Sal forests. Rich mixed forests consisting of Sal (*shorea rubusta*), Saja, Salai, and Dhobin, etc. with dense bamboo thickets occur in many places. These together provide Bandhavgarh its rich biodiversity.

With the tiger at the apex of the food chain, it contains 37 species of mammals. According to forest officials, there are more than 250 species of birds, about 80 species ofbutterflies, a number of reptiles. But many people have the species' list of about 350 birds along with photographs. The richness and tranquility of grasslands invites pairs ofSarus Cranes to breed in the rainy season.

One of the biggest attractions of this national park is the tiger (*panthera tigris tigris*) and its sightings. Bandhavgarh has a very high density of tigers within the folds of its jungles. The 105 km² of park area open to tourists was reported to have 22 tigers, a density of one tiger for every 4.77 km². (Population estimation exercise 2001). The population of tigers in the park in 2012 is about 44-49. There is a saying about the Park that goes: "In any other Park, You are lucky if you see a tiger. In Bandhavgarh, you are unlucky if you don't see (at least) one." But the situation is not like that nowadays. spotting a tiger is rare one out of 10 tourists is able to spot the tiger.

Bandhavgarh tiger reserve is densely populated with other species: the gaur, or Indian bison, are now extinct or have migrated elsewhere; sambar and barking deer are a common sight, and nilgai are to be seen in the open areas of the park.

There have been reports of the Indian Wolf (*canis lupus indica*), hyena, and the caracal the latter being an open country dweller. The tiger reserve abounds with cheetal or the spotted deer (*Axis axis*) which is the main prey animal of the tiger and the leopard (*Panthera pardus*). The Indian bison were reintroduced from Kanha.

Reintroduction of Gaur

Bandhavgarh National Park had small population of Gaur. But due to some disease passed from the cattles to them, all of them died. The project of reintroduction of Gaurs dealt with shifting some Gaurs from Kanha National Park to Bandhavgarh. 50 animals were shifted by the winter of 2012. This project was executed by M.P. Forest dept., Wildlife Institute of India, Taj Safaris and Conservation corporation of Africa by technical collaboration.

Transportation

Air : Though Bandhavgarh do not have the airport facility for main stream Flights but Jabalpur city which is the nearest city to Bandhavgarh has good air connectivity with major cities of India. Private charters can land near to Bandhavgarh National Park, Umaria district is having small air-strip facility for charter planes. Jabalpur Airport (199 km/04:30hrs).direct flights for Delhi and Mumbai. It is the best option for reaching Bandhavgarh National Park as it connected with 02 important cities: Delhi & Mumbai. In between these flight options AirIndia, SpiceJet flight is operating daily

Rail : Katni and Umaria are both major railway stations with good train connectivity across India.

Fauna

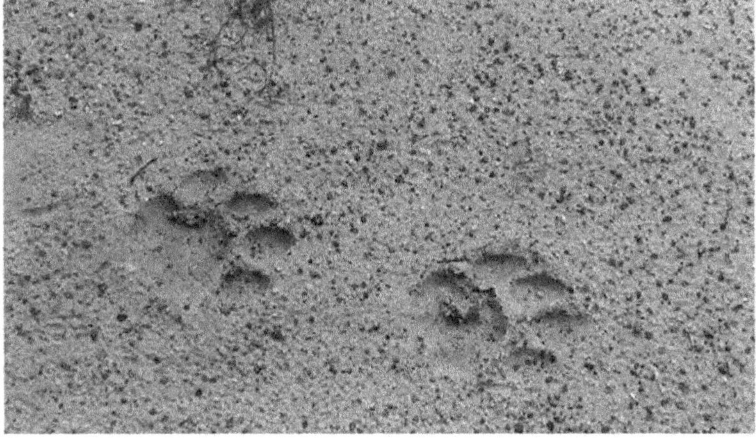

Tiger Paws

With the tiger at the apex of the food chain, it contains 37 species of mammals.

According to forest officials, there are more than 250 species of birds, about 80 species of butterflies, a number of reptiles. But many people have the species' list of about 350 birds along with photographs. The richness and tranquity of grasslands invites pairs of sarus cranes to breed in the rainy season.

FLORA IN BANDHAVGARH NATIONAL PARK

Bandhavgarh National Park is spread across the area of 446 sq km and the Madhya Pradesh Forest Department has considered it as the most vegetative part of the Umaria district. The foliage in Bandhavgarh National Park is mostly of dry deciduous type and is the only region which is quite rich in flora and fauna. The area brings relatively moderate climate and of course the favorable topography that uniquely supports the growth of a rich and varied flora in the park. Along with that the captivating landscapes are being spread over 32 hills, cliffs, plateaus and meadows. The vegetation of Bandhavgarh is specially filled with Sal forest in the valleys and Bamboo stretches on the lower slopes of the region. While half of the forest is being covered with fine trees of Sal and Bamboo, the forest also beholds the mixed species around the higher hills that also includes high grasslands which are the major specialty of the Bandhavgarh jungle.

Naturally, the riverbanks of Bandhavgarh region is extremely fertile and is quite lush that surely brings the reason why at least 300 species of flora can be found at both the core and the buffer region of Bandhavgarh. Moreover, some perennial streams and rivulets flow at different crisscrossed zones of the park creating scenic vistas and budding importance to the jungle. The beautiful sceneries of this Indian Wildlife Park offer picturesque view to the tourists and nature lovers.

Some of the most famous floral species including Sal can be found in Bandhavgarh National Park are:

- Saj (Terminalia tomentosa)
- Dhaora (Anogeissus latifolia)
- Tendu, Arjun (Terminalia arjuna)
- Amla (Emblica officinalis)
- Palas (Butea monosperma)
- Salai (Boswellia serrata)
- Mango (Mangifera indica)
- Jamun (Blackberry) (Syzygium Cumini)
- Babul (Accasia nilotica)
- Banyan (F icus benghalensis)
- Ber (Zizyphus mauritania)
- Dhak or Chila (flame of the forest){Butea monosperma}
- Dhok (Anogeossis pendula)
- Jamun (Syzygium cumini)
- Kadam (Authocephalus cadamba)
- Khajur (Phoenix sylvestris)
- Khair (Accacia catechu)
- Bamboo
- Lagerstroemia
- Boswelia
- Pterocarpus
- Madhuca

Along with that the Bandhavgarh forest is also being filled with lots of contrasting vegetation including:

- Karel (Capparis decidua)
- Mohua (Madhuca indica)
- Khejda (Prosopis specigera)
- Kakera (Flacourtia indica)
- Neem (Azadirachta indica)

THE ECOLOGICAL SYSTEM IN THE BANDHAVGARH NATIONAL PARK

The Flora in Bandhavgarh National Park

Bandhavgarh has a large variety of tree cover. Bandhavgarh has an excellent tree and foliage concentration. About half the Bandhavgarh park is covered with fine trees of Sal, while mixed forests are found in the higher reaches of the hills.

It is only in the slightly higher lands that it changes to a more mixed vegetation of sali, saj, saja, dhobin etc. Stretches of bamboo and grasslands extend to the north. The main wildlife viewing is still done in the core of the park with its 32 picturesque, wooded hills.

Bandhavgarh National Park

Bandhavgarh National Park

The Fauna in the Bandhavgarh National Park

The density of it's big cat population has made Bandhavgarh famous across the globe. Bandhavgarh is blessed with a large variety of natives in terms of animals. It is possible to sight tigers, leopards, gaur (Indian Bison-although some say this is no longer seen), chital (spotted deer), Sambar deer, Dholes,nilgais, wild boars, chinkaras, sloth bears, rhesus macaques, chital, black faced langurs, jungle cats, hyenas, porcupines, jackals, foxes, wild dogs, chausinghas and ratels, among others.

The Avi-fauna in the Bandhavgarh National Park

Despite being famous for it's four legged inhabitants, Bandhavgarh National Park is also a bird lover's paradise.

Keep a look out for white browed fantails, steppe eagles, green pigeons, white rumped shama, grey malabar hornbills, black and white malabar hornbills (quite a rare sighting), blossom headed parakeets, parakeets, blue bearded bee eaters, green bee eaters, white bellied drongos, owls, Jerdon's and gold fronted leaf birds, minivets, woodshrikes and the lovely paradise flycatchers.

SAFARIS IN THE BANDHAVGARH NATIONAL PARK

Jeep & Elephant Safari

One can enjoy exploring the wildlife in Bandhavgarh by two ways - Jeep Safari and Elephant Safari. Jeep safaris are undertaken during the early morning hours till evening. A forest department guide is always their with the visitors on these jeep trips taken inside the park. Elephant safari trips are organised for tiger tracking early in the morning.

Bandhavgarh National Park Travel Circuit

Khajuraho - Bandhavgarh - Kanha - Nagpur

How to Reach the Bandhavgarh National Park

Air : Khajurao at 230 km is the most convenient airport connected to the park by various domestic airline services with Agra, Delhi, Varanasi.

Rail : The nearest railhead Umaria at 30 km is on the Katni-Bilaspur section of South-Eastern Railway. Another convenient railhead Satna (117 km) is on the Bombay-Howrah main line of the Central Railway.

Road : Bandhavgarh National Park is situated on the Satna-Umaria & Rewa-Umaria highway. Madhya Pradesh State Transport Bus Services are also available from Rewa, Satna, Katni and Umaria.

Chinnar Wildlife Sanctuary, Kerala

After the Periyar National Park, Chinnar Wildlife Sanctuary is one of the largest wildlife sanctuaries in Kerala. This sanctuary is located on the Western Ghats and shares its border with Tamil Nadu on the Annamalai Hills. Among the 34 species of mammals found in this sanctuary, Panthers, Spotted Deer, Indian Elephant, Tiger and Nilgiri Tahr are the most spectacular.

It is also the dwelling of Mugger Crocodiles and more than 240 species of exotic birds. The presence of Thoovanam Waterfalls within the forests has made this sanctuary, one of the popular trekking and camping destinations in Kerala.

HISTORY OF CHINNAR WILDLIFE SANCTUARY

Chinnar Wildlife Sanctuary, (CWS), is located 18 km north of Marayoor on SH 17 in the Marayoor and Kanthalloor Panchayats of Devikulam Taluk in the Idukki district of Kerala state in South India. It is one of twelve Wildlife Sanctuaries among the Protected areas of Kerala.

It is under the jurisdiction of and contiguous with Eravikulam National Park to the south. Indira Gandhi Wildlife Sanctuary is to the north and Kodaikanal Wildlife Sanctuary is to the east. It forms an integral part of the 1,187 km² (458 sq mi) block of protected forests straddling the Kerala-Tamil Nadu border in the Annamalai Hills. The Western Ghats, Anamalai Sub-Cluster, including all of Chinnar Wildlife Sanctuary, is under consideration by the UNESCO World Heritage Committee for selection as a World Heritage Site.

Geography

CWS is located between latitude 10°15' - 10°21' N and Longitude 77°5' - 77°16' E. The Munnar – Udumalpet road SH 17passes through the Sanctuary for 16 km and divides it into nearly equal portions. Average annual rainfall is only 500 mm, spread over about 48 days, because it is in the rain shadow region of the southern Western Ghats.

The altitude ranges from 400 meters (1,300 ft) at east end of the Chinnar River to 2,522 meters (8,274 ft) at Kumarikal Malai peak. Other major peaks in the sanctuary are Nandala Malai 2,372 meters (7,782 ft), Kottakombu malai (2,144 meters (7,034 ft)), Vellaikal malai (1,863 meters (6,112 ft)) and Viriyoottu malai 1,845 meters (6,053 ft). In contrast, Anamudi peak 2,695 metres (8,842 ft), located 23 kilometers (14 mi) away in the adjacent Eravikulam National Park, is the highest peak in South India.

The Chinnar River and Pambar rivers are the major perennial water resources in the sanctuary. The Chinnar originates near Kumarikal Malai, follows the interstate boundary along the northwest edge of the sanctuary for 18 km and becomes theAmaravati River in Tamil Nadu.

The Pambar River originates in the Anaimudi Hills and is joined by seasonal rivulets and a few perennial streams originating fromsholas in the upper reaches. It traverses the Turner's Valley in Eravikulam National Park and flows down into the Sanctuary through the Taliar Valley between Kanthalloor and Marayoor Villages and eastwards through the sanctuary. It joins the Chinnar river at Koottar. The spectacular Thoovanam water falls lie deep within the Sanctuary on the Pambar River. This breathtaking cascade is a major tourist attraction. The Chinnar, Pambar, Kabani and Bhavani are the only rivers of the 44 in Kerala that flow eastwards.

Settlements and crops

There are 11 tribal settlements inside the Chinnar WLS, each is well demarcated by temporary stone walls. The main inhabitants are Muthuvas and Pulayars. Cultivation of maize, ragi and lemongrass is practiced in the settlements. The Mudhuvas carry out small scale ganja cultivation for their religious purposes.

FAUNA

34 species of Mammals live here, including many Panthers and Spotted deer, 50 -60 Indian Elephants, Gaur, Tigers, Sambar Deer,Common langur, Bonnet Macaque, Hanuman monkey, threatened Nilgiri Tahr, vulnerable Rusty-spotted Cats and about 240 of the onlyvulnerable Grizzled Giant Squirrels in Kerala. 245 species of birds including Yellow-throated Bulbuls. 52 species of reptiles including 29 species of snakes, Indian Star Tortoise and the largest population of vulnerable Mugger Crocodiles in Kerala live in the Sanctuary. Most common of the 42 species of fishes observed in the Chinnar and Pambar rivers are Garra mullya minnows, River-carp baril, Giant Danio and the endangered hill stream game fish Deccan Mahseer. 22 amphibian species live in the Sanctuary. There are 156 species ofbutterflies.

The Chinnar forests support a diverse variety of mammals, reptiles, birds and butterflies. The star among them is the Grizzled Giant Squirrel, a large tree squirrel. In Kerala, the Grizzled Giant Squirrel is found only in the riparian forest of the Chinnar Sanctuary. The rare Manjampatti White Bison, a gaur noted for its distinctive ash-grey color, is another special inhabitant spotted in the sanctuary.

Other important mammals found are the rare Rusty Spotted Cat, Nilgiri Tahr, Elephant, Tiger, Leopard, Gaur, Wild Boar, Sambar, Spotted Deer, Barking Deer, Porcupine, Wild Dog, Common Langur, Bonnet Macaque, Jackal, Sloth Bear, Nilgiri Langur, Jungle Cat, Bison, Spotted Deer and Sambar.

Leopards also live in the sanctuary but don't assume that the tiger is an inhabitant of the sanctuary if you spot some. They are visitors from the neighboring forests. Bonnet Macaques, Elephants and Gaur are also present. White Bison has been recently sighted in the Chinnar plains. 28 species of mammals have been found in the sanctuary.

Chinnar Sanctuary is home to a wide variety of wildlife. Over 34 species of Mammals including Panthers, Elephants, Gaur, Bonnet Macaque, Spotted deer, Sambar, Common langur, Giant grizzled squirrel, Hanuman monkey, Blacknaped hare, Slender loris, Nilgiri Tahr, Porcupine, Rusty-spotted Cats, Rabbit and about 240 Grizzled Giant Squirrels are the commonly found animals in Chinnar Sanctuary.

Staying overnight at Vasyappara in the tribal huts is best to see Elephants, Peacocks, Langur, Deer and the Giant squirrel.

Till now, about 225 species of birds have been listed in different parts of Chinnar Sanctuary. Some globally threatened and endemic species like the Yellow-throated bulbul and the Nilgiri pipit are also found here.

Report says that this is the only place in Kerala where the Yellow-throated bulbul is found. The other avian fauna such as Rock bush quail , Plum-headed parakeet, Yellow-fronted pied woodpecker, Small green-billed malkoha etc inhabit the Chinnar forests.

The sanctuary also boasts a large reptilian diversity which includes 29 species of snakes, Indian Star Tortoise and the largest population of vulnerable Mugger Crocodiles.

Sighting of crocodiles is possible during the day along the riverside. Most common of the 42 species of fishes observed in the Chinnar are Garra mullya minnows, River-carp baril,Giant Danio, the endangered hill stream game fish Deccan Mahseer and Tor remadevi, a Mahaseer species. 22 amphibian species as well as a large variety of insects and 156 species of butterflies are reported from the sanctuary.

The forest department does not run any safaris inside the Chinnar Sanctuary but they conducts Ecotourism facilities which includes River trekking, trekking to the cultural site, Nature trail to the watch tower., Trek to Thoovanam falls, Interpretation activities and medicinal Garden, Tree house at Chinnar, Machans at Koottar,Karakkad and Champakkad, Trekking and camping at Vasyappara. For trekking bookings contact Eravikulam wildlife warden at the checkpost.

Entry Fee : Indians Rs. 10/-, Foreigners Rs.100/-, Children below 12 years and bonafied students on tour Rs. 5/- .

Video & Movie Camera : Rs. 150/- , Still Camera : Rs. 25/-;

Vehicles : Heavy vehicles Rs. 150/-, Light vehicles Rs. 50/-, Others - Rs. 20/-

Nearest to this park are Eravikulam National Park and Indira Gandhi Wildlife Sanctuary.

How to Reach Chinnar Wildlife Sanctuary:

By Road: Road journeys are considered as the best ways to reach Chinnar Wildlife Sanctuary. The wildlife sanctuary is well-connected to most of the major parts of Kerala, and can be easily reached from popular Kerala tourist destinations like Munnar, Cochin, Ernakulam, and others.

By Train: Pollachi and Alluva railway stations are the nearest railway stations to reach Chinnar Wildlife Sanctuary. While the former is only 60km away from the sanctuary, the latter is around 200km away.

By Air: Coimbatore Airport; at a distance of 115km, and Kochi Airport at a distance of 208km are the two nearest airports to reach Chinnar Wildlife Sanctuary.

Best Time to Visit Chinnar Wildlife Sanctuary:

Chinnar Wildlife Sanctuary enjoys inland climatic conditions; mainly hot and dry. Owing to this, summers are not advisable for a trip to this wildlife park in Kerala. If you are planning for a Kerala trip, you should visit this national park during the winters; November to February.

Safari Timings in Chinnar Wildlife Sanctuary:

Visitors can get into the Chinnar Wildlife Sanctuary by paying minimal fees of INR 100 per head for a day. For students and children below 12 years, the entry fee is INR 10.In order to visit the Chinnar Wildlife Sanctuary, visitors must take official permissions from the Idukki Wildlife Division. Visitors can enjoy Elephant Safari and Hunter Jeep Safaris every day between 06:00AM to 06:00PM.

FLORA

There are 965 species of flowering plants in the sanctuary Ecoregions of the sanctuary comprise mostly grassland and wet grasslands vegetation and some South Western Ghats montane rain forests and high shola at the higher western elevations.

South Western Ghats moist deciduous forestss at mid elevations give way to dry deciduous forests and thorny scrub forests in the lower dryer eastern edges of the valley. The major Xerophyticspecies in the throny scrub forests are Acacia arabica, Acacia leucofolia, Acacia concinna, Prosporis juliflora, and Opuntia stricta.

The Marayoor Sandalwood forest is located here.,

Major attractions include:

Grizzled Giant Squirrel: The riverine forests along with Chinnar and Pambar support a large number of highly endangered Grizzled Giant Squirrels. The sanctuary plays host to the second largest population of Grizzled Giant Squirrels in the world.

Thoovanam Waterfalls: Deep within the sanctuary, the spectacular Thoovanam waterfall is located. The river Pambar flows eastwards through the sanctuary and plummets down from a great height on the river Chinnar. Wildlife Department permit tourists to visit the falls as part of wildlife tourism.

Watch Tower: Standing on the lofty watchtower, one can have a panoramic view of the entire park and the wildlife beauties, adjoining jungles in the neighbouring state of Tamil Nadu and also the magnificent mountains far away.

Things to DO

Tourists can enjoy the natural walk along the Chinnar and Pamber river banks. They can also find the grizzled giant squirrel. This is an amazing place for the trekkers also. They can enjoy the scenic beauty of the nature by moving towards Thooyanam Waterfalls. Tourists can enjoy camping here.

Regional Cooperation

Contiguous protected areas like Chinnar Wildlife Sanctuary and Indira Gandhi Wildlife Sanctuary will benefit from Regional cooperation. Senior officials of the Ministry of Environment and Forests (India), Principal Chief Conservators of Forests of Kerala, Tamil Nadu, Andhra Pradesh and Karnataka, together with other senior forest officials of these states and the Union Territory of Pondicherry, met at Thiruvananthapuram on November 3 and 4, 2006 and resolved several mutual issues concerning conservation and protection of forests and wildlife of the region.

This formalization of interstate cooperation on protected areas administration will improve effectiveness in the areas of daily staff communication including common wireless frequencies, joint enforcement action, boundary survey and demarcation, management of cross border resources like Biosphere Reserves, National Parks, Tiger reserves and Wildlife Sanctuaries, technology, staff and intelligence sharing and coordinated communication with the Govt. of India. A regular conference of the Forest Ministers and forest officials of the southern states are held once a year, in rotation in each State.

Visitor information

Eco-tourism is promoted and organized jointly by the Forest Department and the Eco Development Committees (EDCs) of the local tribal communities, the objective is to empower latter and involve them in the conservation of the forest ecosystem.

Trek paths most commonly used are the Chinnar – Chullipetty and Chinnar – Koottar. Trekking to the Dolmens, the megalithic burial sites of tribal communities in Alampatti, can be arranged. Daytime sighting of crocodiles and boars is possible while hiking along the riverside. The trail will also take you to the enchanting Thoovanam falls and to the watchtower in Jellimalai.

The lofty Chinnar Watch Tower has a panoramic view of the entire sanctuary, and beyond to the jungles of Tamil Nadu to the east and the majestic hills of the Western Ghats in all directions. The watch tower is accessible to the public with the permission of the forest department. The watchtower is a 20-minute walk from the Chinnar check post. A fee of Rs. 15 per person is collected at the tower. A Forest guard and tourist guide accompanies visitors. The guide charges Rs. 100 a day.

Accommodations are available in three suites at the Forest guesthouse for Rs. 400 per room without food. Treetop machans, arranged by the Forest Department, cost Rs. 1,000 for an overnight stay for two. Camping overnight in tribal huts at Vasyappara gives opportunities to sight elephants, peacocks, langur, deer and the giant squirrel. Camping at the Vasyappara huts cost Rs. 2,000 (including dinner, night stay and breakfast). The Forest Department also arranges accommodation at log houses in Churlipatti. Dormitory facilities are also available at Chinnar. However visitiors must be warned that there are no means of buying anything to eat or drink at chinnar except the odd pack of milk biscuits and a few bottles of water.

5

Corbett National Park, Uttarakhand

Among all the national parks in India, the Corbett National Park is the oldest and one of the best among the top 10 national parks in India. It was established in 1936 to protect the imposing Bengal Tigers. Located at the foothills of the Himalayan range of Uttarakhand, Corbett National Park is one of the hot spots of the wildlife lovers.

This park has been named after the popular wildlife story writer Jim Corbett. Beauty and wilderness of this park attracts enthusiasts from various parts of the globe. This wildlife tourist destination of India has also been featured in many wildlife documentaries in order to raise the awareness towards the mighty and stunning Bengal Tigers.

ABOUT JIM CORBETT NATIONAL PARK

Jim Corbett National Park is the oldest national park in India and was established in 1936 as Hailey National Park to protect the endangered Bengal tiger. It is located in Nainital district of Uttarakhand and was named after Jim Corbett who played a key role in its establishment. The park was the first to come under the Project Tiger initiative.

The park has sub-Himalayan belt geographical and ecological characteristics. An ecotourism destination, it contains 488 different species of plants and a diverse variety of fauna. The increase in tourist activities, among other problems, continues to present a serious challenge to the park's ecological balance.

Corbett has been a haunt for tourists and wildlife lovers for a long time. Tourism activity is only allowed in selected areas of Corbett Tiger Reserve so that people get an opportunity to see its splendid landscape and the diverse wildlife. In recent years the number of people coming here has increased dramatically. Presently, every season more than 70,000 visitors come to the park from India and other countries.

Corbett National Park comprises 520.8 km^2 (201.1 sq mi) area of hills, riverine belts, marshy depressions, grasslands and a large lake. The elevation ranges from 1,300 to 4,000 ft (400 to 1,220 m). Winter nights are cold but the days are bright and sunny. It rains from July to September.

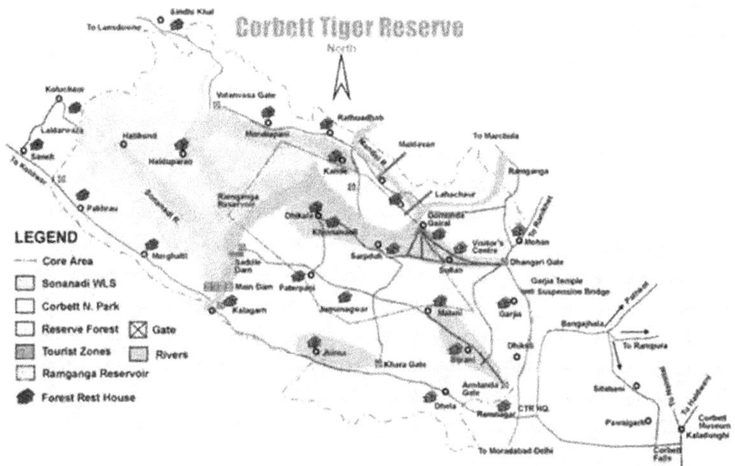

Dense moist deciduous forest mainly consists of sal, haldu, peepal, rohini and mango trees. Forest covers almost 73% of the park, 10% of the area consists of grasslands. It houses around 110 tree species, 50 species of mammals, 580 bird species and 25 reptile species.

HISTORY

Some areas of the park were formerly part of the princely state of Tehri Garhwal. The forests were cleared to make the area less vulnerable to Rohilla invaders. The Raja of Tehri formally ceded a part of his princely state to the East India Company in return for their assistance in ousting the Gurkhas from his domain. The Boksas—a tribe from the Terai—settled on the land and began growing crops, but in the early 1860s they were evicted with the advent of British rule.

Efforts to save the forests of the region began in the 19th century under Major Ramsay, the British Officer who was in-charge of the area during those times. The first step in the protection of the area began in 1868 when the British forest department established control over the land and prohibited cultivation and the operation of cattle stations. In 1879 these forests were constituted into a Reserve Forest where restricted felling was permitted.

In the early 1900s several Britishers, including E. R. Stevans and E. A. Smythies, suggested the idea of setting up of a national park on this soil. The British administration considered the possibility of creating a game reserve there in 1907. It was only in the 1930s that the process for demarcation of such an area got underway, assisted by Jim Corbett, who knew the area well. A reserve area known as *Hailey National Park* covering 323.75 km^2 (125.00 sq mi) was created in 1936 when Sir Malcolm Hailey was Governor of United Provinces, and Asia's first national park came into existence. Hunting was not allowed in the reserve, but only timber cutting for domestic purposes. Soon after the establishment of the reserve, rules prohibiting killing and capturing of mammals, reptiles and birds within its boundaries were passed.

Indian Monitor lizards have long necks, powerful tails and claws, and well-developed limbs

The reserve was renamed in 1954–55 as *Ramganga National Park* and was again renamed in 1955–56 as *Corbett National Park*. The new name honours the well-known author and wildlife conservationist Jim Corbett, who played a key role in creating the reserve by using his influence to persuade the provincial government to establish it.

Tiger Cub - JCTR, the cub of very famous tigress 'Paarwali' - the local guides and drivers give the names to the tigers.

The park fared well during the 1930s under an elected administration. But during the Second World War, it suffered from excessive poaching and timber cutting. Over time the area in the reserve was increased—797.72 km^2 (308.00 sq mi) were added in 1991 as a buffer for the Corbett Tiger Reserve. The 1991 additions included the entire Kalagarh forest division, assimilating the 301.18 km^2 (116.29 sq mi) area of Sonanadi Wildlife Sanctuary as a part of the Kalagarh division. It was chosen in 1974 as the location for launching Project Tiger, an ambitious and well known wildlife conservation project. The reserve is administered from its headquarters in the district of Nainital.

Corbett National Park is one of the thirteen protected areas covered by World Wildlife Fund under their Terai Arc Landscape Programme. The programme aims to protect three of the five terrestrial flagship species, the tiger, the Asian elephant and the Great One-horned Rhinoceros, by restoring corridors of forest to link 13 protected areas ofNepal and India to enable wildlife migration.

GEOGRAPHY

The park is located between 29°25' to 29°39'N latitude and 78°44' to 79°07'E longitude. The average altitude of the region ranges between 360 m (1,181 ft) and 1,040 m (3,412 ft). It has numerous ravines, ridges, minor streams and small plateaus with varying aspects and degrees of slopes. The park encompasses the *Patli Dun* valleyformed by the Ramganga river. It protects parts of the Upper Gangetic Plains moist deciduous forests and Himalayan subtropical pine forests ecoregions. It has a humid subtropical and highland climate.

Banks of the Ramganga reservoir in the Dhikala grasslands of Corbett Tiger Reserve.

The present area of the Reserve is 1,318.54 square kilometres (509.09 sq mi) including 520 square kilometres (200 sq mi) of core area and 797.72 square kilometres (308.00 sq mi) of buffer area. The core area forms the Jim Corbett National Park while the buffer contains reserve forests (496.54 square kilometres (191.72 sq mi)) as well as the Sonanadi Wildlife Sanctuary (301.18 square kilometres (116.29 sq mi)).

The reserve, located partly along a valley between the Lesser Himalaya in the north and the Shivaliks in the south, has a sub-Himalayan belt structure. The upper tertiary rocks are exposed towards the base of the Shiwalik range and hard sandstone units form broad ridges. Characteristic longitudinal valleys, geographically termed *Doons,* or *Duns* can be seen formed along the narrow tectonic zones between lineaments.

CLIMATE

The weather in the park is temperate compared to most other protected areas of India. The temperature may vary from 5 °C (41 °F) to 30 °C (86 °F) during the winter and some mornings are foggy. Summer temperatures normally do not rise above 40 °C (104 °F).

Rainfall ranges from light during the dry season to heavy during the monsoons.

FLORA

Dense forest inside the park

A total of 488 different species of plants have been recorded in the park. Tree density inside the reserve is higher in the areas of *Sal* forests and lowest in the *Anogeissus-Acacia catechu* forests. Total tree basal cover is greater in Sal dominated areas of woody vegetation. Healthy regeneration in sapling and seedling layers is occurring in the *Mallotus philippensis, Jamun* and *Diospyros tomentosa* communities, but in the Sal forests the regeneration of sapling and seedling is poor.

FAUNA

More than 586 species of resident and migratory birds have been categorised, including the crested serpent eagle, blossom-headed parakeet and the red junglefowl — ancestor of all domestic fowl. 33 species of reptiles, seven species of amphibians, seven species of fish and 36 species of dragonflies have also been recorded.

Friendly tussle of tuskers at Dhikala grassland

Bengal tigers, although plentiful, are not easily spotted due to the abundance of camouflage in the reserve. Thick jungle, the Ramganga river, and plentiful prey make this reserve an ideal habitat for tigers who are opportunistic feeders and prey upon a range of animals. The tigers in the park have been known to kill much larger animals such as buffalo and even elephant for food. The tigers prey upon the larger animals in rare cases of food shortage. There have been incidents of tigers attacking domestic animals in times when they are in a shortage of prey.

Leopards are found in hilly areas but may also venture into the low land jungles. Small cats in the park include the jungle cat, fishing catand leopard cat. Other mammals include barking deer, sambar deer, hog deer and chital, Sloth and Himalayan black bears, Indian grey mongoose, otters, yellow-throated martens,

Himalayan goral, Indian pangolins, and langur and Rhesus macaques. Owls and Nightjars can be heard during the night.

In the summer, Indian elephants can be seen in herds of several hundred. The Indian python found in the reserve is a dangerous species, capable of killing a chital deer. Local crocodiles and gharials were saved from extinction by captive breeding programs that subsequently released crocodiles into the Ramganga river.

ECOTOURISM

Young Indian elephant bull charging a jeep

Though the main focus is protection of wildlife, the reserve management has also encouraged ecotourism. In 1993, a training course covering natural history, visitor management and park interpretation was introduced to train nature guides. A second course followed in 1995 which recruited more guides for the same purpose. This allowed the staff of the reserve, previously preoccupied with guiding the visitors, to carry out management activities uninterrupted. Additionally, the Indian government has organised workshops on ecotourism in Corbett National Park and Garhwal region to ensure that the local citizens profit from tourism while the park remains protected.

Patil & Joshi (1997) consider summer (April–June) to be the best season for Indian tourists to visit the park while recommending the winter months (November–January) for foreign tourists. According to Riley & Riley (2005): "Best chances of seeing a tiger to come late in the dry season- April to mid June-and go out with mahouts and elephants for several days."

As early as 1991, the Corbett National Park played host to 3237 tourist vehicles carrying 45,215 visitors during the main tourist seasons between 15 November and 15 June. This heavy influx of tourists has led to visible stress signs on the natural ecosystem. Excessive trampling of soil due to tourist pressure has led to reduction in plant species and has also resulted in reduced soil moisture. The tourists have increasingly used fuel wood for cooking. This is a cause of concern as this fuel wood is obtained from the nearby forests, resulting in greater pressure on the forest ecosystem of the park. Additionally, tourists have also caused problems by making noise, littering and causing disturbances in general. In 2007, young naturalist and photographer – Kahini Ghosh Mehta – took up the challenge of promoting healthy tourism in Corbett National Park and made the first comprehensive travel guide on Corbett. The film titled – Wild Saga of Corbett – showcases how tourists can contribute in their own small way in conservation efforts. The film is loaded with all information needed by a tourist before planning a visit to the park along with tips from senior park officials, nature guides and naturalists. Tourists can get a DVD copy of this film from the Bombay Natural History Society (BNHS).

OTHER ATTRACTIONS

- Dhikuli is a well-known destination in the park and situated at the fringes of Patli Dun valley. There is a rest house, which was built hundred of years ago. Kanda ridge forms the backdrop, and from Dhikala, one can enjoy the spectacular natural beauty of the valley.
- Jeep Safari is the most convenient way to travel within the national park; jeeps can be rented for park trips from Ramnagar.
- Treks: tourists are not allowed to walk inside the park, but only to go trekking around the park in the company of a guide. The winter season is cold, so tourists should make proper arrangements for their clothing, if they are travelling in the winter season.
- Kalagarh Dam is dam located in the south-west of the wildlife sanctuary. This is one of the best places for a bird watching tour. Lots of migratory waterfowl comes here in the winters.
- Corbett Falls is a 20 m (66 ft) water fall situated 25 km (16 mi) from Ramnagar, and 4 km (2.5 mi) from Kaladhungi, on the Kaladhungi–Ramnagar highway. The water falls is surrounded by dense forests and pin drop silence.

Location

Corbett National Park is situated in Ramanagar in the district of Nainital, Uttarakhand.

Area: 521 km^2.

Route: The town of Ramnagar is the headquarters of Corbett Tiger Reserve.

There are overnight trains available from Delhi to Ramnagar. Also, there are trains from Varanasi via Lucknow and Allahabad via Kanpur to Ramnagar. Reaching Ramnagar, one can hire a taxi to reach the park and Dhikala.

Ramnagar is also well connected by road with Kanpur, Lucknow, Bareilly, Nainital, Ranikhet, Haridwar, Dehradun and New Delhi.

One can also drive from Delhi (295 km) via Gajraula, Moradabad, Kashipur to reach Ramnagar. A direct train to Ramnagar runs from New Delhi. Alternatively, one can come up to Haldwani/Kashipur/Kathgodam and come to Ramnagar by road.

Best Time to Visit: Mid-November to Mid-June.

Challenges

Past

A major incident in the history of the reserve followed the construction of a dam at the Kalagarh river and the submerging of 80 km^2(31 sq mi) of prime low lying riverine area.

The consequences ranged from local extinction of swamp deer to a massive reduction in hog deer population. The reservoir formed due to the submerging of land has also led to an increase in aquatic fauna and has additionally served as a habitat for winter migrants.

Two villages situated on the southern boundary were shifted to the Firozpur–Manpur area situated on Ramnagar–Kashipur highway during 1990–93; the vacated areas were designated as buffer zones. The families in these villages were mostly dependent on forest products. With the passage of time, these areas began to show signs of ecological recovery. Vines, herbs, grasses and small trees began to appear, followed by herbaceous flora, eventually leading to natural forest type. It was observed that grass began to grow on the vacated agricultural fields and the adjoining forest areas started recuperating. By 1999–2002 several plant species emerged in these buffer zones. The newly arisen lush green fields attracted grass eating animals, mainly deer and elephants, who slowly migrated towards these areas and even preferred to stay there throughout the monsoon.

There were 109 cases of poaching recorded in 1988–89. This figure dropped to 12 reported cases in 1997–98. In 1985 David Hunt, a British ornithologist and birdwatching tour guide, was killed by a tiger in the park.

Present

The habitat of the reserve faces threats from invasive species such as the exotic weeds *Lantana, Parthenium* and *Cassia.* Natural resources like trees and grasses are exploited by the local population while encroachment of at least of 13.62 ha (0.05 sq mi) by 74 families has been recorded.

The villages surrounding the park are at least 15–20 years old and no new villages have come up in the recent past. The increasing population growth rate and the density of population within 1 km (0.62 mi) to 2 km (1.24 mi) from the park present a challenge to the management of the reserve.

Incidents of killing cattle by tigers and leopards have led to acts of retaliation by the local population in some cases. The Indian government has approved the construction of a 12 km (7.5 mi) stone masonry wall on the southern boundary of the reserve where it comes in direct contact with agricultural fields.

In April 2008, the National Conservation Tiger Authority (NCTA) expressed serious concern that protection systems have weakened, and poachers have infiltrated into this park.

Monitoring of wild animals in the prescribed format has not been followed despite advisories and observations made during field visits. Also the monthly monitoring report of field evidence relating to tigers has not been received since 2006. NCTA said that in the "absence of ongoing monitoring protocol in a standardised manner, it would be impossible to forecast and keep track of untoward happenings in the area targeted by poachers."

A cement road has been built through the park against a Supreme Court order. The road has become a thoroughfare between Kalagarh and Ramnagar.

Constantly increasing vehicle traffic on this road is affecting the wildlife of crucial ranges like Jhirna, Kotirau and Dhara. Additionally, the Kalagarh irrigation colony that takes up about 5 square kilometres (1.9 sq mi) of the park is yet to be vacated despite a 2007 Supreme Court order.

HOW TO REACH CORBETT NATIONAL PARK

The Corbett National Park, an oldest national park of India, is the prime wildlife destination for the wildlife loving as well as nature loving tourists from all over the world. The park is located in the Ramnagar, a city of Uttrakhand state of India, around 260 km from New Delhi. Being in the proximity of the National Capital City of India, the park is easily accessible through the Railway and Roadway routes. Here, you will find the detailed information on how to reach Corbett National Park-

The best road route from Delhi to Corbett

The Roadway is the best option to commute from Delhi to Corbett as the road trip has its own allure, especially, in the pleasant weather. The Delhi to Corbett road distance is around 245 km and 6 hours of drive. You can either travel in your private vehicle or take the car/ tempo traveler/ Bus service which is easily available from Delhi. Below is the detailed Road route to reach Corbett-

Delhi - Gajrola - Moradabad - Kashipur - Ramnagar (around 245 km)

Whether you are traveling by your private vehicle or by the hired vehicle, this is the easiest and shortest road route to reach Corbett from Delhi. Start your journey from Delhi and by crossing the Ghaziabad or Noida road, hit the NH24 to drive towards Hapur.

Crossing the Hapur, Gajrola and Garhmukeshwar you will reach Moradabad. Here, at Moradabad, do not enter into the city instead take the right turn to Muradabad bypass road and crossing the Thakurdwara and then Kashipur you will finally reach the Ramnagar

From Ramnagar, you can either directly reach the entry gate of the Corbett Park or visit at your pre-booked hotel or resort to stay. The whole distance will be around 245 km which will take nearly 6 hours to cover. The roads are in decent conditions except for the little stretch of state road near Ramnagar.

Here are the few other road routes which you can prefer to take if you are visiting the Corbett Park from places other than Delhi-

If you are starting your journey from Bareilly or nearby places, then choose the following route- Bareilly - Kichha - Haldwani - Ramnagar (around 160 km)

If you are visiting Corbett from Nainital then hit the route below- Nainital - Ramnagar (Via Kaladhungi) (62 Km).

For Lucknow to Corbett road trip, go for the given route- Lucknow - Bareilly - Kicha - Rudrapur - Kashipur - Ramnagar (435 km)

By Rail: Delhi To Ramnagar

The nearest railway station from Corbett is Ramnagar which is around 12 km from the park and the station is directly connected to the railway stations in Delhi. A direct train named Ranikhet Express runs from Delhi to Ramnagar which is the best train to reach Corbett from Delhi. You can catch the Ranikhet express at 10:50 pm at Delhi to reach Ramnagar at 04:35 am next day, and again return by catching the same train at Ramnagar at 09:05 pm to reach Delhi at 05:00 am next day. The train operates on a daily basis. However, Ramnagar station is the best option to reach Corbett but alternatively, you can also arrive at the Kathgodam station and visit Ramnagar by taxi or cab which will take around 3 and half hours by road.

6

Dudhwa National Park, Uttar Pradesh

The Dudhwa National Park, a part of Dudhwa Tiger Reserve, is situated in Uttar Pradesh. History of this park lies back into 1958, when it was declared as a wildlife sanctuary for Swamp Deer. Later, in 1978, it was declared as a Tiger Reserve due to its large number of tigers.

HISTORY OF DUDHWA NATIONAL PARK

The Dudhwa National Park is a national park in the Terai of Uttar Pradesh, India, and covers an area of 490.3 km²(189.3 sq mi), with a buffer zone of 190 km² (73 sq mi). It is part of the Dudhwa Tiger Reserve. It is located on the Indo-Nepalborder in the Lakhimpur Kheri District, and has buffer of reserved forest areas on the northern and southern sides. It represents one of the few remaining examples of a highly diverse and productive Terai ecosystem, supporting a large number of endangered species, obligate species of tall wet grasslands and species of restricted distribution.

History

The area was established in 1958 as a wildlife sanctuary for Swamp deer. Thanks to the efforts of 'Billy' Arjan Singh the area was notified as a national park in January 1977. In 1987, the park was declared a Tiger Reserve and brought under the purview of the 'Project Tiger'. Together with the Kishanpur Wildlife Sanctuary and the Katarniaghat Wildlife Sanctuary it forms the Dudhwa Tiger Reserve.

The Post-Independence era witnessed tremendous encroachment towards the Dudhwa jungle. As a result the forest was converted in an agricultural land. Additionally, due to its location on the Indo-Nepal border the chances of poaching and hunting enhanced to greater extent and the trading of the wild animals increased to a massive extent who sell their products in Nepal, which being a tourist place gives them a huge market for these things. It was the perfect money-making place for the poachers but it was "Billy" Arjan Singh whose single handed efforts made this park to reach at its richness. The great conservationist initiated an idea of converting this land into a wildlife sanctuary in the year 1965 and thus received a lot of appraisal from the wildlife conservationists and wildlife lovers across the world. In 1977, Arjan Singh approached the erstwhile prime minister, Indira Gandhi to declare the forest as a National park. In 1984-85, seven rhinos were relocated from Assam and Nepal to Dudhwa to rehabilitate a rhino population which lived here 150 years ago. Four years later, it was declared a Tiger Reserve under the Project Tiger and currently is a major habitat for tigers in India.

Deer in Dudhwa

Climate

Like most of northern India, Dudhwa has an extreme Humid Subtropical with dry winter (CWa) type of climate. Summers are hot with temperatures rising up to 40 °C (104 °F). During winters from mid-October to mid-March, temperatures hover between 20 and 30 °C (68 and 86 °F). The months of February to April are ideal for visiting the park.

Prevalent winds are westerly. The hot wind Loo blows strongly from mid-April up to end of May. Monsoon starting in mid-June and lasting up to September accounts for 90% of the annual rainfall of 150 cm (59 in). Temperatures range from between a minimum of9 °C (48 °F) in winter to a maximum of up to 45 °C (113 °F) in peak summer.

Habitat

The area of the park falls within the Upper Gangetic plains and is a vast alluvial plain ranging in altitude from 150 m (490 ft) in the farthest southeast to 182 metres (597 ft) in the extreme north.

The park's mosaic of high forest interspersed with grasslands is characteristic of the Terai ecosystems in India and the area is, probably, the last prominent remnant of this type of ecosystem. The forests, especially the sal forests, have always been very dense and can be categorized into Northerntropical semi-evergreen forest, Northern Indian moist deciduous forest, tropical seasonal swamp forest and Northern tropicaldry deciduous forest.

The main flora comprises sal, asna, shisham, jamun, gular, sehore and bahera. The grasslands comprise about 19% of the park. The wetlands constitute the third major habitat type and include the rivers, streams, lakes and marshes. While many of the major wetlands are perennial with some amount of surface moisture retained round the year, some dry up during hot summer.

The park is home to one of the finest forests in India, some of these trees are more than 150 years old and over 70 ft (21 m) tall.

Fauna

Major attractions of Dudhwa National Park are the tigers (population 98 in 1995) and Swamp Deer (population over 1,600). Billy Arjan Singh successfully hand-reared and reintroduced zoo-born tigers and leopards into the wilds of Dudhwa. Some rare species inhabit the park. Hispid hare, earlier thought to have become extinct, was rediscovered here in 1984.

In the mid 1980s, Indian rhinoceros was reintroduced into Dudhwa from Assam and Nepal.

The other animals to be seen here include Swamp deer, Sambar deer, barking deer, spotted deer, hog deer, tiger, Indian rhinoceros, sloth bear, ratel, jackal, civets, jungle cat,fishing cat, leopard cat.

Dudhwa National Park is a stronghold of the barasingha. Around half of the world's barasinghas are present in Dudhwa National Park. Smaller than the sambar deer, the barasinghas have 12 antlers that collectively measure up to 100 cm (39 in). One can spot herd of these rare animals passing through open grasslands. Around half of the surviving population of Barasinghas is found in the park. These animals are smaller than sambar deer and weigh around 180 kg. Due to their slightly woolly, dark brown to pale yellow cloak, the grasslands acts as the perfect camouflage.

Birds

The park has a rich bird life, with over 350 species, including the Swamp Francolin, Great Slaty Woodpecker and Bengal Florican. Dudhwa also boasts a range of migratory birdsthat settle here during winters. It includes among others, painted storks, black and white necked storks, Sarus Cranes, woodpeckers, barbets, kingfishers, minivets, bee-eaters,bulbuls and varied night birds of prey.

Drongos, Barbets, Cormorants, Ducks, Geese, Hornbills, Bulbuls, Teal, Woodpeckers, Heron, Bee Eaters, Minivets, Kingfishers, Egrets, Orioles, plenty of painted storks, sarus cranes, owls and more. One can also spot rare species like the Bengal florican.

Dudhwa's birds in particular are a delight for any avid bird watcher. The marshlands are habitat for about 400 species of resident and migratory birds including the Swamp Francolin, Great Slaty Woodpecker, Bengal Florican, plenty of Painted Stork, Sarus Crane, several species of owl, Asian barbet, woodpecker and minivets. Much of the park's avian fauna is aquatic in nature and found around Dudhwa's lakes such as Banke Tal.

WILDLIFE

Dudhwa being spread over an expanse of approximately 811 sq km of marshes, grasslands and dense forests, is an ideal and protected home for over 38 species of mammals, 16 species of reptiles and numerous species of birds.

Tiger, Rhinoceros, Swamp deer, Elephant, Sambar, Hog deer, Cheetal, Kakar, Wild pig, Rhesus monkey, Langur, Sloth bear, Blue bull, Porcupine, Otter, Turtles, Python, Monitor lizard, Mugger, Gharial etc.

Of the nearly 1300 birds found in the Indian subcontinent, over 450 species can be seen in Dudhwa Reserve. These include Hornbill, Red Jungle Fowl, Pea fowl, Bengal Florican, Fishing eagle, Bengal Florican, Serpent eagle, Osprey, Paradise flycatcher, Woodpeckers, Shama, Indian Pitta, Orioles, Emerald dove etc. During winter the vastand varied water bodies attract a large variety and number of migratory birds making the reserve a favorite haunt of bird watchers.

Flora of Dudhwa

Dudhwa Reserve represents some of the best natural forests and grasslands left in the Terai district of Uttar Pradesh. The vegetation is of the North Indian Moist Deciduous type, containing some of the finest examples of Sal forests (Shorea robusta) in India, as well the most extensive tracts of moist grasslands that remain in this region.

Attractions in Dudhwa

Frog Temple : From Dudhwa national Park, the tourists can make a fine excursion towards the unique Frog Temple at Oel town which is 12 kms from Lakhimpur on the route from Lakhimpur to Sitapur. This is one of its kind of temple based on the Maduk Tantra and was built by the former king of Oel state during 1860-1870. The temple is actually dedicated to Lord Shiva and is believed to be built on the back of a large frog. The Temple is constructed within an octagonal lotus. The Shivling installed in the temple was brought from the Banasur Prati Narmdeshwar Narmada Kund. The architecture of this temple is based on Tantra Vidya with its main gate opening in the east and another gate in the south as an exit.

Surat Bhawan Palace : Built in 1894, the Surat Bhawan Palace near Dudhwa National Park is made in Indo-Sarasenic style and is composed of ten bedrooms, one large dining room with pantry and two lounges. The palace set in a large green, nine acre retreat is eight kms away from the park with its eastern entrance facing the reserve.

Excursions

Lucknow - the city of the nawabs is the most visited place for the tourists coming to Dudhwa Reserve where the tourists can find multiple attractions in the name of Bara Imambara, Chattar Manzil, Jama Masjid, Rumi Darwaza, Moti Mahal and much more. The main hub of multiple facets of industries Lucknow is best known for the ancient historical importance.

Safari in Dudhwa Tiger Reserve

Safari in Dudhwa is the best option for the wildlife lovers to catch the amazing species of the dense ambience. Jeep safari in Dudhwa could prove as the perfect option for a wildlife safari. But for the sake of information and convenience, it is to remind that the forest officials do not provide any jeep safari or guides for assistance. One has to arrange privately for safari conveyance. Elephant rides through the Park are also offered and the mahouts or Elephant drivers also act as guides.

Safari Timing : - Daily jeep safaris in Open 4WD safari vehicles, 7:00 AM to 10:00 AM and 3:00 PM to 6:00 PM.

Park Opening Time : (Nov till May) the best time to visit the Dudhwa Tiger Reserve is from February to April. You can also visit during mid November to mid June.

Other activities to be enjoyed in the park:

- Guided jungle walks
- Elephant safari
- Bird Watching in the area
- Tribal village walk
- Excursion to Katarniaghat Wildlife Sanctuary

Travel Information

By Air : Lucknow is the nearest airport at a distance of 238 km.

By Rail : Dudhwa Railway station at a distance of 4 kms is the nearest railhead. It is well- connected to Lucknow and Nainital via Mailani (37 km.) on the metre gauge.

Another option is to undertake a 301 km. journey from Delhi to Shahjahanpur by rail, and then proceed by road to Dudhwa, which is another 107 km.

By Road : The nearest town is Palia at a distance of 5 kilometers which is linked to Lucknow directly from the distance of 238 km.

UPSRTC and private buses ply between Palia and Lakhimpur-Kheri, Shahjahanpur, Bareilly (260 km.) and Delhi (430 km).

Hotels in/around Dudhwa Tiger Reserve

Dudhwa Reserve which is quite closer to the city of the Nawabs- Lucknow provides the ample amount of reasons for staying at this region.

The other major attractions also allure the tourists to spread their magnanimous moods during their stay at this region. And the provision of different hotels and resorts make the journey more wonderful at its excellent level.

Not so far away from the city's crowd, the accommodation options are accosted with beneficiary services and luxury amenities. Find the best one that suits your needs and enhances your pleasure during your stay in the Dudhwa Reserve area.

MAIN ATTRACTION

Spread over 490 square kilometres, the Dudhwa National Park has a treasure of wildlife for its visitors, but there are certain species which deserve a spot on visitors' must watch list. On the open stretches of grasslands, move the eye-balls in all possible directions to catch a sight of a Tiger, Rhinoceros, Barasingha (Swamp Deer), Crocodile and Bengal Florican. These make up the big five of the national park.

The national park is also inhabited by rattling diversity of birds, including Swamp Francolin, Bengal Florican and Great Slaty Woodpecker. Also, one can get to see sarus cranes, cormorants, heron, minivets, kingfishers, orioles, and bulbuls.

Location

The Dudhwa National Park, on the border shared between India and Nepal in the district of Lakhimpur-Kheri, Uttar Pradesh, is one of the three national parks of the Dudhwa Tiger Reserve. The other two are the Kishanpur Wildlife Sanctuary and the Katarniaghat Wildlife Sanctuary.

How to Reach

The Dudhwa National Park can be reached by road, train or plane. The Dudhwa Railway Station is situated in proximity, at a distance of about 4 km, while the nearest Airport is that of Lucknow. From the airport or the railway station, one can hire a taxi to get to the national park.

If one is travelling to the national park from Delhi, it will take about 8-9 hours drive or one can avail the train to Shahjehanpur and then take a 3-hour drive. Also, one can go to Lucknow first and then head towards Dudhwa, which is around 245 km away from Lucknow.

Climate

In summer season, visiting the national park will make one work into a lather. The temperature goes as high as 45 degrees centigrade in summers, while it drops up to 2 degrees in winter season. The period from mid June to mid November is the rainy season in the region.

Best Time to Visit

The park is opened for visitors from 15 November to 15 June. However, for grabbing the best draws of the spot, one must plan the trip between February and April.

Hotels and accommodation

Perhaps to avoid disturbance to the natural setting, there are not many hotels or restaurants around the park. However, to facilitate its visitors, the park has well-maintained and green accommodation options available within the premises. But in that case, one must get the bookings done at the office of the Chief Wildlife Warden in advance.

7

Gir National Park and
Sasan Gir Sanctuary, Gujarat

The Gir National Park and the Sasan Gir Sanctuary of Gujarat are the only wildlife sanctuaries in India that have Asiatic Lions. October-June is the ideal time to visit the place and watch these majestic beasts strolling in their territories.

The park was established on 18th September 1965 and it is one of the largest and elegantly preserved areas for the Asiatic Lions. Rivers and streams flowing through this national park remain occupied by the dwellers of the park.

SUBTLE GLIMPSES OF MAJOR ATTRACTIONS AT SASAN GIR

Animals:The entire forest area of the Gir National Park is dry and deciduous which provides best habitat for Asiatic Lions. As per the new statics of 2015, the entire Saurashtra Region is inhabited by 523 Lions and more than 300 Leopards. Apart from these two animals the park is a home to two different species of Deer.

The Sambar is counted largest Indian Deer. The Gir forest is also known for the Chowsingha – the world's only four horned antelope. The Jackal, striped Hyena and India Fox are some of the smaller carnivores found in Gir Forest.

Birds: The exotic flora of Gir National Park gives shelter to more than 200 species of birds and moreover the sanctuary has been declared an important bird area by the Indian Bird Conservation Network. Gir is also habitat of raptors like critically endangered white-backed and long-billed vultures.

Reptiles:Sasan Gir is blessed with more than 40 species of reptiles and amphibians. Kamleshwar – a large reservoir in the sanctuary is the best spot where Marsh Crocodile can be seen in large numbers. Park has even many species of snake including King Kobra, the Russell's viper, Saw-scaled viper and the Krait.

Gir Interpretation Zone, Devaliya: Devaliya Safari Park is enclosed area of the Sanctuary that offers a good opportunity for visitors to experience a rustic beauty and wilderness of the area. The safari tour is conducted in a mini bus that takes visitors to another cross section of the Gir. Travelers can watch here a good variety of wildlife in just 20 to 30 minutes tour including Asiatic Lion.

How to Reach Gir National Park Gir: National Park attracts large number of tourists to witness the Asiatic lion, as this is the sole place all across the world where these creatures are presently found. Once extinct, numbers have been recovered owing to the conservation efforts. The Sanctuary is open for tourism from 16th October to 15th June every year.

Junagadh is perhaps the best approach to the park. The railway station in Junagadh receives trains from different cities like Ahmedabad and Rajkot and other major cities. Then, from here it takes approximately one and half hour to reach Sasan Gir National Park.

From Rajkot-On reaching Rajkot Railway Station or Airport you can take a cab or bus and to reach a Limda chowk. There are a number of privately operated that go to Junagadh at frequent intervals. Junagadh is nearly 105 Kms from the city Rajkot and it takes nearly 2 and a half to 3 hours to cover the distance.From this point you have two options. First one is either you take a bus from gate number 11or 12 to Sasan Gir or travel by taxi that is accessible bang opposite the taxi stand. The taxi will take nearly one and half an hour and will charge reasonably and will drop you to Sasan Gir.

From Somnath to Gir National Park: Road Distance or the driving distance from the Gir National Park to Somnath is approximately 50 Kms and it takes nearly 1 hour to cover this distance. GSRTC buses and quite a few private buses ply between both the cities and take you directly to Sasan Gir Forest.

From Diu To Sasan Gir Park: Diu airport is closest to the Gir National Park. From here you can hire that are present just outside the airport which will take you to Sasan Gir. Sasan Gir is nearly 110 kms airport of Diu and takes approximately 2 hours to cover this distance. If you have a late afternoon flight it is better to take a halt at Diu or can visit Somnath Temple which is nearly 80 kms from Diu and the road too is good except in little patches.

It just takes an hour to reach Somnath from Diu. Next morning you can move on to Sasan Gir which is just 40 kms from here and just takes half an hour to cover this distance.Some other routes to reach Sasan Gir by road is from Keshod which also has an airport and is 45 kms, Veraval is 40 kms away, Junagadh is 55kms, Rajkot is 160Kms, Ahemedabad is 410Kms. The closeby railway stations are Sasan which is 40 Kms and Rajkot which is 160 Kms.

If you can't afford a taxi there are frequent buses that are playing throughout the day. The park is easily accessible from the beautiful beaches of Diu which is about two hours drive don't want to take a taxi, pubic buses run regularly to Sasan Gir from both places during the day. People prefer private buses as it conveniently drops them to the Guest houses you want to reach. So in this way they are more convenient than the buses. No prior booking is required as the buses are available on any part of the day. So, come and enjoy the beautiful flora and fauna of Sasan Gir National Park and take home some of the most treasured moments back home.

HISTORY OF GIR FOREST NATIONAL PARK

The Gir Forest National Park and Wildlife Sanctuary is a forest and wildlife sanctuary in Gujarat, India. Established in 1965, with a total area of 1412 km² (about 258 km² for the fully protected area (the national park) and (1153 km² for the Sanctuary), the park is located 43 km in the northeast from Somnath, 65 km to the southeast of Junagadh and 60 km to south west of Amreli.

It is the sole home of the Asiatic Lions (*Panthera leo persica*) and is considered to be one of the most important protected areas in Asia due to its supported species. The ecosystem of Gir, with its diverse flora and fauna, is protected as a result of the efforts of the government forest department, wildlife activists and NGOs. The forest area of Gir and its lions were declared as "protected" in the early 1900s by the Nawab of the princely state of Junagadh. This initiative assisted in the conservation of the lions whose population had plummeted to only 15 through slaughter for trophy hunting.

The April 2010 census recorded the lion-count in Gir at 411, an increase of 52 compared to 2005. The lion breeding programme covering the park and surrounding area has bred about 180 lions in captivity since its inception.

GENERAL

In Gir you touch the history of India before humanity itself. Before monuments, temples, mosques and palaces. Or rather, a history as humanity was emerging, when humans coexisted with lions, before the former had overrun the continent (and the world) and pushed the latter to the brink of extinction.

Many come to Gir because, outside of Africa, it is the only place with wild lions. But to truly experience Gir and the lions, you must explore their natural habitat, with everything from tiny wild birds, not easily seen, but heard singing in the forest canopy, to crocodiles floating in the marsh waters.

Driving around, you are uncommonly aware you are in someone else's territory. You stay in your vehicle because you are in the home of lions, leopards, hyenas, crocodiles; you remember that humans do not rule the world, and however "advanced" we think we are, most of us would not survive very long on our own in a place like Gir.

That is not to say that all humans are out of place. The local Maldhari community has lived here for generations and coexists magnifcently with the wilderness. They sustain themselves by grazing their livestock and harvesting what they need from the forest. The sizeable portion of their herds lost to lions and other predators is considered prasad, offered in exchange for living in another's homeland.

How many of us are aware, let alone as concientious as the Maldharis about the impact of our lifestyle on other species? How can we be, if we so distance ourselves from the habitats that are ravaged to feed our material appetites? When you visit Gir, try to see the Maldharis not with nostalgia for a picturesque past, but as crucial teachers for a better present and future. You don't have to be a shepherd living with wild lions to learn from their way of life. Ask yourself why we have reached the point where National Parks like Gir are neccessary; what happened to these lions who used to inhabit everywhere from Greece to Bangladesh. If you begin to understand the deeper implications of these questions, you will return home, whether home is a hut in the countryside, or a high-rise apartment, whether in Mumbai or Berlin, charged with new inspiration for evolution in your own life.

Gir is a place that deserves time and involvement. Your chances of spotting wildlife in a few hours is small, especially in the middle of the day; to truly experience the wonders of the Gir forest, and hopefully see a wide variety of its diverse wildlife, three or four days is recommended, particularly with a knowledgeable guide. This will vastly improve the depth of your visit. Contact the Park for information about hiring a guide (phone number below.)

While Gir is most famous for its lions, the park is one of the most diverse places in Gujarat, both in flora and fauna.

GEOGRAPHY

The seven major perennial rivers of the Gir region are *Hiran, Shetrunji, Datardi, Shingoda,Machhundri, Godavari* and *Raval*. The four reservoirs of the area are at four dams, one each on Hiran, Machhundri, Raval and Shingoda rivers, including the biggest reservoir in the area, the *Kamleshwar Dam*, dubbed 'the lifeline of Gir'.

During peak summer, surface water for wild animals is available at about 300 water points. When drought hits the area following a poor rainfall, surface water is not available at a majority of these points, and water scarcity becomes a serious problem (mainly in the eastern part of the sanctuary). Ensuring the availability of water during peak summer is one of the major tasks of the Forest Department staff.

FLORA

More than 400 plant species were recorded in the survey of Gir forest by *Samtapau & Raizada* in 1955.

The Botany department of M.S. University of Baroda has revised the count to 507 during their survey. According to the 1964 forest type classification by *Champion & Sheth*, the Gir forest falls under "5A/C-1a—very dry teak forest" classification.Teak occurs mixed with dry deciduous species. The degradation stages (DS) sub-types are thus derived as:

1. 5/DS1-Dry deciduous scrub forest and
2. 5/DS1-Dry savannah forests (Locally known as "vidis"). It is the largest dry deciduous forest in western India.

Teak bearing areas are mainly in the eastern portion of the forest, which constitutes nearly half of the total area.

The forest is an important biological research area with considerable scientific, educational, aesthetic and recreational values. It provides nearly 5 million kilograms of green grass by annual harvesting, which is valued approximately at Rs. 500 million (US$10 million). The forest provides nearly 123,000 metric tons worth of fuel wood annually.

Most of the area is rugged hills, with high ridges and densely forested valleys, wide grassland plateaus, and isolated hilltops. Around half of the forested area of the park is teak forest, with other trees such as khair, dhavdo, timru, amla, and many others. The other half is non-teak forest, with samai, simal, khakhro and asundro jambu, umro, amli, vad and kalam; mostly broadleaf and evergreen trees. The river Hiran is the only one to flow year-round; the rest are seasonal. There are also areas of the park with open scrub and savannah-type grassland.

Deer and Antelope

This variety of vegetation provides for a huge array of animals. The most-sighted animal in the park, the chital, or Indian spotted deer, inhabits the dry and mixed deciduous forest, with a population of over 32,000. The more reclusive sambar, the largest of the Indian deer species, weighing 300-500 kg, lives in the wetter western part of the park. Both the sambar and the chausingha, the world's only 4-horned antelope (chau= four, singha= horns), are very dependent on water, and rarely found far from a water source. Another one-of-a-kind is the chinkara, the only gazelle in the world with horns in both males and females. The fastest of the Indian antelopes, the blackbuck, also lives in Gir, but has a relatively small population here compared to Velavadar National Park (near Bhavnagar), as it prefers open grasslands to forests.

Wild Cats

Along with the famous lions, who number around 350, the park is also home to four other wild cats. There are around 300 leopards, though they are nocturnal and thus harder to spot. Of the three smaller wildcats, the jungle cat is the most widespread, and lives in deciduous scrub and riverine areas. The mysterious desert cat is almost never seen. The rusty spotted cat, previously thought to only live in the Dangs of southeast Gujarat, has only recently been found in Gir.

Other animals and reptiles

The top and middle canopies of the dry, mixed and riverine decidous forests are home to troops of hanuman langur monkeys. The striped hyena is usually seen scavenging alone in the grasslands and scrub forest, far more solitary than the African hyena. Wild boars rooting into the ground for tuber provide aeration of the soil. If you look closer, you may see smaller mammals like pangolins, pale hedgehogs, Indian hares, or grey musk shrews. The ratel or honey badger is renowned for its snake-killing exploits, earning it the "most fearless animal" title in the Guinness Book of World Records. Another snake-killer in Gir is the ruddy mongoose; the snakes they contend with include the common krait, russell's viper, and the saw-scaled viper. The Kamaleshwar reservoir now houses the largest population of marsh crocodiles in the country. Other reptiles include the soft-shelled turtle, star tortoise, Indian rock python and monitor lizard (which grows to over 1.5 m long; don't look for the lizards that live in your yard.)

Birds

Gir is also home to more kinds of birds than any other park in Gujarat, yet somehow is not known for its birdlife. While it may not have the half-million flamingoes found in Kutch during breeding season, Gir is home to over 300 species of birds, many of which can be seen year-round, from the Malabar whistling thrush to the Paradise flycatcher, from the crested serpent eagle to the king vulture, from pelicans to painted storks. The noted ornithologist Dr. Salim Ali said that if there were no lions here, Gir would be well-known as one of the best bird sanctuaries in western India.

The Asiatic Lion

Until the early 19th century, Asiatic lions roamed an immense area of South and Southwest Asia, as far east as Greece and as far west as modern Bangladesh. As humanity has lived in this region for millennia, people coexisted with lions for thousands of years, but in the last few centuries, the growth of the human population has come at the cost of the lions' habitat. Like the Bengal Tiger and the Asiatic Cheetah, lions saw a dramatic decline in population as their preferred habitat of grasslands and semi-forested areas became overrun with humans. Beyond just habitat reduction, though, once guns arrived and became widespread, from 1800-1860, nearly all the lions remaining outside Gujarat were hunted and killed. The last Asiatic lions in India outside of Gir forest were killed in 1886 at Rewah, and the last wild lion sighted the world outside Gir was in Iran in 1941.

In 1901, Lord Curzon was offered to be taken lion hunting while visiting

Junagadh. Noting that these were the only lions left in Asia, he declined, and reportedly suggested to the Nawab of Junagadh that it would be better to conserve the lion population than to hunt it. The Nawab began what was probably the first institutional wildlife conservation effort in India and one of the earliest in the world (though various human societies have been operating in ways that conserve wildlife throughout the ages), banning all lion hunting entirely. From a population reported to be as low as 20 in 1913 (considered exaggerated by some wildlife experts, noting that the first official census in the 1930s found over 200 lions), the lions have rebounded to now number 359 in the most recent census of 2005. This is due almost entirely to the Nawab's conservation efforts, and the Indian Government's post-independence ban on lion killing in 1955.

Though the lions have maintained a small healthy population, their habitat continues to shrink, and they remain a critically endangered species. The Gir forest area, which covered over 3000 square km in 1880, was reduced to just over 2500 square km by the mid-20th century, and only 1400 square km today. Of that, a mere 258 square km make up the National Park itself. While the population has grown due to successful conservation programs in the park, the park is too small for the number of lions it now houses, and lions are straying outside to seek further living space, often not surviving well in the other areas.

Locally called sher or sinh, the Asiatic lion is over two and a half meters long, weighs 115 to 200 kg, and can run short distances at 65 km/h to chase down the sambar, chital, nilgai, and chinkara that are its preferred prey. However, when not hungry, it will never attack an animal; after a lion makes a kill, it will gorge itself on up to 75 kg of meat, and then not worry about eating for a few days, so it is not unusual to see a well-fed lion lounging calmly beside a herd of grazing deer. The lions prefer open scrub and deciduous forest areas, and are very bold, not shy around humans. So even if they seem tame or timid, do not approach them, they are still very powerful wild animals.

Humans and Gir

Humans' relationship with Gir is long and mixed. The very existence of a sanctuary is testament to the dire need of a protected area, given the rapid expanse of civilization that has completely taken over everywhere else around (see above section on the lion.) After India's independence in 1947, the rapid push for food independence led much wild grassland to be converted to agriculture. This had major effects on the wildlife of Saurashtra, but also on the human population; as large-scale farming spread across the region, those peoples who traditionally herded livestock in wild grasslands were pushed further and further into much more limited regions. Faced with this situation, the Maldhari community migrated into the Gir forest despite obvious dangers and a total lack of infrastructure, in order to maintain their way of life. When the park was declared, they were allowed to remain and continue their traditional practices; in fact, Gir forest is now virtually the only area where the Maldharis still live as they wish.

As herders, they shepherd their cattle and buffalo around the park, which opponents (including the Forest Department) claim overgrazes the area and makes it harder for the wild deer, antelope, and other species to graze as well. However, recent studies have shown that between 25 and 50% of the Gir lions' diet is made up of Maldhari livestock, meaning that the presence of the Maldharis is vital to the survival of the lions. In fact, the Maldharis apparently consider livestock lost to predators as payment for living in their territory. Furthermore, as vegetarians, the Maldharis are never poachers.

Compare this attitude with that of farmers near the park, who have killed many lions who they say "encroached on their land," not realizing that they have in fact encroached on the lions' land, and the lions of course cannot know where people have drawn the park boundary line. The humans who do know this, however, often graze cattle illegally inside the park adding further pressure on the ecosystem from the 97 villages within 5 km of the park. For these reasons and many others, the Gir forest and the critically endangered lions are under increasing threat from human activity.

Tourism itself is a growing threat to Gir. Clearly, the genuine visitor is beneficial, but tens of thousands of people visit the park every year simply as an afterthought to their trip to Somnath or Junagadh, stopping in for a few hours to snap a photograph of the lions in captivity. These visitors create a huge demand for infrastructure but do little of benefit to the park or the lions, not even staying long enough to really experience it or learn much at all. The presence of several temples inside the park also puts strain on the ecosystem, as visitors to them also demand accommodation and infrastructure that often conflicts with the park's conservation goals, leading to great controversy and political tension between park management and temple management. While all of these threats may have distinct immediate origins, they are in fact all the result of having reached a point where wild natural environments are confined to extremely limited areas, and human civilization, industry and economy has overtaken everything else. The problem is not, in fact, that the lion population has grown "too big for the park," but that the park is far too small for the lions. As a visitor, let this be an opportunity to spark your imagination on the question of shifting the priorities of humanity towards re-integrating ourselves with the rest of life.

For shorter visits, the Gir Interpretation Zone, at Devalia, 12 km west of Sasan Gir, has some lions in captivity, but this is not the same as visiting them in the wild. After all, to see a lion in captivity you can visit a local zoo; come to Gir to see them in the wild. Entry fees for the Interpretation Centre (different from the park itself) are, for Indians Rs. 75/- Mon.-Fri, Rs.95/- Sat.-Sun, Rs. 115/- on Holidays and for foreigners US$20, payable only in rupees.

WILDLIFE

The count of 2,375 distinct fauna species of Gir includes about 38 species of mammals, around 300 species of birds, 37 species of reptiles and more than 2,000 species of insects.

The carnivores group mainly comprises Asiatic lions, Indian Leopards, Sloth bears, Indian Cobras, Jungle cats, Striped Hyenas, Golden Jackals, Indian Mongoose, Indian Palm Civets, and Ratels. Desert cats and Rusty-spotted cats occur but are rarely seen.

The main herbivores of Gir are Chital, Nilgai (or Bluebull), Sambar, Four-horned Antelope, Chinkara and Wild boar. Blackbucks from the surrounding area are sometimes seen in the sanctuary.

Among the smaller mammals, Porcupine and Hare are common but the Pangolin is rare. The reptiles are represented by the Marsh crocodile hir Tortoise and the Monitor Lizard in the water areas of the sanctuary. Snakes are found in the bushes and forest. Pythons are sighted at times along the stream banks. Gir has been used by the Gujarat State Forest Department which adopted the Indian Crocodile Conservation Project in 1977 and released close to 1000 Marsh crocodile reared in Gir rearing centre into the *Kamaleshwar lake* and other reservoirs and small water bodies in and around Gir. The plentiful avifauna population has more than 300 species of birds, most of which are resident. The scavenger group of birds has 6 recorded species of Vultures. Some of the typical species of Gir include Crested Serpent Eagle, endangered Bonelli's Eagle, Crested Hawk-eagle, Brown Fish Owl, Indian Eagle-Owl, Rock Bush-Quail, Pygmy Woodpecker, Black-headed Oriole, Crested Treeswift andIndian Pitta. The Indian Grey Hornbill was not found from the last census of 2001.

Asiatic Lion habitat, distribution and population

The Asiatic Lion's habitat is dry scrub land and open deciduous forest. These lions were once found across northern Africa, south west Asia and northern Greece. Now there are only around 411 left in the wild and all of them are in or around the Gir Forest National Park. The first modern day count of lions was done by Mark

Alexander Wynter-Blyth, the Principal of Rajkumar College, Rajkot sometime between 1948 to 1963, probably early in his tenure as the Principal during that period. Even though the Gir Forest is well protected, there are instances of Asiatic Lions being poached. They have also been poisoned for attacking livestock. Some of the other threats include floods, fires and the possibility of epidemics and natural calamities. Gir nonetheless remains the most promising long term preserve for them.

The lion breeding programme and lion-counting

Year	Count	Male : Female : Cub
1968	177	-
1974	180	-
1979	261	76:100:85
1984	252	88:100:64
1990	249	82:100:67
1995	265	94:100:71
2000	327	-
2005	359	-
2010	411	97:162:152

The Lion Breeding Programme creates and maintains breeding centres. It also carries out studies of the behaviour of the Asiatic lions and also practices artificial insemination. One such centre has been established in the Sakkarbaug Zoo at the district headquarters ofJunagadh, which has successfully bred about 180 lions. 126 pure Asiatic lions have been given to zoos in India and abroad.

The census of lions takes place every five years. Previously indirect methods like using pugmarks of the lion were adopted for the count. However, during the census of April 2005 (which originally was scheduled for 2006, but was advanced following the reports and controversy over vanishing tigers in India), "Block-Direct-Total Count" method was employed with the help of around 1,000 forest officials, experts and volunteers.

It means that only those lions were counted that were "spotted" visually. Use of "live bait" (a prey that is alive and used as a bait) for the exercise, though thought to be a traditional practice, was not used this time. The reason believed to be behind this is the Gujarat High Court ruling of 2000 against such a use of animals.

Gir Interpretation Zone, Devalia

Gir National Park and Sanctuary does not have a designated area for tourists. However, to reduce the tourism hazard to the wildlife and to promote nature education, an Interpretation Zone has been created at Devalia within the sanctuary. Within its chained fences, it covers all habitat types and wildlife of Gir with its feeding-cum-living cages for the carnivores and a double-gate entry system.

GIR ANIMALS

The Gir National park has variety of gir animals which are found in Sasan Gir National Park. Sasan Gir is very good place for bird-watching. Sasan Gir holds a large number of lions with leopards, which makes one of the big-cat concentrations in India. Sambar and chital, nilgai, chousingha ,Indian gazelle and wild boar thrive in Gir. Jackal, striped hyena, jungle cat, rusty-spotted cat, langur, porcupine, black-naped Indian hare are other animals of Gir Forest.There are only 411 Asiatic Lions are left out in the Gir National Park and all of them are in or around the Gir Forest National Park. That is why Gir Animals are famous for its Only Asiatic Lions.

Gir Animals Fauna

The ecology of Sasan Gir holds about 38 species of mammals, and around 300 species of birds, 2000 species of insects and 37 species of reptiles. Animals of gir forest are carnivores that includes Asiatic Lion, Hyeana, Mongoose, Civet cat Leopard, Jackal, Jungle cat and ratel.Some of the gir forest animals are seen very rarely which are desert cats and rusted spotted cats. Some of the gir animals are herbivores which includes Sambhar, Chital, Spotted deer, Nilgai, Chinkara and wild boar with a small population of black buck.

Including all these gir forest animals there are smaller mammals which are the porcupines and hares and the rare pangolin. The reptilian fauna is represented by crocodile, the star tortoise, the monitor lizard and a number of species of snakes. Along with the stream banks Python is also found. It is estimated that highest population of marsh crocodiles is found in gir forest. The Gir National park has number of 250 birds and 50 other species of gir animals which includes endangered lesser florican and saras crane that were recorded in the grassl along the wildlife sanctuary. The main scavenger bird is the vulture of which about 6 species have been recorded. Gir animals of species like sandgrouse, grey francolin, quails, Asian paradise flycatcher, black-naped monarch, Pygmy woodpecker, black headed oriole, crested swift, grey-headed flycatcher, verditer flycatcher, tickell's blue flycatcher, white-browed fantail, sambhar, Asian brown flycatcher, greenish warbler, white-eye, coppersmith barbet, common and marshal's iora, spotted deer, rufous treepie, yellow-footed green pigeon have been spotted by our guests around the lodge itself. Gir animals like Long-billed vulture, black buck, Indian white-backed vulture, red-headed (king) vulture, and Indian Pitta have been seen in the Gir Wildlife Sanctuary.

Gir Animals Asiatic Lions

The Sasan Gir is recognized as the home of the Asiatic lion. The Junagadh Zoo was built in 1863 then Nawab of Gujarat had set up this zoo in order to save the Asiatic Lion. Gir forest animals are recognized for only the Asiatic Lions. The Asiatic Lions had vanished from all over the world except Sasan Gir. The probable years of its extermination region wise was Bihar in 1840, Delhi 1834, Bhavalpur 1842, Eastern Vindhyas and Bundelkhand 1865, Central India and Rajasthan 1870 and western Aravalis in 1880. It was reported in 1884 that last animal existing in the wild outside Saurashtra. The Nawab of sasan gir provided sufficient protection for the gir animals-Lions and after than their population increases in year of 1904 to 1911. After the passing of the Nawab 12 more lions were shooted but after year 1911 shooting was severely restricted by the British Government. In the year of 1913, one of the officer reported a population about 20 lions in Sasan Gir. Animals of gir forest are now preserved and safe from danger.

HOW TO REACH GIR NATIONAL PARK

Being the only reserve forest in the world for the endangered Asiatic Lion, the Gir National Park attracts a large number of Lion lovers for the Jungle safari, which is organized by the park administration. The Asiatic Lion was once considered extinct in the Gir forest due to the heavy poaching and a reduction in the forest habitat and declared as the endangered species. However, with the proper implementation of the conservation methods, the number of Lions has been increased tremendously in the recent times, which also enhanced the tourism activity in the park. The park organizes Jeep safari in three shifts every day from 16th October to 15th June every year. There are many commuting options available for tourists to reach the Gir National Park. Below is the detailed information about it-

By Air- The nearest airports to the Gir National Park are Keshod airport and Rajkot airport. The Keshod airport is located around 70 km from the park, whereas the Rajkot airport is at a distance of around 160 km. Take a cab or bus service to reach the Gir national park from any of these two airports. However, the best way to reach Gir National Park from overseas is by using the Mumbai International Airport. One can reach the Diu airport from the Mumbai airport via air route and then take the cab from Diu airport to Gir national park, which is at around drive of 2 hours by a cab. You can also opt to reach the Porbandar airport from the Mumbai airport and then take a cab or taxi to reach the Gir national park by road. It will take around 2 to 2 and half hour to drive from Porbandar to Gir.

By Rail- Junagadh and Veraval railway stations are the nearest railway station from the Gir national park, located at around the same distance from the park. Both the railway stations are on the main railway line of the state and connected to all the major location of the country by the direct trains. Take a cab or taxi or state bus to reach Gir from any of these two railway stations which will take around one and a half hour to 2 hours by road. The other nearest railway station is the Rajkot railway station, which is located at around 165 km from the Gir forest and takes around 3 and a half hours to 4 hours by road. The Rajkot railway station is also a major station and connected to major cities by direct or connecting trains.

By Road- The roadways traveling is always an appealing journey and the best than any other commuting option. The conditions of the roads in Gujarat are comparatively good and the road journey can be comfortable and enjoyable in the state. The Gir National Park is properly connected to most of the prominent cities of Gujarat via a good road. There are state bus transport service and private bus service, which offer frequent bus service to Gir from various parts of the state. The cab and taxi are also available easily at major cities in Gujarat to commute to the Gir National Park.

8

Kanha National Park, Madhya Pradesh

Kanha National Park is another sought after destination in the list of national parks of Madhya Pradesh. Established in the year 1955, this park has gained a lot of attention due to its efforts in saving the rare and almost extinct species of the Swamp Deer, also known as 'Barasingha'. It is also one of the well-maintained parks in Asia.

Kanha National Park is nestled in the Maikal range of Satpuras in Madhya Pradesh, the heart of India that forms the central Indian highlands.The national park is being popularized as the Tiger reserve and interestingly is being declared as one of the finest wildlife areas in the world. Spreading across two revenue districts the Mandala and the Kalaghat, Kanha National Park was declared a reserve forest in 1879 and revalued as a wildlife sanctuary in 1933. Its position was further upgraded to a national park in 1955.

The Kanha National Park is spread across the area of 940 sq km in the Maikal chain of hills. By bringing up the buffer and core zone all together, the Kanha Tiger Reserve has the total area of 1945 sq km.

The landscapes and the surrounding luxurious meadows along with the wooded strands and the dense maroons of forests offer magnanimous sightseeing experiences for the nature lovers. Making the land more beautiful and adorable, the crystal clear streams amidst the dense jungle cleanses the surroundings and makes the wildlife unrivalled. This vivacious land has been the source of inspiration for Rudyard Kipling, a famous writer for his outstanding creation- "The Jungle Book".

The Kanha National Park is the ideal home for wide ranges of wild creatures; right from the mighty tigers to the most populated Barasingha and the countless species of plants, birds, reptiles and insects. This reserve has fascinated many travelers around the corners of the world with its well developed infrastructure specially meant for them. The best location here to enjoy the most is the Bammi Dadar, also known as the Sunset Point.

The other feature of the Kanha National Park is its sunset point called Bamni Dadar. Almost the entire park can be seen from this point. It offers the most eye-catching views of the animals in their natural habitat.

HISTORY OF KANHA NATIONAL PARK

Kanha National Park is one of the biggest park in Madhya Pradesh, India. 'Kanha National Park' is a national park and a Tiger Reserve in the Mandla and Balaghat districts of Madhya Pradesh, India. In the 1930s, Kanha area was divided into two sanctuaries, Hallon and Banjar, of 250 and 300 km². Kanha National Park was created on 1 June 1955. Today it stretches over an area of 940 km² in the two districts Mandla and Balaghat. Together with a surrounding buffer zone of 1,067 km² and the neighboring 110 km² Phen Sanctuary it forms the Kanha Tiger Reserve. This makes it the largest National Park in Central India.

The park has a significant population of Royal Bengal Tiger, leopards, the sloth bear, Barasingha and Indian wild dog. The lush sal and bamboo forests, grassy meadows and ravines of Kanha provided inspiration to Rudyard Kipling for his famous novel "Jungle Book "

Flora

Kanha National Park is home to over 1000 species of flowering plants. The lowland forest is a mixture of sal (*Shorea robusta*) and other mixed forest trees, interspersed with meadows. The highland forests are tropical moist dry deciduous type and of a completely different nature with bamboo on slopes (*Dendrocalamus strictus*). A very good looking Indian ghost tree can also be seen in the dense forest.

Meadows at Kanha

Kanha Tiger Reserve abounds in meadows or *maidans* which are basically open grasslands that have sprung up in fields of abandoned villages, evacuated to make way for the animals.

Kanha meadow is one such example. There are many species of grass recorded at Kanha some of which are important for the survival of Barasingha (*Cervus duvauceli branderi*).

Dense forested zones with good crown cover has abundant species of climbers, shrubs and herbs flourishing in the understory. Aquatic plants in numerous "tal" (lakes) are life line for migratory and wetland species of birds.

Fauna

Kanha national park has species of tiger, leopards, wild dogs, wild cats, foxes and jackals. Among the deer species Swamp Deer or Hard Ground Barasingha is pride of the place as it is the only sub species of swamp deer in India (Cervus duavcelli branderi). The animal is adapted to hard ground unlike swamp deer of the North which live in marshy swamps. Kanha National Park has been instrumental in rescuing the "Swamp Deer" from extinction. Indian Gaur (Bos guarus), belonging to the ox genus, is found in Kanha but seen mostly as winter ends. In summer gaur inhabit meadows and water holes in the park.

Other commonly seen animals in the park include the spotted deer, sambar, barking deer and the four-horned deer. The latter can be seen at Bamni Dadar climb. Recently, mouse deer have also been discovered in the tiger reserve. Black buck were once found in Kanha, but became very rare for unknown reasons. They vanished completely, but have been reintroduced recently inside a fenced area in the park.

Nilgai can still be seen near the Sarahi Gate, while the Indian Wolf once commonly seen at Mocha is a rare sight now. Hyena and sloth bear are seen occasionally. Langurs and wild boars are common, but the pugnacious rhesus macaque is seen less often.

Nocturnal animals like fox, hyena, jungle cat, civets, porcupine, ratel or honey badger and hares can be seen outside the park confines.

Reptiles like pythons, cobras, krait, rat snakes, vipers, keelbacks and grass snakes are nocturnal animals, and are therefore rarely seen. There are many species of turtles as well as amphibians found in or near the water bodies. Kanha and Satpura forest being a part of Gondwana, now famous as tiger reserve, once upon a time were ruled by wild Indian Elephants.

Tigers of Kanha

Currently one of the dominant male tigers of Kanha National Park is a tiger named Munna. Munna is famous for his large size, big head and has symbol "CAT" written on his head.

Transport & facilities

Jabalpur, the most convenient place to approach the Park from, has the nearest airport (175 km), Nagpur (260 km) and Raipur (219 km) have other airports, Mandla (70 km) has a good connection with Kanha and there is a tourist taxi service from Jabalpur to the national park.

From Jabalpur, the best way to travel is via Mandla and Nainpur - perhaps with an overnight stop - then taking the diversion at Bamhni.

Mandla, Nainpur and Seoni all have sports clubs, Internet cafes, guides, Christian churches and some beautiful temples.

There are three gates for entrance into the Park. The Kisli gate is best accessed from Jabalpur and stops at the village Khatia, inside the buffer area. The second gate is at Mukki and the third, most recently opened, gate is at Serai.

Reintroduction of Barasingha

An exciting conservation effort in this national park is the reintroduction of Barasingha. The Gaur will be relocated to Bandhavgarh and some Barasingha will be relocated to Satpura Tiger reserve The objective of this project is to introduce about 500 Barasingha in this national park to eight or nine different locations. There is also a project to capture about twenty tigers and relocate them to Satpura Tiger reserve.

KANHA TREES

The plateaux, though essentially grasslands, have sporadic growth of fruit - bearing trees such as achar (Buchanania lanzan), aonla (Emblica Officinalis) and tendu (Diospyros melanoxylon). The nalas are moist, shady and cools with thick bamboo (Dendrocalamus strictus) breaks and tall mango (Mangifera indica), jamun (Syzygium cumini) and arjun (Terminalia arjuna) trees.

The upper slopes carry mixed jungle with numerous mahul (Bauhinia vahlii) climbers crowning the trees with foliage and their swinging stems spanning the spaces between the trees.

The treetops look white when mahul is in flower in summer. There are many tree speices, of which bija (Pterocarpus marsupium) and dhaura (Anogeissus latifolia) are specially remarkable. The forest on the upper slopes are particularly picturesque in winter.

Bamboo , the Great Grass

Bamboo is really a species of grass ! They say you can see a bamboo shoot growing taller by many centimetres every day. When monsoon is well set bamboo is among the fastest growing plant species.

Like a true grass, bamboo dies on seeding. In kanha, bamboo flowers gregariously only once in 40 to 60 years. However, the entire bamboo patch does not flower and die at the same time:clumps of different seed origins flower and seed at different times. there is a carpet of bamboo seedlings in the year of gregarious flowering as soon as monsoon breaks.

Bamboo is abundant and nutritious, and animals and birds feed on it.

GENERAL INFORMATION

- Area: (core) 940 km²
- Terrain: sal and bamboo forests, plateaus, meadows and meandering streams
- Best Season: February to June
- Morning Visiting Hours: 6:30 am to 12:00 noon
- Evening Visiting Hours: 3:00 pm to 6:00 pm
- Closed: 1 July to 15 October

Transportation

Air : Jabalpur Airport (175 km/04:30hrs). direct flights for Delhi and Mumbai. It is the best option for reaching kanha National Park as it connected with 02 important cities: Delhi & Mumbai. In between these flight options Air India, SpiceJet flight is operating daily

Rail : Jabalpur is major railway stations with good train connectivity across India.

HOW TO REACH KANHA

Kanha National Park is situated at Mandla & Balaghat Districts of Madhya Pradesh State in Central India. Kanha National Park has excellent Air, Road & train connections from most parts of India. There are two key locations of Kanha National park, Khatia & Mukki Entrance gate. Khatia entrance gate falls on Mandla district & Mukki on Balaghat district of M. P. State. From Khatia Entrance gate one can explore Kisli, Kanha & Sarhi zones of Kanha national park & Mukki entrance gate covers Mukki range of the national park. Khatia Entrance gate is well connected from Jabalpur & Nagpur & Mukki entrance gate is from Jabalpur, Raipur & Nagpur.

By Train: The Nearest Railway Stations for accessing Kanha National Park is Gondia & Jabalpur. Gondia railway station is 145kms / 03:00 hrs drive from Kanha (Khatia Entrance Gate). Jabalpur railway station is 160kms / 04:00 hrs drive from Kanha (Mukki Entrance Gate)

By Air: The Nearest Airport for Kanha National Park are Jabalpur 160 Kms, Raipur 250 Kms & Nagpur 300 Kms.

9

Kaziranga National Park, Assam

Kaziranga National Park is the only natural habitat of the endangered One-Horned Rhinos in India as well as in the world. Located in the Golaghat district of Assam, Kaziranga National Park is one of the largest wildlife sanctuaries to explore the wildlife of Northeast India. It is also a highly visited park among the top 10 national parks in India.

This park also boasts of its number of tigers and other wildlife species. Due to the noteworthy number of tigers, Kaziranga National Park has been declared as Tiger Reserve Forest in 2006. Other wildlife consists Elephants, Wild Buffaloes and Swamp Deer. The park also witnesses a large number of migratory birds during the winters.

ABOUT KAZIRANGA NATIONAL PARK

Kaziranga National Park is a national park in the Golaghat and Nagaon districts of the state of Assam, India. A World Heritage Site, the park hosts two-thirds of the world's Great One-horned Rhinoceroses.

Kaziranga boasts the highest density of tigers amongprotected areas in the world and was declared a Tiger Reserve in 2006. The park is home to large breeding populations of elephants, wild water buffalo, and swamp deer.

Kaziranga is recognized as an *Important Bird Area* by Birdlife International for conservation of avifaunal species. Compared to other protected areas in India, Kaziranga has achieved notable success in wildlife conservation. Located on the edge of the Eastern Himalaya biodiversity hotspot, the park combines high species diversity and visibility.

Kaziranga is a vast expanse of tall elephant grass, marshland, and dense tropical moist broadleaf forests, crisscrossed by four major rivers, including the Brahmaputra, and the park includes numerous small bodies of water. Kaziranga has been the theme of several books, songs, and documentaries. The park celebrated its centennial in 2005 after its establishment in 1905 as areserve forest.

Kaziranga National Park is the only natural habitat of the endangered One-Horned Rhinos in India as well as in the world. Located in the Golaghat district of Assam, Kaziranga National Park is one of the largest wildlife sanctuaries to explore the wildlife of Northeast India. It is also a highly visited park among the top 10 national parks in India. Don't forget to witness the wildness of this place on your next tour to the Northeast.

HISTORY

The history of Kaziranga as a protected area can be traced back to 1904, when Mary Curzon, Baroness Curzon of Kedleston, the wife of the Viceroy of India, Lord Curzon of Kedleston, visited the area. After failing to see a single rhinoceros, for which the area was renowned, she persuaded her husband to take urgent measures to protect the dwindling species which he did by initiating planning for their protection. On 1 June 1905, the Kaziranga Proposed Reserve Forest was created with an area of 232 km^2 (90 sq mi).

Over the next three years, the park area was extended by 152 km^2 (59 sq mi), to the banks of the Brahmaputra River. In 1908, Kaziranga was designated a *Reserve Forest.*

In 1916, it was redesignated as a game sanctuary—*The Kaziranga Game Sanctuary*—and remained so till 1938, when hunting was prohibited and visitors were permitted to enter the park.

The Kaziranga Game Sanctuary was renamed the Kaziranga Wildlife Sanctuary in 1950 by P. D. Stracey, the forest conservationist, in order to rid the name of hunting connotations. In 1954, the government of Assam passed the Assam (Rhinoceros) Bill, which imposed heavy penalties for rhinoceros poaching. Fourteen years later, in 1968, the state government passed the Assam National Park Act of 1968, declaring Kaziranga a designated national park.

The 430 km^2 (166 sq mi) park was given official status by the central government on 11 February 1974. In 1985, Kaziranga was declared a World Heritage Site by UNESCO for its unique natural environment.

Kaziranga has been the target of several natural and man-made calamities in recent decades.

Floods caused by the overflow of the river Brahmaputra, leading to significant losses of animal life. Encroachment by people along the periphery has also led to a diminished forest cover and a loss of habitat.

An ongoing separatist movement in Assam led by the United Liberation Front of Asom (ULFA) has crippled the economy of the region, but Kaziranga has remained unaffected by the movement; indeed, instances of rebels from the United Liberation Front of Assam protecting the animals and, in extreme cases, killing poachers, have been reported since the 1980s.

The park celebrated its centenary with much fanfare in 2005, inviting descendants of Lord and Lady Curzon for the celebrations. In early 2007, elephants and two rhinoceroses were relocated to Manas National Park, the first recorded instance of elephants being moved from one national park in India to another.

Etymology

One horned Indian rhinos grazing at swamp area near Bagori range under Kaziranga National Park in Nagaon district of Assam, India on Thursday. For years, rhinos have been widely slaughtered for their horn, a prized ingredient in traditional Asian medicines. Destruction of their habitat over the years has brought the rhinos to the brink of extinction. These animals are among the world's most endangered species.

Although the etymology of the name Kaziranga is not certain, there exist a number of possible explanations derived from local legends and records. According to one legend, a girl named Ranga, from a nearby village, and a youth named Kazi, from Karbi Anglong, fell in love. This match was not acceptable to their families, and the couple disappeared into the forest, never to be seen again, and the forest was named after them. According to another legend, Srimanta Sankardeva, the sixteenth century Vaisnava saint-scholar, once blessed a childless couple, Kazi and Rangai, and asked them to dig a big pond in the region so that their name would live on.

Greater one-horned rhinoceros

Testimony to the long history of the name can be found in some records, which state that once, while the Ahom king Pratap Singha was passing by the region during the seventeenth century, he was particularly impressed by the taste of fish, and on asking was told it came from Kaziranga. Kaziranga also could mean the *"Land of red goats (Deer)"*, as the word *Kazi* in the Karbi language means "goat", and *Rangai* means "red".

Some historians believe, however, that the name Kaziranga was derived from the Karbi word *Kajir-a-rang*, which means *"the village of Kajir"* (kajiror gaon).

Among the Karbis, Kajir is a common name for a girl child, and it was believed that a woman named Kajir once ruled over the area. Fragments of monoliths associated with Karbi rule found scattered in the area seem to bear testimony to this assertion.

Geography

Kaziranga is located between latitudes 26°30' N and 26°45' N, and longitudes 93°08' E to 93°36' E within two districts in the Indian state of Assam—the Kaliabor subdivision of Nagaon district and the Bokakhat subdivision of Golaghat district.

The park is approximately 40 km (25 mi) in length from east to west, and 13 km (8 mi) in breadth from north to south. Kaziranga covers an area of 378 km^2 (146 sq mi), with approximately 51.14 km^2 (20 sq mi) lost to erosion in recent years.

A total addition of 429 km^2 (166 sq mi) along the present boundary of the park has been made and designated with separate national park status to provide extended habitat for increasing the population of wildlife or, as a corridor for safe movement of animals to Karbi Anglong Hills. Elevation ranges from 40 m (131 ft) to 80 m (262 ft). The park area is circumscribed by the Brahmaputra River, which forms the northern and eastern boundaries, and the Mora Diphlu, which forms the southern boundary. Other notable rivers within the park are the Diphlu and Mora Dhansiri.

Kaziranga has flat expanses of fertile, alluvial soil, formed by erosion and silt deposition by the River Brahmaputra. The landscape consists of exposed sandbars, riverine flood-formed lakes known as, *beels*, (which make up 5% of the surface area), and elevated regions known as, *chapories*, which provide retreats and shelter for animals during floods.

Many artificial *chapories* have been built with the help of the Indian Army to ensure the safety of the animals. Kaziranga is one of the largest tracts of protected land in the sub-Himalayan belt, and due to the presence of highly diverse and visible species, has been described as a *"biodiversity hotspot"*. The park is located in the Indomalaya ecozone, and the dominant biomes of the region are Brahmaputra Valley semi-evergreen forests of the tropical and subtropical moist broadleaf forests biome and a frequently flooded variant of the Terai-Duar savanna and grasslands of the tropical and subtropical grasslands, savannas, and shrublands biome.

Climate

The park experiences three seasons: summer, monsoon, and winter. The winter season, between November and February, is mild and dry, with a mean high of 25 °C (77 °F) and low of 5 °C (41 °F). During this season, *beels* and *nallahs* (water channels) dry up. The summer season between March and May is hot, with temperatures reaching a high of 37 °C (99 °F). During this season, animals usually are found near water bodies. The rainy monsoon season lasts from June to September, and is responsible for most of Kaziranga's annual rainfall of 2,220 mm (87 in). During the peak months of July and August, three-fourths of the western region of the park is submerged, due to the rising water level of the Brahmaputra. The flooding causes most animals to migrate to elevated and forested regions outside the southern border of the park, such as the Mikir hills. 540 animals, including 13 rhinos and mostly hog deers perished in unprecedented floods of 2012. However, occasional dry spells create problems as well, such as food shortages and occasional forest fires.

Fauna

Kaziranga contains significant breeding populations of 35 mammalian species, of which 15 are threatened as per the IUCN Red List. The park has the distinction of being home to the world's largest population of the Great Indian One-Horned Rhinoceros (1,855), Wild Asiatic Water Buffalo (1,666) and Eastern Swamp Deer (468). Significant populations of large herbivores include elephants (1,940), gaur (30) and sambar (58). Small herbivores include the Indian Muntjac, wild boar, and hog deer. Kaziranga has the largest population of the Wild water buffalo anywhere accounting for about 57% of the world population.

Kaziranga is one of the few wild breeding areas outside Africa for multiple species of large cats, such as Indian Tigers and Leopards. Kaziranga was declared a Tiger Reserve in 2006 and has the highest density of tigers in the world (one per five km²), with a population of 118, according to the latest census. Other felids include the Jungle Cat, Fishing Cat, and Leopard Cats. Small mammals include the rare Hispid Hare, Indian Gray Mongoose, Small Indian Mongooses, Large Indian Civet, Small Indian Civets, Bengal Fox, Golden Jackal, Sloth Bear, Chinese Pangolin, Indian Pangolins, Hog Badger, Chinese Ferret Badgers, and Particolored flying squirrels.

Nine of the 14 primate species found in India occur in the park. Prominent among them are the Assamese Macaque, Capped, Golden Langur, as well as the only ape found in India, the Hoolock Gibbon. Kaziranga's rivers are also home to the endangered Ganges Dolphin.

Kaziranga has been identified by Birdlife International as an Important Bird Area. It is home to a variety of migratory birds, water birds, predators, scavengers, and game birds. Birds such as the Lesser White-fronted Goose, Ferruginous Duck, Baer's Pochard duck and Lesser Adjutant,Greater Adjutant, Black-necked Stork, and Asian Openbill stork migrate from Central Asia to the park during winter. Riverine birds include the Blyth's Kingfisher, White-bellied Heron, Dalmatian

Pelican, Spot-billed Pelican, Nordmann's Greenshank, and Black-bellied Tern. Birds of prey include the rare Eastern Imperial, Greater Spotted, White-tailed, Pallas's Fish Eagle, Grey-headed Fish Eagle, and the Lesser Kestrel.

Kaziranga was once home to seven species of vultures, but the vulture population reached near extinction, supposedly by feeding on animal carcasses containing the drug Diclofenac. Only the Indian Vulture, Slender-billed Vulture, and Indian White-rumped Vulturehave survived. Game birds include the Swamp Francolin, Bengal Florican, and Pale-capped Pigeon.

Other families of birds inhabiting Kaziranga include the Great Indian Hornbill and Wreathed Hornbill, Old World babblers such as Jerdon's and Marsh Babblers, weaver birdssuch as the common Baya Weaver, threatened Finn's Weavers, thrushes such as Hodgson's Bushchat and Old World warblers such as the Bristled Grassbird. Other threatened species include the Black-breasted Parrotbill and the Rufous-vented Prinia. Two of the largest snakes in the world, the Reticulated Python and Rock Python, as well as the longest venomous snake in the world, the King Cobra, inhabit the park. Other snakes found here include the Indian Cobra, Monocled Cobra, Russell's Viper, and the Common Krait.

Monitor lizard species found in the park include the Bengal monitor and the Water Monitor. Other reptiles include fifteen species of turtle, such as the endemic Assam Roofed Turtle and one species of tortoise, the Brown Tortoise. 42 species of fish are found in the area, including the Tetraodon.

Flora

Grasslands and deciduous forests of Kaziranga

Four main types of vegetation exist in this park. These are alluvial inundated grasslands, alluvial savanna woodlands, tropical moist mixed deciduous forests, and tropical semi-evergreen forests. Based on Landsat data for 1986, percent coverage by vegetation is: tall grasses 41%, short grasses 11%, open jungle 29%, swamps 4%, rivers and water bodies 8%, and sand 6%.

View of a leafless tree viewed from a watch tower in Kaziranga National Park with the backdrop of the grasslands and the forest in the distance

There is a difference in altitude between the eastern and western areas of the park, with the western side being at a lower altitude. The western reaches of the park are dominated by grasslands. Tall elephant grass is found on higher ground, while short grasses cover the lower grounds surrounding the beels or flood-created ponds. Annual flooding, grazing by herbivores, and controlled burning maintain and fertilize the grasslands and reeds. Common tall grasses are sugarcanes, spear grass, elephant grass, and the common reed. Numerous forbs are present along with the grasses. Amidst the grasses, providing cover and shade are scattered trees—dominant species including kumbhi, Indian gooseberry, the cotton tree (in savanna woodlands), and elephant apple (in inundated grasslands).

Thick evergreen forests, near the Kanchanjhuri, Panbari, and Tamulipathar blocks, contain trees such as *Aphanamixis polystachya, Talauma hodgsonii, Dillenia indica, Garcinia tinctoria, Ficus rumphii, Cinnamomum bejolghota*, and species of Syzygium. Tropical semi-evergreen forests are present near Baguri, Bimali, and Haldibari. Common trees and shrubs are *Albizia procera, Duabanga grandiflora, Lagerstroemia speciosa, Crateva unilocularis, Sterculia urens, Grewia serrulata, Mallotus philippensis, Bridelia retusa, Aphania rubra, Leea indica*, and *Leea umbraculifera.*

There are many different aquatic floras in the lakes and ponds, and along the river shores. The invasive water hyacinth is very common, often choking the water bodies, but it is cleared during destructive floods. Another invasive species, *Mimosa invisa*, which istoxic to herbivores, was cleared by Kaziranga staff with help from the Wildlife Trust of India in 2005.

Administration

The Wildlife wing of the forest department of the Government of Assam, headquartered at Bokakhat, is responsible for the administration and management of Kaziranga. The administrative head of the park is the director, who is a Chief Conservator-level officer. A divisional forest officer is the administrative chief executive of the park. He is assisted by two officers with the rank of assistant conservator of forests. The park area is divided into five ranges, overseen by range forest officers. The five ranges are the Burapahar, Baguri, Central, Eastern and North Bank. They are headquartered at Ghorakati, Baguri, Kohora, Agoratoli and Biswanath respectively. Each range is further sub-divided into beats, headed by a forester, and sub-beats, headed by a forest guard.

The park receives financial aid from the State Government as well as the Ministry of Environment and Forests of Government of Indiaunder various Plan and Non-Plan Budgets. Additional funding is received under the Project Elephant from the Central Government. In 1997–1998, a grant of US$ 100,000 was received under the Technical Co-operation for Security Reinforcement scheme from the World Heritage Fund. Additional funding is also received from national & international Non-governmental organizations.

Conservation management

Kaziranga National Park has been granted maximum protection under the Indian law for wildlife conservation. Various laws, which range in dates from the *Assam Forest Regulation of 1891* and the *Biodiversity Conservation Act of 2002* have been enacted for protection of wildlife in the park. Poaching activities, particularly of the rhinoceroses for its horn, has been a major concern for the authorities.

Between 1980 and 2005, 567 rhinoceroses were hunted by poachers. Following a decreasing trend for the past few years, 18 one-horned rhinoceroses were killed by poachers in 2007. Reports have suggested that there are links between these poaching activities and funding of terrorism#Organisation. But these could not be substantiated in later years. Preventive measures such as construction of anti-poaching camps and maintenance of existing ones, patrolling, intelligence gathering, and control over the use of firearms around the park have reduced the number of casualties. Since 2013, the park used cameras on drones which are monitored by security guards to protect the rhino from armed poachers.

Perennial flooding and heavy rains have resulted in death of wild animals and damage to the conservation infrastructures. To escape the water-logged areas, many animals migrate to elevated regions outside the park boundaries where they are susceptible to hunting, hit by speeding vehicles, or subject to reprisals by villagers for damaging their crops. To mitigate the losses, the authorities have increased patrols, purchased additional speedboats for patrol, and created artificial highlands for shelter.

Several corridors have been set up for the safe passage of animals across National Highway–37 which skirts around the southern boundary of the park. To prevent the spread of diseases and to maintain the genetic distinctness of the wild species, systematic steps such as immunization of livestock in surrounding villages and fencing of sensitive areas of the park, which are susceptible to encroachment by local cattle, are undertaken periodically.

Water pollution due to run-off from pesticides from tea gardens, and run-off from a petroleum refinery at Numaligarh, pose a hazard to the ecology of the region. Invasive species such as Mimosa and wild rose have posed a threat to the native plants in the region. To control the growth and irradiation of invasive species, research on biological methods for controlling weeds, manual uprooting and weeding before seed settling are carried out at regular intervals. Grassland management techniques, such as controlled burning, are effected annually to avoid forest fires.

Visitor activities

Observing the wildlife, including birding, is the main visitor activity in and around the park. Guided tours by elephant or Jeep are available. Hiking is prohibited in the park to avoid potential human-animal conflicts. Observation towers are situated at Sohola, Mihimukh, Kathpara, Foliamari, and Harmoti for wildlife viewing.

The Lower Himalayan peaks frame the park's landscape of trees and grass interspersed with numerous ponds. An interpretation centre is being set up at the Bagori range of Kaziranga, to help visitors learn more about the park. The park remains closed for visitors from mid-April to mid-October due to monsoon rains. Four tourist lodges at Kohora and three tourist lodges inside the park are maintained by the Department of Environment and Forests, Government of Assam.

Private resorts are available outside the park borders. Increase in tourist inflow has led to the economic empowerment of the people living at the fringes of the park, by means of tourism related activities, encouraging a recognition of the value of its protection. A survey of tourists notes that 80 percent found rhino sightings most enjoyable and that foreign tourists were more likely to support park protection and employment opportunities financially, while local tourists favored support for veterinary services.

Transport

Authorised guides of the forest department accompany all travellers inside the park. Mahout-guided elephant rides and Jeep or other4WD vehicles rides are booked in advance. Starting from the Park Administrative Centre at Kohora, these rides can follow the three motorable trails under the jurisdiction of three ranges— Kohora, Bagori, and Agaratoli. These trails are open for light vehicles from November to mid-May. Visitors are allowed to take their own vehicles when accompanied by guides.

Buses owned by Assam State Transport Corporation and private agencies between Guwahati, Tezpur, and Upper Assam stop at the main gate of Kaziranga on NH 37 at Kohora. The nearest town is Bokakhat 23 kilometres (14 mi) away. Major cities near the park are Guwahati (217 kilometres (135 mi)) and Jorhat (97 kilometres (60 mi)). Furkating 75 kilometres (47 mi), which is under the supervision of Northeast Frontier Railway, is the nearest railway station. Jorhat Airport at Rowriah (97 kilometres (60 mi) away), Tezpur Airportat Salonibari (approx 100 kilometres (62 mi) away), and Lokpriya Gopinath Bordoloi International Airport in Guwahati (approximately 217 kilometres (135 mi) away) are the nearby airports.. Transportation is also available from Guwahati to Kaziranga National Park and other places in Assam.

In popular culture

Kaziranga has been the theme of, or has been mentioned in, several books, songs, and documentaries. The park first gained international prominence after Robin Banerjee, a physician turned photographer and filmmaker, produced a documentary titled *Kaziranga*, which aired onBerlin television in 1961 and became a runaway success. American science fiction and fantasy author, L. Sprague de Camp wrote about the park in his poem, *"Kaziranga, Assam"*. It was first published in 1970 in *Demons and Dinosaurs*, a poetry collection, and was reprinted as *Kaziranga* in *Years in the Making: the Time-Travel Stories of L. Sprague de Camp* in 2005.

Kaziranga Trail, a children's storybook by Arup Dutta about rhinoceros poaching in the national park, won the Shankar's Award. The Assamese singer Bhupen Hazarika refers to Kaziranga in one of his songs. The BBC conservationist and travel writer, Mark Shand, authored a book and the corresponding BBC documentary *Queen of the Elephants*, based on the life of the first female mahout in recent times—Parbati Barua of Kaziranga. The book went on to win the 1996 Thomas Cook Travel Book Award and the Prix Litteraire d'Amis, providing publicity simultaneously to the profession of mahouts as well as to Kaziranga.

KAZIRANGA NATIONAL PARK AND TIGER RESERVE

All those who have thought Indian one-horned rhinoceros only existed in Jurassic-era, then a trip to Kaziranga is a must for them. One of the most sought after wildlife holiday destinations in India, Kaziranga National park's 430 square kilometer area sprinkled with elephant-grass meadows, swampy lagoons, and dense forests is home to more than 2200 Indian one-horned rhinoceros, approximately 2/3rd of their total world population. Formed in 1908 on the recommendation of Mary Curzon, the park is located in the edge of the Eastern Himalayan biodiversity hotspots - Golaghat and Nagaon district.

In the year 1985, the park was declared as a World Heritage Site by UNESCO. It is said when Mary Curzon, the wife of the Viceroy of India - Lord Curzon of Kedleston, visited the park to see Indian one-horned rhinoceros; she wasn't able to found even one. Then she persuaded her husband to take urgent measures to protect the dwindling species which he did by initiating planning for their protection. After a series of meetings and documentations, the Kaziranga Proposed Reserve Forest was created with an area of 232 km2 (90 sq mi) in 1905.

Along with the iconic Greater one-horned rhinoceros, the park is the breeding ground of elephants, wild water buffalo, and swamp deer. Over the time, the tiger population has also increased in Kaziranga, and that's the reason why Kaziranga was declared as Tiger Reserve in 2006. Also, the park is recognized as an Important Bird Area by BirdLife International for the conservation of avifaunal species. Birds like lesser white-fronted goose, ferruginous duck, Baer's pochard duck and lesser adjutant, greater adjutant, black-necked stork, and Asian Openbill stork specially migrate from the Central Asia during the winter season.

Undoubtedly, the park is known for its good population of animals but more than that its the wildlife conservation initiatives that take place in the park are more popular. With its amazing wildlife conservation activities, the park has successfully managed to grow the population of Greater one-horned rhinoceros, an endangered species.

The vast expanse of tall elephant grass, marshland, and dense tropical moist broadleaf forests undoubtedly makes the park look beautiful but it's the presence of Brahmaputra river, which makes it look enigmatic.

Flora

Due to the difference in altitude between the eastern and western areas of the park, here one can see mainly four types of vegetation' like alluvial inundated grasslands, alluvial savanna woodlands, tropical moist mixed deciduous forests, and tropical semi-evergreen forests. Kumbhi, Indian gooseberry, the cotton tree, and elephant Apple are amongst the famous trees that can be seen in the park. Also, a good variety of aquatic flora can be seen in lakes, ponds, and along the river shores.

Fauna

The forest region of Kaziranga Park is home to world's largest population of Indian Rhinoceros. Other animals that can be seen in the elephant grass, marshland and dense tropical moist broadleaf forests of Kaziranga are Hoolock Gibbon, Tiger, Leopard, Indian Elephant, Sloth Bear, Wild water buffalo, swamp deer, etc.

With increase in tiger population every year, the government authorities declared Kaziranga as a Tiger Reserve in the year 2006. Also here one can find good number of migratory bird species from Central Asia.

Best Time to Visit

Kaziranga Park remain closed from 01 May till 31 Oct every year for the visitors. Therefore November to April is the best time to visit Kaziranga National Park.

Summer (April to May): During this time of the year, the climate remains dry and windy; one can find animals around the water bodies.

Monsoon (June to September): From June till September, the region receives heavy rain, approximately 2,220 millimeters (87 in); thus the climate remains hot and humid. The park remains closed from May to October due to warnings of Brahmaputra river floods.

Winter (November to February): Perhaps the best time to visit the Kaziranga National Park as the climate is mild and dry. Chances of spotting rhinos are more in winter as the grass burn off and the background becomes clearer.

Safari Timing

To promote wildlife tourism in Assam, Kaziranga Park authorities organizes a jeep and elephant safari tour.

- Morning Jeep Safari: 8:00 AM to 10:00 AM
- Afternoon Jeep Safari: 02:00 PM to 04:00 PM

Elephant Safari Timing

- Morning- 05:30 / 06:30
- Morning- 06:30 / 07:30

Safari Gate/Zones

Sprawling over an area of 430 sq km, the park alias the hotspot of diversity is split into four areas; each has its own distinguish feature regarding grasslands, the density of mammals & bird, land topography, terrains. Below are some points of the pre-defined tourist circuits where the jeep safari takes place:

- Mihimukh in Central Range at Kohora
- Bagori in Western Range at Bagori
- Agaratoli in Eastern Range at Agaratoli
- Ghorakati in Burapahar Range at Ghorakhati

Major Attractions in & Around the Park

To enjoy the best of the park, it would be good to take a jeep or elephant but what apart from these options? Fortunately around Kaziranga, one can find an ample number of nature getaways options like wildlife sanctuaries, parks for bird watching and hill stations. So, if, by chance, tourists have some extra days at their disposal than go to the list of places mentioned below to make the holiday even memorable. Below are some places to visit around Kaziranga National Park:

- Orang National Park (114 kms)
- Hoollongapar Gibbon Sanctuary
- Addabarie Tea Estate
- Kakochang fall (46 kms)
- Deopahar (51 kms)

If on an extended trip to Kaziranga, tourists can visit:

- Shillong
- Guwahati
- Dibru-Saikhowa National Park
- Nameri National Park
- Manas National Park.

10

Keoladeo Ghana National Park, Rajasthan

Keoladeo Ghana National Park is one of the man-made wetlands in India that has been declared as a National Park. It was formerly called as 'Bharatpur Bird Sanctuary'.

This park hosts a large number of avifauna during the summers and is considered as one of the best national parks to observe exotic migratory birds and other birds of India. Located in Bharatpur district of Rajasthan, this park serves as a primary centre for ornithologists and other zoological studies.

HISTORY OF KEOLADEO NATIONAL PARK

The Keoladeo National Park or Keoladeo Ghana National Park formerly known as the Bharatpur Bird Sanctuary in Bharatpur, Rajasthan, India is a famous avifauna sanctuary that plays host to thousands of birds especially during the winter season. Over 230 species of birds are known to have made the National Park their home. It is also a major tourist centre with scores of ornithologists arriving here in the hibernal season. It was declared a protected sanctuary in 1971. It is also a declaredWorld Heritage Site.

Keoladeo Ghana National Park is a man-made and man-managed wetland and one of the national parks of India. The reserve protects Bharatpur from frequent floods, provides grazing grounds for village cattle and earlier was primarily used as awaterfowl hunting ground. The 29 km^2 (11 sq mi) reserve is locally known as Ghana, and is a mosaic of dry grasslands, woodlands, woodland swamps, and wetlands. These diverse habitats are home to 366 bird species, 379 floral species, 50 species of fish, 13 species of snakes, 5 species of lizards, 7 amphibian species, 7 turtle species, and a variety of other invertebrates. Every year thousands of migratory waterfowl visit the park for wintering breeding etc. The Sanctuary is one of the richest bird areas in the world. It is known for nesting of its resident birds and visiting migratory birds including water birds. The rare Siberian cranes used to winter in this park but this central population of Siberian Cranes is now extinct. According to Sir Peter Scott Keoladeo Sanctuary is the world's best bird area.

History

The sanctuary was created 250 years ago and is named after a Keoladeo (Shiva) temple within its boundaries. Initially, it was a natural depression; and was flooded after the *Ajan Bund* was constructed by Maharaja Suraj Mal, the then ruler of the princely state of Bharatpur, between 1726–1763.

The bund was created at the confluence of two rivers, the Gambhir and Banganga. The park was a hunting ground for the maharajas of Bharatpur, a tradition dating back to 1850, and duck shoots were organised yearly in honor of the British viceroys. In one shoot alone in 1938, over 4,273 birds such as mallards and teals were killed by Lord Linlithgow, the then Governor-General of India.

The park was established as a national park on 10 March 1982. Previously the private duck shooting preserve of the Maharaja of Bharatpur since the 1850s, the area was designated as a bird sanctuary on 13 March 1976 and a Ramsar site under the Wetland Convention in October 1981. The last big shoot was held in 1964 but the Maharajah retained shooting rights until 1972. In 1985, the Park was declared a World Heritage Site under the world Heritage Convention. It is a reserve forest under the Rajasthan Forest Act, 1953 and therefore, is the property of the State of Rajasthan of the Indian Union. In 1982, grazing was banned in the park, leading to violent clashes between local farmers and the government.

Getting There

The nearest airports are in Delhi, and Jaipur. Daily flights are available between Delhi, Jaipur, Mumbai, Varanasi, and Lucknow. The nearest railway station is Bharatpur Junction (5 km). Bharatpur is connected with other parts of the nation by very good roads. One can travel through own vehicle too. There are regular bus services from Delhi (184 km), Mathura (39 km), Jaipur (176 km), Alwar (117 km), Agra(56km) and adjoining areas. Many trains from New Delhi (New Delhi – Mumbai and Agra – Jaipur route) stop at Bharatpur. Bharatpur is easily reached by train or bus, although private taxis from New Delhi or Agra can be employed. The Park gate is close to the bus stand and railway station.

Geography

Keoladeo (Bharatpur) National Park (27°10'N, 77°31'E) is a World Heritage Site situated in eastern Rajasthan. The park is 2 kilometers (km) southeast of Bharatpur and 50 km west of Agra. The Park is spread over approx 29 square kilometer area.

One third of the Keoladeo National Park habitat is wetland systems with varying types of microhabitats having trees, mounds, dykes and open water with or without submerged or emergent plants. The uplands have grasslands (savannas) of tall species of grass together with scattered trees and shrubs present in varying density.

A similar habitat with short grasses, such as *Cynodon dactylon* and *Dicanthium annulatum* also exists. Woodlands with thickets of huge Kadam trees (*Neolamarckia cadamba*) are distributed in scattered pockets. Richness and diversity of plant life inside the Park is remarkable. The Park's flora consists of 379 species of flowering plants of which 96 are wetland species. The Wetland is a part of the Indo-Gangetic Great Plains.

In an area characterized by sparse vegetation, the park is the only spot which has dense vegetation and trees. The principal vegetation types are tropical dry deciduous forests intermixed with dry grasslands. Where the forest has degraded, the greater part of the area is covered with shrubs and medium sized trees. The park is a fresh water swamp and is flooded during the monsoon. For most part of the year, effective wetland is only 10 km^2. The rest of the area remains dry.

Dykes divide the wetland into ten units. Each unit has a system of sluice gates to control its water level. Depth of water ranges from 1 metre to 2 metre during rains (July, August and September). In subsequent months, October to January, the level gets lowered.

The area starts drying from February. In May and June, the entire area dries. Water remains only in some depressions. This alternate wetting and drying helps to maintain the ecology of the fresh water swamp, ideal for water-fowl and resident water birds. Arrangement to pump water from deep tube wells to fill small depressions to save seeds, spores and other aquatic life also exist. They are also helpful in extreme years of drought.

Climate

During 1988, mean maximum temperature ranged from 20.9° Celsius (C) in January to 47.8°C in May, while the mean temperature varied from 6.8°C in December to 26.5°C in June. The diurnal temperature variation ranged from 5°C in January to 50°C in May. Mean relatively humidity varied from 62% in March to 83.3% in December. The mean annual precipitation is 662 millimeters (mm), with rain falling on an average of 36 days per year. During 1988 only 395mm of rain fell during 32 wet days.

Local observers have noted the shrinking of habitat for aquatic plant species in the Keoladeo National Park in Bharatpur, Rajasthan, northern India, after a number of years of drought and upstream water abstraction. The Keoladeo Naturalists Society invited U.S. Geological Survey (USGS) research ecologist Beth Middleton to visit the park to make observations of aquatic species of concern (Technical Assistance Agreement T-09-763b). The Keoladeo Naturalists Society (a.k.a. "The Barefoot Naturalists") is a group of local nature guides and rickshaw pullers. Middleton is a researcher who studies the impact of climate change, drought, and hurricanes on coastal wetlands; because of this expertise, she was asked to look at the impact of droughts on the Keoladeo National Park wetlands.

Middleton did her Ph.D. research in India 20 years previously, so she was familiar with the park under conditions of more normal flooding. Upon her return in April 2009, the park looked very different after several years of drought. The aquatic areas of the park appeared to be smaller than during the 1980s; however, at least one positive observation is that park managers have enlisted local villagers to remove the invasive mesquite plant, *Prosopis juliflora*, within upland savanna habitats.

Biology

A semi-arid biotype, the park is the only area with significant vegetation, hence the term 'Ghana' meaning 'thicket'.

The principal vegetation types are tropical dry deciduous forest, intermixed with dry grassland in areas where forest has been degraded. Apart from the artificially managed marshes; much of the area is covered by medium-sized trees and shrubs.

Forests, mostly in the northeast of the park, are dominated by kalam or kadam (*Mitragyna parvifolia*), jamun (*Syzygium cumini*) and babul (*Acacia nilotica*). The open woodland is mostly babul with a small amount of kandi (*Prosopis cineraria*) and ber (*Zizyphus*).

Scrublands are dominated by ber and kair. It is unlikely that the site would support such numbers of waterfowl as it does without the addition of water from Ajan Bund, a man-made impoundment. Soils are predominantly alluvial – some clay has formed as a result of the periodic inundations. The mean annual precipitation is 662mm, with rain falling on an average of 36 days per year.

The open woodland is mostly babul with a small amount of kandi and ber. Scrublands are dominated by ber and kair (*Capparis decidua*).

Piloo (*Salvadora oleoides* and *Salvadora persica*) also present in the park and happens to be virtually the only woody plants found in areas of saline soil. The aquatic vegetation is rich and provides a valuable food source for waterfowl.

Fauna

Macro invertebrates such as worms, insects and mollusks, though more abundant in variety and numbers than any other group of organisms, are present mostly in aquatic habitats.

They are food for many fish and birds, as well as some animal species, and hence, constitute a major link in the food chain and functioning of the ecosystem. Land insects are in abundance and have a positive effect on the breeding of land birds.

Waterfowls

The park's location in the Gangetic Plain makes it an unrivalled breeding site for herons, storks and cormorants, and an important wintering ground for large numbers of migrant ducks. The most common waterfowl are gadwall, shoveler, common teal, cotton teal,tufted duck, comb duck, little cormorant, great cormorant, Indian shag, ruff, painted stork, white spoonbill, Asian open-billed stork, oriental ibis, darter, common sandpiper, wood sandpiper and green sandpiper. Sarus crane, with its spectacular courtship dance, is also found here.

Landbirds

Among landbirds are a rich assortment consisting of warblers, babblers, bee-eaters, bulbuls, buntings, chats, partridges and quails. TheIndian grey hornbill and Marshall's iora are also present. There are many birds of prey including the osprey, peregrine, Pallas' sea eagle,short-toed eagle, tawny eagle, imperial eagle, spotted eagle and crested serpent eagle. The Greater spotted eagle has recently been recorded breeding here, a new breeding record for the species in India.

Mammals

Mammalian fauna of Keoladeo National Park is equally rich with 27 identified species. Nilgai, feral cattle, and chital deer are common while sambar are few. Wild boar and Indian porcupine are often spotted sneaking out of the Park to raid crop fields. Two mongoosespecies, the small Indian mongoose and the common Indian gray mongoose, are occasionally found. Cat species present include thejungle cat and the fishing cat. The Asian palm civet and the small Indian civet are also present, but rarely sighted. The smooth-coated otter can be seen attacking birds such as coots and at times crossing the woodlands. Jackals and hyenas are also sighted and have taken up the role of predators and feed on birds and rodents. Many species of rats, mice, gerbils and bats are also found in the park.

Other Species

Fish fauna of the park comprises 43 species, of which 37 enter the park along with the water from Ajan Bund, and six species are breeding residents. During a good rainy season the park receives around 65 million fish fry and fingerlings. The fish population and diversity are of high ecological importance as they form the food source of many birds.

The herpetofauna of Keoladeo National Park is diverse. Out of the ten species of turtles that are seen in Rajasthan, seven are present in this park. Besides this, there are five lizard species, thirteen snake species and seven species of amphibians. The bullfrog and skipper frog are commonly found in the wetlands. It is often easy to see a python out of its burrow and basking in the sun on a sunny winter day. The common monitor lizard, Indian porcupine and Bi-colored leaf-nose Bat have been seen in the same burrow as that of the python. The poisonous snakes found in the park are krait, cobra and Russell's viper. Primates include the rhesus macaque and langurs. Large predators are absent, leopards having been deliberately exterminated by 1964, but small carnivores include Bengal fox, jackal, striped hyena, common palm civet, small Indian civet, Indian grey mongoose (*Herpestes edwardsi*), fishing cat, leopard cat, jungle cat andsmooth-coated otter. Ungulates include blackbuck, chital, sambar, hog deer, nilgai and wild boar and feral cattle. Other mammals include Indian porcupine and Indian hare. During the year 2007–2008 attempts have been made to eradicate the mesquite *Prosopis juliflora* and specimens of the asteraceous genus *Cineraria* to prevent the park being overrun with these invasive species and to assist natural vegetation in recovering.

World Heritage Site

To be included on the World Heritage List, sites must be of outstanding universal value and meet at least one out of ten selection criteria. These criteria are explained in the Operational Guidelines for the Implementation of the World Heritage Convention which, besides the text of the Convention, is the main working tool on World Heritage. The criteria are regularly revised by the Committee to reflect the evolution of the World Heritage concept itself. The UNESCO convention for listing goes on to explain the criteria the selection of Keoladeo Ghana National Park as a World Heritage Site under the Natural Criteria iv of Operational Guidelines 2002 and the description which follows is that the park is a "Habitat of rare and endangered species. The park is a wetland of international importance for migratory waterfowl. It is the wintering ground for the rare Siberian Crane and habitat for large numbers of resident nesting birds." According to the revised Operational Guidelines of 2005, the park falls under Criteria (x) which states that to be conferred the status of World Heritage, the site should "contain the most important and significant natural habitats for in-site conservation of biological diversity, including those containing threatened species of outstanding universal value from the point of view of science or conservation."

Management

The management objective is to allow the area to flood and dry out annually, rather than be maintained as a system of permanent marshes. Water for the wetlands is supplied from the dam outside the park boundaries. Usually some 14.17 million cubic meters of water is the estimated annual requirement of the park. The water level inside the park is regulated by means of dykes and artificial embankments. The alternative arrangement of water in case of emergencies such as danger of marshes and water bodies drying out completely is ensured through four boreholes so that survival of the aquatic flora and fauna is not endangered before the arrival of monsoon. The boundaries of the park are clearly delineated by a thirty two Kilometer long boundary encircling the park restricting the encroachment of humans and domestic cattle inside the perimeters of the park. The road from Bharatpur town which used to intersect the park was also closed and relocated outside the boundary to reduce the disturbance by visitors from the town which helped in bringing down the levels of pollution inside the park considerably. As opposed to most of the national parks in India and elsewhere, Bharatpur Bird sanctuary has no buffer zone. Due to the heavy density of population and more than 15 villages settled on the periphery of park, it was impossible for authorities to create a buffer zone around the bird sanctuary. Grazing and collection of firewood and grass was phased out from the park as far back as 1983.

Constraints

The Siberian crane, which formerly lived throughout the entire Indo-Gangetic plains of India, is reported to no longer be found in the area. Its absence has been attributed to hunting by nomadic tribes along the species' 5,000 mile migration route from Siberia to Bharatpur.

Some 2,500 cattle and water buffalo were allowed in the area up until November 1982 when grazing was banned. Predictably, the ban led to a buildup of local resentment, resulting in an attempted forced entry into the park. Police opened fire and eight people were killed: tensions still remain high. The absence of grazing is causing management problems as vegetation, principally Paspalum distichum, a perennial amphibious grass, blocks up the channels. The Rajasthan government has rejected a proposal from the Bombay Natural History Society to allow limited grazing, since this conflict with the law. Furthermore, recycled nutrients from the large quantity of dung deposited by livestock probably supported considerable numbers of insects.

The presence of some 700 feral cattle within the park is cause for concern as they compete with wildlife for valuable forage. Larvae of the Lepidopteran *Parapoynx diminutalis*has also been a serious pest, and considerably inhibited the growth of *Nymphoides cristatum* during June–July 1986. High levels of pollutants in Ajan Bund are believed to be responsible for the increasing number of piscivorous birds seen in a dazed state and unable to fly. Fewer birds were recorded in 1984 than in previous years.

Four Sarus cranes and 40 ring doves were found dead outside the park during 1988 and early 1989, possibly due to pesticide poisoning, and a study of the impact of pesticide use in surrounding areas on the park has been initiated in addition to studies on heavy metal contamination. Disturbance from visitors can be a cause for concern, especially during the December and January when visitors come to see the cranes.

A non-native water hyacinth Icornia species was introduced in 1961, and has now proliferated to the extent that it is blocking the artificial waterways and filling the impoundments. This is significantly altering the habitat for many bird species, and is a serious management problem. Attempts to control the species have been ineffectual upto date.

Tourism & Visitor facilities

By virtue of being one of the best bird watching sites of Asia, more than 100,000 visitors come to the park every year. The range of visitors varies from very serious birdwatchers to school children. Of the visitors, 45,000 are foreign tourists.

In addition the location of the park is such that tourists visiting Agra, Fatehpur Sikri and Jaipur invariably stop over at Bharatpur. The Park opens from sunrise to sunset around the year. The ticket is Rs200 per foreign visitor and Rs50 for Indian visitor. Vehicles are not permitted inside the park, but you need to park them in the designated parking are for 100rs for four wheeler. After this you can choose to walk, bicycle, or go by cycle rickshaw, Tonga or boat when the water level is high.

Jent's standard bicycle is available for 25 rs and Ladies cycle is available for 40 rs. Do check that the bicycle is in good condition(The staff is very helpful and will advise you to do so). For all services including parking you will have to pay and take a token from the counter at the main gate.

There is no charge to get your photo or video camera inside the park.

If you do not wish to drive bicycle or walk, then take a rickshow for 100rs per hour. The cycle rickshaw wallah's displaying yellow plate meaning authorized double up as guides also carry binoculars. Hotels do supply packed lunches and you can get a bite at a canteen on the second gate and even at Forest Lodge.

Food and accommodation facilities are available within the precincts of the park. The only accommodation inside the Keoladeo National Park is available in the property of government Bharatpur Forest Lodge and lesser expensive Shanti Kutir, which is maintained and run by the ITDC. Bharatpur Forest Lodge is a quaint hotel in the vicinity of natural treasure trove of the park and has a total of 16 rooms to offer to visitors. Circuit house and Dak bungalow also offer good accommodation options.

Visitors coming to Bharatpur can also stay in palaces, havelis and other heritage properties converted into hotels. It's always advisable to have one's accommodation pre-booked, especially so during winters. An array of 3 star hotels and resorts are also located in the vicinity of the park where visitors can stay cozily.

Besides the normal tourism activities and self arranged bird watching tours of the Keoladeo National Park, visitors can also opt for a tour of this birding destination by selecting from an array of luxury tourist train services. Luxury trains like Palace on Wheels include Bharatpur Bird Sanctuary in its tour itinerary.

Scientific Research and Facilities

The Bombay Natural History Society has done considerable work in the area, including the ringing of birds for the last 40 years. The society has recently intensified its operations and has established a hydro-biological station to monitor the ecology of the wetland. Particular attention will be given to any in dramatic change in the vegetation following the ban on grazing. Limnological studies have been carried out by the Zoology Department of the University of Rajasthan, Jaipur. The park authorities are monitoring the bird populations. A documentary film 'Indian birds of the monsoon' was produced by S. and B. Breeden in 1979–1980. The park has considerable potential for education, more so than other wetland sites in India, in view of it being relatively near to the cities of Agra, Delhi and Jaipur.

Between December 1992 and January 1995, a collaborative project between the Governments of India and Russia, International Crane Foundation and Wild Bird Society of Japan was set up to save the Siberian crane. The project focused on releasing captivity bred cranes into the wild, tracking migratory routes of common cranes, and building up the resident crane population in the park. Although the project did not yield the desired results, the successful survival of introduced cranes in the park has given sufficient hope to develop a viable resident population in the future.

Crises of 2007

A proposal for water supply to Keoladeo National Park, Bharatpur was forwarded by the Government of Rajasthan seeking assistance from Planning Commission as advised and approved by the Ministry of Environment and Forests. Keeping in view the uniqueness of the eco system and the capacity to attract a variety of migratory birds the project was thought to be approved in principal with the caveat that the cost be firmed up after a visit to the site by an expert team. The park is in danger of being removed as a Ramsar Site as well as UNESCO World Heritage Site, due to severe drought and abandoning of the park mid way by nesting birds in the year 2007.

A proposal for water supply to Keoladeo National Park, Bharatpur was forwarded by the Government of Rajasthan seeking assistance from Planning Commission as advised and approved by the Ministry of Environment and Forests (MoEF) vide their letter dated 10.04.2008. As per the MoEF, the proposal is beyond the purview of the existing centrally sponsored scheme of the MoEF, seems to be viable and has the potential to put an end to the eternal water scarcity in Bharatpur National Park.

The Keoladeo National Park (KNP) is a Ramsar Wetland Site and a World Heritage site. Due to acute water scarcity the ecosystem of the Park has been affected badly and this has resulted in reduction in the arrival of migratory birds in the National Park. Water supply is essential for the National Park, which is a wetland and a Ramsar site facing acute shortage of water for the last few years.

Currently apart from rain fall the Park receives water from "Ajan Bund", a temporary reservoir via the Dakan canal. Through a small canal dug last year water from Khokhar Weir (Bees Mora) is also available. The total requirement of water for the Park is estimated at about 14.17 Million cubic meters (500 MCft). The supply from Ajan Bund is irregular and subject to the bund being full to the extent of reservoir level at 8.5 meters. During the last several years either water is not supplied or supplied insufficiently.

The project had been prepared keeping in view the need for 400 MCFT of water during late July to August, for a period of 30 days to the Park which is to be had by diverting and lifting flood waters of Yamuna. The project thus covered diversion of water during monsoon through underground pipes with lifting arrangements over a length of 16 km. from the off-take point of Goverdhan drain near Santruk village.

The estimated cost of the project as proposed by the State Government was to the tune of Rs650 millions. The project proposed was to channelize water from Govardhan drain to meet the water deficit of KNP during the months of July to September at the time of requirement. The major components of the project were construction of a head regulator with control gate at the drain located in the state, raw water reservoir with capacity of 13,000 m, 3 pump houses, DG sets for pumping station and laying and testing of /PCC/MS pipelines.

11

Nagarhole National Park, Karnataka

Nagarhole National Park is located in Mysore district of Karnataka and is a popular destination for Tiger spotting. It is also known as 'Rajiv Gandhi National Park'. With quite a large number of Tigers, this park also has a significant number of Indian Bison, Leopard, Sloth Bear and Elephant.

Forests of this park are extremely rich with several species of high commercial valued trees. Teak, Sandalwood and Silver Oak are the major trees found in this park. Along with the endangered Mugger Crocodile, this park also has more than 250 species of birds, 96 species of Dung Beetles and 60 species of Ants.

HISTORY OF NAGARHOLE NATIONAL PARK

Nagarhole National Park (also known as Rajiv Gandhi National Park), is a national park located in Kodagu district and Mysore district in Karnataka state in South India. This park was declared the thirty seventh Project Tiger tiger reserve in 1999.

It is part of the Nilgiri Biosphere Reserve. TheWestern Ghats Nilgiri Sub-Cluster of 6,000 km² (2,300 sq mi), including all of Nagarhole National Park, is under consideration by the UNESCO World Heritage Committee for selection as a World Heritage Site.

The park has rich forest cover, small streams, hills, valleys and waterfalls. The park has a healthy tiger-predator ratio, with manytigers, Indian bison and elephants.

Location

The park ranges the foothills of the Western Ghats spreading down the Brahmagiri hills and south towards Kerala state. It lies between the latitudes 12°15'37.69"E and longitudes 76°17'34.4"N. The park covers 643 km² (248 sq mi) located to the north-west of Bandipur National Park. The Kabini reservoir separates the two parks. Elevations of the park range from 687 to 960 m (2,254 to 3,150 ft). It is 50 km (31 mi) from the major city of Mysore.

Together with the adjoining Bandipur National Park (870 km² (340 sq mi)), Mudumalai National Park (320 km² (120 sq mi)) andWayanad Wildlife Sanctuary (344 km² (133 sq mi)), it forms the largest protected area in Southern India, totalling 2,183 km²(843 sq mi).

History

Nagarhole name has been derived from two Kannada name, Nagar means "snake" and hole meaning streams. Genuinely, the name strikes the true meaning to this national park where few serpentine streams fork through the rich tropical forests running eastwards through its center. The birth of Nagarhole National Parkcan be traced by the stretching area of 258 sq km when it was a hunting reserve for the Maharajas of Mysore. That time it included some of the areas of the forest like Arkeri, Hatgat and Nalkeriin Kodagu. Subsequently in the year 1974 some other reserve forests from the adjoining areas of Mysore district were added to bring the area as Nagarhole Game Reserve and then was updated into the national park extending by the area 643.39 sq km in the year 1988.

The park was declared as a tiger reserve in the year 1999 to exemplify rich forest cover, small streams, hills, valleys and waterfalls. The park has a healthy tiger-predator ratio, with many tigers, Indian bison and elephants.

The park derives its name from *naga*, meaning snake and *hole*, referring to streams. The park was an exclusive hunting reserveof the kings of the Wodeyar dynasty, the former rulers of the Kingdom of Mysore. It was set up in 1955 as a wildlife sanctuary and later its area increased to 643.39 km (399.78 mi). It was upgraded into a national park in 1988. The park was declared a tiger reserve in 1999.

Young Gray Langur at Nagahole, Mysuru

Climate and Ecology

The park receives an annual rainfall of 1,440 millimetres (57 in). Its water sources include the Lakshmmantirtha river, Sarati Hole, Nagar Hole, Balle Halla, Kabini River, four perennial streams, 47 seasonal streams, four small perennial lakes, 41 artificial tanks, several swamps, Taraka Dam and the Kabini reservoir.

Flora

The vegetation here consists mainly of North Western Ghats moist deciduous forests with (*teak* and *rosewood* predominating in the southern parts. There is Central Deccan Plateau dry deciduous forests with Pala indigo and thorny wattle towards the east. There are some sub-montane valley swamp forests with several species of the Eugenia genus.

The main trees found are here are the commercially important rosewood, teak, sandalwood and silver oak. Species of trees of the dry deciduous forest include *crocodile bark, Lagerstroemia lanceolata* (Crepe myrtle), Indian Kino Tree, Grewia tilaefolia, *rosewoodand* axlewood. Other tree species that are seen in the forests are *Lagerstroemia microcarpa* (Crepe myrtle), Kadam, cotton tree,*Schleichera trijuga* and some species of Ficus.

In the understorey, species found growing include *Kydia calycina*, Indian gooseberry and beechwood, Shrubs like horse nettles, tick clover, *Helicteres* species and invasive species like lantana and bonesets are found in abundance.

These forests have some conspicuous tree species such as golden shower tree, Flame of the Forest and *clumping bamboo.*

Fauna

The park protects the wildlife of Karnataka. The important predators and carnivors in the Nagarhole National Park are tiger, leopard, wild dog (dhole or Cuon alpinus), sloth bear and the hyena (Hyaena hyaena). The herbivores are spotted deer, sambar, barking deer, four-horned antelope (Tetracerus quadricornis), gaur (Bos gaurus), wild boar (Sus scrofa) and elephant. Nagarhole National Park provides an opportunity to see some of the southern population of Gaur (jungle Bison).

Also, this park in Karnataka is a good place to see elephants in the luxuriant forests and bamboo thickets which they most enjoy. Their total population in southern India is now about 6500, nearly all living in the area where Karnataka, Tamil Nadu and Kerala adjoin in the shadow of the Western Ghats.

Other mammalian miscallany includes the common langur (Presbytes entellus), Bonnet macaque (Macaca radiata), jungle cat, slender Loris (Loris tadigradus), leopard-cat (Felis bengalensis), civet cat (Viverricula indica and Paradoxurus hermaphroditus), mongoose (Herpestes fuscus and Herpestes vitticollis), common otter (Lutra lutra), giant flying squirrel (Petaurista petaurista), giant squirrel (Ratufa indica), porcupine, jackal, mouse-deer (Tragulus meminna), hare and pangolin (Manis crassicaudata). Over 250 species of birds are found at Nagarhole National Park.

Besides the enormous variety of woodland birds, there are large congregations of water fowl in the Kabini river. Birds range from blue-bearded bee-eater, scarlet minivet and Malabar whistling thrush to the more common ospreys, herons and ducks.

Flora

The vegetation is comprised mainly of North Western Ghats, moist deciduous forests with (teak and rosewood predominating in the southern parts. The presence of Central Deccan Plateau, dry deciduous forests with Pala indigo and thorny wattle towards the east bring the topography more ardent for lushly foliages. There are some additional sub-montane valleys, swamp forests with several species of the Eugenia genus.

The main trees found here are the commercially important rosewood, teak, sandalwood and silver oak. Species of trees of the dry deciduous forest include crocodile bark, Lagerstroemia lanceolata (Crepe myrtle),Grewiatilaefolia, Indian Kino Tree, rosewood and axlewood. Other tree species that are seen in the forests are Lagerstroemia microcarpa (Crepe myrtle), Schleicheratrijuga, Kadam, cotton tree and some species of Ficus.

Along with that some other species may also be found germinating at Nagarholeto include Kydiacalycina, Indian gooseberry and Beachwood, Shrubs like horse nettles, tick clover, Helicteres species and invasive species like lantana and bonesets are found in abundance.

Forests of the reserve area may also have some conspicuous tree species such as golden shower tree, Flame of the Forest and clumping bamboo for more wildernesses.

Places of Interest

Kutta : Presiding not so far way from Nagarhole National Park, the place is named after Kutta, the son of Goddess Kali. It is believed that Goddess Kali came to this place and resided here with low-caste Kurubas. It is here that she had a son named Kutta. A major festival celebrated here to honor the goddess that can be witnessed on the occasion.

Irppu Falls : Yet another crowd puller near Nagarhole National Park, this spot is extremely scenic. As the water gushes down Brahmagiri, a fall is formed at this spot which is termed as Irppu Falls.

Ishwara Temple : This is an important pilgrim and tourist center near Nagarhole, where legends trails that a Shivalinga was placed by Lord Rama himself. The temple is flocked by devotees in the mornings and is closed during the afternoon.

Nearby Places

Nagarhole is the place which is located at the most juncture of all the rest of the national parksin the area. So let's find some other national parks and sanctuaries around Nagarhole National Park

Bandipur National Park : Famous for its tigers, Bandipur National Park hosts a variety of exotic flora and fauna. It is one of the protected areas within Nilgiri Biosphere Reserve, located 123 kms from Nagarhole to hardly carry for next two hours to reach the place.

Wayanad National Park : Simply 52 kms away from Nagarhole wildlife area, this is the second largest wildlife sanctuary in Kerala.

Wayanad Wildlife sanctuary hosts a rich collection of endangered wildlife species which is also home to large herds of elephants. The national park also comes under Project Elephant.

Ranganathittu Bird Sanctuary : Situated 80 km from the park, Ranganathittu Bird Sanctuary is a small sanctuary hosting some of the best avian species such as wooly necked stork, common spoonbill, Asian open bill stork and more, apart from some floral and mammal species too.

Bramhagiri Wildlife Sanctuary : This is a popular wildlife sanctuary separated from Nagarhole National Park by Kabini River. It hosts a great variety of flora and fauna. Animals like jungle cat, sloth bear, tiger, elephant, gaur, etc. can be spotted in the park.

Mudumalai National Park : The Madumalai National Park is most famous for its elephant population. It also boasts a good number of tiger populations and has been declared a tiger reserve. Panther, sambar, spotted deer, blackbuck, common langur, etc. are other wildlife species that can be spotted in the park. Interestingly, 13% of all mammal species in India are found in Mudumalai National Park.

Kabini Lake is another prime attraction situated 13 km outside the national park where the tourists can have the refreshing walk and some lucrative moments.

Safaris

Nagarhole is the place where the safari experience can be felt with great surprises. With the presence of abundance of wildlife, this place brings tremendous crowd of wildlife lovers for sighting of elephants, sambhar, spotted deer, gaur, wild boar, sloth bear, wild dogs, etc. which is quite assured. And if anyone is very lucky for sure, he/she can also have a fascinating encounter with a tiger or a panther too. The tourists are really permitted to shoot; yes they are, but not with the guns, with their cameras and videos and that truly bring a rewarding experience.

Vehicle Safari

During the boat safari, you can see many large and small herbivores such as Asiatic Elephant. Further, you can also get a chance to spot the predators like the Leopardare and Tiger.

Timing:

Morning Safari: Between 05:30 AM to 10:00 AM

Evening Safari: Between 03:00 PM to 07:00 PM

Boat Safari

While enjoying the boat safari, you will go upstream on the River Kabini from the resort and arrive at the area which divides the Bandipur and Nagarhole

National Parks. Apart from witnessing many animals on the shore of the river, you can also witness the Marsh Crocodile and many other water birds.

Timing:

Morning Safari: Between 06:30 AM to 09:15 AM

Evening Safari: Between 03:30 PM to 06:15 PM

Coracle ride (On River Kabini)

Coracle is a traditional round shaped boat designed to take ride on Indian Rivers. You can ride on a Coracle and slowly drift down the Kabini River while holding close to the shoreline. During this adventures journey, you will have an incredible experience of connecting with the river indirectly. With many slow drifts, you will come to know about many interesting facts about the river.

Timing:

Morning Safari: Between 09 AM to 11 AM

Evening Safari: Between 05 PM to 06:00 PM

Travel Information

Nagarhole National park is well connected to the adjoining areas of Karnataka. The motorable highways are linked to the park to the towns of Madikere (90 km) and Mysore (96 km). The journey from both places will stretch the timingsup to 2 hours. Similarly, the nearest well-connected railway junction is Mysore, while the nearest international airport is Bangalore (220 km). Advantageously, various airlines also connect Bangalore to the rest of the nation.

The best time to view the animals is during the heat of April& May, when the waterholes are dry and the animals come out and visit the lake. However, the weather is more pleasant from November to February.

Travel Tips

One must arrive at the park gates well before dusk, for the road through the park that leads to the lodges is prone to elephant blocks and closes at 6 pm. Those interested in trekking should avoid visiting the park during monsoons as floods wash out most of its dirt tracks and leeches render trekking impossible.

Hotels

The Nagarhole Tiger Reserve area is extenuated with great residing options in the area so as to make the jungle tour more adventurous and thrilling with the advancements of comfy services. One can stay in the Nagarhole Forest Guest house with prior booking from Wildlife department in Mysore. Besides, number of private lodges and guest houses are available at Kutta, the area available just at the outskirt of the park on the way to Irrupu Falls. Murkal is also the most demanding place in the Nagarhole vicinity to get a number of private lodges and resorts.

Mammals

Flagship species like tiger (*Panthera tigris*), Indian bison or gaur (*Bos gaurus*) and Asian elephants (*Elephas maximus*) are found in large numbers inside the park. A study carried out by Dr. Ullas Karanth of the Wildlife Conservation Society has shown that the forests of Nagarhole have three species of predators i.e. tiger, leopard (*Panthera pardus*) and wild dogs (*Cuon alpinus*) present at an equivalent density.

The park also has a good number of jackals (*Canis aureus*), grey mongoose (*Herpestes edwardsi*), sloth bears (*Melursus ursinus*),striped hyena (*Hyaena hyaena*), spotted deer or chital (*Axis axis*), sambar (*Cervus unicolor*), barking deer (*Munitacus muntjak*), four-horned antelopes (*Tetracerpus quadricornis*) and wild boar (*Sus scrofa*).

Other mammalian inhabitants include the common palm civet (*Paradoxurus hermaphroditus*), brown mongoose (*Herpestes brachyurus*), striped-necked mongoose(*Herpestes vitticollis*), black-naped hare (*Lepus nigricollis*), mouse deer, Indian pangolin (*Manis crassicaudata*), red giant flying squirrel (*Petaurista petaurista*), Indian porcupine (*Hystrix indica*) and Indian giant flying squirrel (*Petaurista philippensis*).

Birds

Recognised as an Important Bird Area the park has over 270 species of birds including the 'Critically endangered' Oriental white-backed vulture (*Gyps bengalensis*), 'Vulnerable' lesser adjutant (*Leptopilos javanicus*), greater spotted eagle (*Aquila changa*) and the Nilgiri wood-pigeon (*Columba elphinstonii*).

'Near threatened' species like darters (*Anhniga melanogaster*), oriental white ibis (*Threskiornis melanocephalus*), greater grey headed fish eagle (*Icthyophaga ichthyaetus*) and red headed vulture (*Sarcogyps calvus*) too can be found here. Endemics include the blue winged parakeet (*Psittacula columboides*), Malabar grey hornbill (*Ocyceros griseus*) and the white bellied treepie (*Dendrocitta leucogastra*).

Seven of the 15 Biome-10 (Indian Peninsula Tropical Moist Forest) and 21 of the 59 Biome-11 (Indo-Malayan Tropical Dry Zone) species have been noted from here.

Some of the birds that can be sighted here include the white cheeked barbet (*Megalaima viridis*), Indian scimitar babbler (*Pomatorhinus horsfieldii*) and Malabar whistling thrush (*Myiophonus horsfieldii*).

Birds commonly seen in drier regions like painted bush quail (*Pendicula erythrorhyncha*), Sirkeer malkhoa (*Phaenicophaeus leschenaultia*), ashy prinia (*Prinia socialis*), Indian robin (*Saxicoloides fulicata*), Indian peafowl (*Pava cristatus*) and yellow legged green pigeon (*Treron phoenicoptera*) can be found here.

Reptiles

Reptiles commonly found here are mugger(*Crocodylus palustris*), common vine snake (*Ahaetulla nasutus*), common wolf snake (*Lycodon aulicus*), rat snake (*Ptyas mucosus*), bamboo pit viper (*Trimeresurus gramineus*), Russell's viper (*Daboia russellii*), common krait (*Bangarus caeruleus*), Indian rock python (*Python molurus*), Indian monitor lizard (*Varanus bengalensis*) and the common toad (*Bufo melanostictus*).

Insects

Extensive studies on the biodiversity of the insect population have been carried out by researchers from the Ashoka Trust for Research in Ecology and the Environment, Bangalore. The insect biodiversity of this park includes over 96 species of dung beetles and 60 species of ants. Unusual species of ants that have been identified include the jumping ants such as *Harpegnathos saltator*, which are known to jump up to a metre high.

The ant species *Tetraponera rufonigra* may be useful as a marker for the health of the forests because these ants feed on termites and are abundant in places where there are lots of dead trees. Species of dung beetles identified include the common dung beetle (*Onthophagus dama*), India's largest beetle, *Heliocopris dominus* which breeds only in elephant dung and *Onthophagus pactolus*, a very rare species of dung beetle.

Tribal and Native Inhabitants

The Jenu Kurubas, primary inhabitants of this forest area, are a tribe in Karnataka state and their traditional practices and rituals are slowly disappearing. The government is restricting their entry inside the National park and forest due to multiple factors including but not limited conservation efforts and bringing the community to the mainstream society.

The Ministry of Home Affairs, Government of India, identified the Jenu Kuruba and the Koraga as tribal groups in Karnataka. The Jenu Kurubas are traditional food gatherers and honey collectors. In Kannada, the term 'Jenu' means 'honey' and the term 'kuruba' generally mean 'shepherd'. It is derived from the Kannada word 'kuri' which means 'sheep'. The term kuruba is also associated with non-shepherd communities. They speak a variant form of Kannada commonly known as Jenu-nudi within their family kin group, and Kannada with others. They use Kannada script. According to the Census of 1981, the population of Jenu Kuruba community is 34,747 out of which 17,867 are male and 16,880 are female.

The Jenu Kurubas are found scattered in the jungles as with other tribal groups. They are excellent climbers of tree and are skilled in the use of sling, bows and arrows. They demonstrate a strong emotional attachment to the forest as their mother deity and represents a whole way of life. Their food, dress, worship, house, medicine storing articles furniture etc. all are linked with forest. Parts of the tribe which have resisted exposure to modernization still live in thatched huts made of mud, leaves and grass.

The Jenu Kurubas mainly depend on forest for their day to day life. They occupy forested regions where for a long period in their history, they lived in isolation but in harmony with nature. They demonstrate significant knowledge of the forest including varied species of flora and fauna and relate to the forest very well. Collecting honey, wax and other forest produce like roots and tubers has been the mainstay of their survival and in recent times they have been found selling them in the market through organized trade groups, both legal and illegal which has led to a furore of angst amongst the conservationists.

Many of the cultural traits they have are common with the neighbouring tribes such as Betta Kuruba / Kadu Kuruba. In the forest the tribes also practice agriculture, the main crops grown are Ragi, Cow gram, Bengal gram, Horse gram and black gram.

In the recent years, a lot of commercialization has occurred due to increase in tourism and fragmentation of forest ranges leading to severe. The tribal communities have long since given up the traditional ways of life and have easily indulged in poaching activities and indiscreet hunting of birds and forest animals. Numerous cases of such assistance provided by the tribal folk to poachers in trying to sell game, live or dead, medicinal herbs have been observed and controlled by the forest department leading to a clash between the tribal communities protected by law and law enforcement agencies. To resolve this conflict and imminent threat to the bio-diversity in this forest, numerous relocation efforts and anti-poaching efforts have been made in the last decade. An increase in poaching was attributed to the tribal support received by poachers in getting guidance from the tribal groups to navigate the forest and tracking game, in exchange for money or other supply of necessities.

Relocation efforts

In the last decade there has been enormous activity undertaken both by the Government and certain NGOs to relocate tribals to the periphery of the forests. The relocation efforts are part of a larger focus to conserve the existing Tiger populations and elephant habitats which were under serious threat due to change in lifestyles of the tribal folk resident within the forests.

There has been much resistance to relocation efforts from the oldest groups of tribals but success has been met in last few years. Many schools and houses with basic amenities like lighting, hospitals and roads being built to support the relocated tribal population.

Threats and Conservation efforts

Timber Smuggling

Threats to the national park come from large scale cutting of sandalwood and teak trees. Timber smuggling, especially sandalwood smuggling, happens quite extensively here. Timber felling has been reported from plantation areas in Kollihadi, Vaddara Modu, Tattikere in Veerahosanahalli and Mettiupe in Kalahalli. Other places where timber felling has been reported include Arekatti, Badrikatte, Bidurukatte, Veerana Hosahalli and Marhigodu ranges. In July 2002 hundreds of trees were cut down in the Veeranahosalli range. Local non-governmental organisations (NGOs) like Kodagu Ekikarana Ranga (KER), Budakattu Krishikara Sangha (BKS) and Budakattu Hakku Sthapana Samiti (BHSS) are working to stop tree felling.

Cattle disease

Disease outbreaks among the cattle have been recorded. An outbreak of rabies that resulted in four cattle deaths and affecting 25-30 cattle was reported in the first week of September 2005 at G M Halli on the border of Antharasanthe Forest Range in the park.

Poaching

Poaching of birds and other mammals is another serious issue. A high number of elephant deaths have been reported from this park, with nearly 100 elephants dying between 1991–92 and 2004-05 in the Kodagu and Hunsur Forest Division. Elephants are killed for their ivory. A study carried out by Wildlife First! found that nearly 77 elephants were reported dead between 1 January 2000 and 31 October 2002. Another study carried out by the Institute for Natural Resources,

Conservation, Education, Research and Training (INCERT) in 2002 revealed that as many as seven elephants had been killed earlier that year.

A study carried out by Dr. Ullas Karanth and Madhusudan between 1996-97 revealed that hunting was the biggest threat to wildlife in Kudremukh and Nagarhole National Parks. The survey carried out on 49 active and 19 retired hunters revealed that 26 species of wildlife were hunted at an average intensity of 216 hunter days per month per village. As much as 48% of the hunters reported hunting for the 'thrill'. The study showed that in Nagarhole, 16 mammal species weighing over 1 kg were regularly hunted with shotguns and also by traditional methods used by tribal communities.

Non-payment of forestry staff

A report submitted by The Project Tiger Steering Committee stated that barely 25% of the park's staff were involved in vigilance work, thus putting the park at high risk of both, poaching and tree felling. Irregular payment to the forestry staff has been reported in both Bandipur and Nagarhole National Parks and there have also been reports of improper use of project funds.

Forest fire

In January, 2012, there was a catastrophic forest fire that destroyed over 6,000 acres (2,400 ha) of forest. Huge trees were reduced to cinder.

Burnt remains of snakes, monitor lizards, giant malabar squirrels lay scattered on the charred remains of what was once a verdant patch of moist-deciduous forest.

Forest fires and seasonal droughts coupled with water shortage have caused many wild animals to migrate to other greener spaces.

Human wildlife conflict

Human-wildlife conflicts due to raids by wild animals and elephants on nearby villages along with the consequent retaliation by the villagers is another important threat to the parks wildlife. In 2001, the Karnataka state government sanctioned Rs 2 crores to dig elephant proof trenches and install solar fencing around the park to prevent elephants from straying into the farmer's fields.

Human habitations

In 1997, tribal activist groups won a public interest litigation in the Karnataka High Court to halt the setting up of a resort called the Gateway Tusker Lodge planned to be set up by the Taj Group of Hotels. With nearly 125 villages present inside the park, NGOs actively working to protect the tribal communities include,

Living Inspiration for Tribals (LIFT), Coorg Organisation of Rural Development (CORD), DEED, FEDINA-VIKASA and Nagarhole Budakattu Janara Hakkustapana Samithi. In 2000, the first relocation attempts initiated by a World Bank funded eco-development project of the local tribal population was begun with 50 tribal people. The relocated families were given land possession certificates for five acres of land and houses at Veeranahosalli, near Hunsur. The state and union government planned to relocate 1,550 tribal families at a cost of Rs. 15.5 crores.

WILDLIFE

Nagarhole is flourished with important predators and carnivorous to bring the most wildering effects on the wildlife lovers where they can witness tremendous counts of tiger, leopard, wild dog (dhole or Cuonalpinus), sloth bear and the hyena (Hyaenahyaena).

Even the girded area is also adhered with many herbivores like spotted deer, sambar, barking deer, four-horned antelope (Tetracerusquadricornis), gaur (Bosgaurus), wild boar (Susscrofa) and elephant.

Nagarhole National Park provides an opportunity to see some of the southern population of Gaur (jungle Bison). Also, this park in Karnataka is a good place to see elephants in the luxuriant forests and bamboo thickets which they most enjoy.

Their total population in southern India is now about 6500, nearly all living in the area where Karnataka, Tamil Nadu and Kerala adjoin in the shadow of the Western Ghats.

Other mammalian miscellany includes the, Bonnet macaque (Macacaradiata), jungle cat, slender Loris (Loris tadigradus), common langur (Presbytes entellus), civet cat (Viverriculaindica, leopard-cat (Felisbengalensis) and Paradoxurushermaphroditus), mongoose (Herpestesfuscus and Herpestesvitticollis), common otter (Lutralutra), giant flying squirrel (Petauristapetaurista), giant squirrel (Ratufaindica), porcupine, jackal, mouse-deer (Tragulusmeminna), hare and pangolin (Maniscrassicaudata). Over 250 species of avians can also be traced in the Nagarhole vicinity wherethe enormous variety of woodland birds can be explicitly found.

Besides, there are large congregations of water fowl in the KabiniRiver along with other ranges of Nagarhole birds from blue-bearded bee-eater, scarlet minivet and Malabar whistling thrush to the more common ospreys, herons and ducks.

The most commonly found reptiles are the marsh crocodile, monitor lizard, rock python and several other species can be represented in the area. Aquatic and terrestrial tortoises, frogs, toads and tree frogs and myriad insects, including some very colorful butterflies, adorn this lovely southern jungle of India.

CONSERVATION HISTORY OF NAGARHOLE NATIONAL PARK

The Nagarhole national park was once the hunting reserve of Maharaja of Mysore. Hyder Ali tried to use this reserve to train elephants in the wild into domestic ones. He tried a lot to capture wild elephants but it was not easy.

After years of trial and failure, he left an inscription of a stone that no one would be able to do so. In 19th century, Captain Sanderson tried and succeeded in the mission. Those camps can be still seen inside the park. It was just 258 square kilometer in area. This reserve included forest areas of Nalkeriin Kodagu, Arkeri, Hatgat and others. In 1974, other areas of reserved forest were joined with the hunting reserve and was announced as Nagarhole national park.

The park covered 643.39 square kilometer in 1988. In 2008, the park was recognized as a tiger reserve.

From 1870 to 1980, 14% of the park was cleared to plant teak trees. In 1955, laws against hunting large mammals was passed. Still illegal hunting and other activities are common inside the park.

HOW TO REACH NAGARHOLE NATIONAL PARK

The nearest airports are located in Mysore and Bangalore. Bangalore is the nearest international airport to the park. It is located 236 km away from Nagarhole national park.

Mysore airport is located just 96 km from the park. Tourists usually enter India via Bangalore airport and then take up a connecting flight to Mysore. From Mysore airport, a lot of cabs, buses and other transportations are available to reach Nagarhole national park.

The nearest railway station is located in Mysore. The railway station is just 80 km away from the Nagarhole national park. There are train services from various parts of the country to Mysore. From the railway station, one can hire cab or bus to reach the park.

Buses to Nagarhole national park are available from Mysore, Bangalore, Madikere and others. Taxi services are also available. A taxi ride from Bangalore to the park would cost around INR 5,000 and from Mysore, the cost is approximately 2000 INR.

Distance between major cities and Nagarhole National Park
- Madikere and Nagarhole national park – 90 km
- Mysore and Nagarhole national park – 80 km
- Bangalore and Nagarhole national park – 220 km

- Coorg and Nagarhole national park – 75 km
- Coimbatore and Nagarhole national park – 288 km
- Palakkad and Nagarhole national park – 235 km
- Kutta and Nagarhole national park – 10 km

Best places to stay in Nagarhole

Inside Nagarhole national park, a forest guesthouse is located where tourists can stay. Prior booking is required for accommodation. Getting accommodation during peak season is rare due to high demand.

- Kabini river lodge, Nagarhole national park
- Jungle Inn, Nagarhole national park
- Kabini Plantation, Karapura
- Ramam Water Wood, Karapura
- Machaan resort, Nagarhole national park
- Bison Manor resort, Coorg
- Red Earth, Kabini
- Waterwoods, Kabini
- Orange County resort, Kabini
- Spice Glade home stay, Kutta
- Wild life resort, Kalpetta
- Coorg guest house, Srimangala.

12

Panna National Park, Madhya Pradesh

Panna National Reserve was established in the year 1981 by the Government of India. This 22nd tiger reserve of India that was recognized under the project tiger was also declared as a Project Tiger Reserve in the year 1994. The area of Panna also included some of the major parts of the former Gangau Wildlife Sanctuary which was created in the year 1975. The reserved forests of the Reserve in Panna district and some protected forests on Chhatarpur district were the hunting preserves of the erstwhile rulers of Panna, Chhatarpur and Bijawar princely states. Today the area of Ganagu Sanctuary is the part of the territorial forests of the present North Panna Forest division to which a portion of the Chattrapur Forest division was also added later.

It was in the year 2008 that the real story starts when the reserve area of Panna lost all its tigers to poaching leaving only 2-4 tigers left. Gradually, it caused the loss of the morale of the staff of Panna jungle authority and so in the following year, i.e. in 2009 Mr. R. Shreenivasa Murthy, IFS as field director of Panna Tiger Reserve initiated the task of reintroducing tigers into the park. In collaboration with WWF and PATA, Murthy introduced two tigers to Panna, one from Bandhavgarh and the other from Panna Tiger Reserve with intricate scientific inputs.

Under this project Mr. Murthy and his team translocated one male from Pench and a tigress from Kanha with proper monitoring and protection, where they achieved successful breeding to bring four litters to them. Since then, the officials are focusing on the reproduction of more and more cubs in the area to maintain the previous counts of the tigers in Panna. Panna National Park is one of the best maintained National Parks of India. Declared as a Tiger Reserve Forest of India in 1994, this park suffered a heavy downfall in the number of Tigers due to poaching.

Among other animals found in this park, Chital, Chinkara, Sambhar and Sloth Bear are found abundantly in this park. Bar-headed Goose and King Vultures are the most commonly found birds among the 200 species of its avifauna.

HISTORY OF PANNA NATIONAL PARK

Panna National Park is a national park located in Panna and Chhatarpur districts of Madhya Pradesh in India. It has an area of 542.67 km² (209.53 sq mi). It was declared in 1994 as the twenty second Tiger reserve of India and the fifth in Madhya Pradesh, Panna was given the *Award of Excellence* in 2007 as the best maintained national park of India by the Ministry of Tourism of India. It is notable that by 2009, the entire tiger population had been eliminated by poaching with the collusion of forest department officials.

Biome

Panna National Park and the surrounding territorial forest area of North and South Panna forest division is the only large chunk of wildlife habitat remaining in North Madhya Pradesh in the otherwise fragmented forest landscape of the region.

The National Park is situated at a point where the continuity of the Tropical and subtropical dry broadleaf forests belt, which starts from Cape Comorin in South India, is broken and beyond this the Upper Gangetic Plains moist deciduous forests of the great Indo-Gangetic Plain begins. This area is the northernmost tip of the natural teak forests and the easternmost tip of the natural 'Kardhai' *Anogeissus pendula* forests. The forests of Panna National Park along with Ken Gharial

Wildlife Sanctuary and adjoining territorial divisions form a significant part of the catchment area of the 406 km (252 mi) Ken River which runs northeast for about 72 km (45 mi) through the park.

FAUNA

Among the animals found here are the tiger, chital, chinkara, sambhar and sloth bear. The park is home to more than 200 species of birds including the Bar-headed Goose, Honey Buzzard, King Vulture and Blossom-headed Parakeet.

TIGER RESERVE

Panna National Park was declared as one of the Tiger reserves of India in 1994/95 and placed under the protection of Project Tiger. The decline of tiger population in Panna has been reported several times. Two female tigers were relocated there from Bandhavgarh National Park and Kanha National Park in March 2009. However, the last male tiger had already disappeared. A committee to look into the disappearance of the tigers was formed.

In June 2009, it was officially announced that the Reserve, which had over 40 tigers six years ago, has no tiger left and only two tigresses, which were brought in a while ago In February 2012, three years after the entire tiger population of the reserve was eliminated, the Madhya Pradesh government had not determined responsibility for the debacle, nor had it passed the inquiry to the Central Bureau of Investigation in spite of requests from the Ministry of Environment and Forests and the Prime Minister's Office.

The Ministry of Environment and Forests (MoEF) approved a proposal to translocate two tigers and two tigresses to the reserve.

One female each from Bandhavgarh National Park (coded T1) and Kanha National Park (T2) were translocated to Panna Tiger Reserve. A tiger male, coded T3, was brought from Pench Tiger Reserve but strayed out of the park shortly thereafter, in November 2009 The tiger started walking towards its home in Pench National Park, indicating homing instinct.

It moved steadily through human dominated landscape without causing any conflict. Forest department staff tracked it continuously for over a month and finally brought it back to the Panna Tiger Reserve.

It then settled well, established territory and started mating. The tigress, T1, translocated from Bandhavgarh National Park, gave birth to four cubs in April 2010 of which 2 survive till date. The second tigress, T2, translocated from Kanha National Park gave birth to four cubs several months later and all four survive till date. A third tigress, coded T4, an orphaned cub was reintroduced to Panna in March 2011. She learnt hunting skills with the help of the male and mated with him. She was found dead on 19 September 2014 of an infection caused by its radio collar. Her sister T5 was released in Panna in November 2011.

Thus four tigers and around 10 cubs of up to 2 years are settled in Panna Tiger Reserve at present and their progress is being regularly monitored by the Forest Department.

WILDLIFE IN PANNA

Mammals

Today Panna is the most outstanding, well-managed habitat for all those miscellaneous wildlife creatures of India. The national park is an ideal home to variety of flora and fauna including vultures, cheetals, chinkaras, sambhar and sloth bears. Panna is also an ideal home to the king of the jungles- the royal tigers (Panthera tigris) along with his fellow beings leopard (Panthera pardus), wild dog (Cuon alpinus), wolf (Canis lupus), hyaena (Hyaena hyaena), caracal (Felus caracal) and other smaller cats.

The wooded areas are dotted with sambar, the largest of Indian deers, chital and chowsingha. One can easily see nilgai and chinkara in most open areas in the grasslands, especially on the periphery.

Avifauna

The number of bird species found in Panna is 200 that include the migratory counts. One can find the species like white necked stork, bareheaded goose, honey Buuzzard, King vulture, Blossom headed Parakeet, Paradise flycatcher, Slaty headed Scimitar babbler for the most chirping and wildering effects in Panna.

Reptiles

Panna also boasts variety of snakes, including the python and other reptiles in the vicinity.

Flora in Panna Tiger Reserve

The areas of Panna Tiger Reserve have dry and hot climate. Such climate brings the dry Teak and dry mixed forest by coupling with shallow Vindhyan soils. The dominating vegetation type is miscellaneous dry deciduous forest inter spread with grassland areas. Other major forest types are open grasslands, open woodlands and riverines with tall grasses and thorny woodlands. The characteristic floral species discovered in this area are Tectona grandis, Diospyros melanoxylon,

Madhuca indica, Buchnania latifolia, Anogeissus latifolia, Anogeissus pendula, Lannea coromandelica, Bosswelia serrata etc.

Places of Interest

Raneh Falls : one of the prominent waterfalls in the Panna Reserve area that emerges from the confluence of Ken and Khuddar rivers. This waterfall is being named after King Rane Pratap who was the erstwhile ruler of the region. Raneh Falls forms the 30 m deep and 5 km long canyon to get down into the regions of the Ken Gharial Sanctuary. The surroundings of the falls are adorned with crystalline granite, which is present in varying shades ranging from pink, red and grey. Apart from the large and small falls that are formed at the confluence, some seasonal falls also appear during monsoon season which is really worth-watching.

Ken Gharial Sanctuary : one of the prominent sanctuaries in Panna outskirts to be established with an objective to conserve the endangered species of Indian Gharials. Ken Gharial Sanctuary is being placed at the assemblage of Khuddar and Ken rivers in Panna, Chattrapur district. The sanctuary is stretched across an area of 13.5 sq km and was established in the year 1985.

Open for the tourists from sunrise to sunset, the sanctuary serves as a natural habitat to various other species of reptiles including 6 m long fish-eating gharial. Surrounded by dense forests, the sanctuary is also being flourished with 45 km of river stretch with sand banks and offers shelter to wild boar, chinkara, blue bull, peacock and chitals.

Mahamati Prannathji Temple : Mahamati Prannathji Temple is an important pilgrimage of Pranamis and attracts number of devotees during Sharada Purnima. The legendary story tells that Mahamati Prannathji lived at this site for 11 years after which he took samadhi inside one of the domes of this temple. The temple was built in the year 1692 with unique Muslim and Hindu architectural styles in its domes and the lotus formations. The temple is divided into six parts namely Shri Gummatji, Shri Bangalaji, Shri Sadguru Mandir, Shri Baijurajji Mandir, Shri Chopada Mandir and Shri Khijada Mandir.

The premier attraction of this pilgrimage site is Shri Gummatji, which is a circular building with nine marble domes. Eight of these domes represent the eight directions and central dome has a divine golden Kalasha. Apart from this, Kaman Darwaza is a famous temple gate, which is constructed in silver metal.

Nearby Places / Excursions

Madla : Madla is a picturesque village on the banks of the River Ken in Panna District. Located simply about 20 km away from Panna, this village is the true highlight of the densest jungle patterns of the area with traditional attractions of the area. The nearest airport to Madla is Civil Airport Khajuraho (30 km). Satna Railway Station (91 km) is the closest railhead. State Highway 6 connects this village with the airport and the park. The Jugal Kishore temple and the Pran nath Temple are the attractions a visitor should not miss out around Madla.

Ajaygarh Fort : This is an old fort elevated at a height of 688 meters and was the capital of the Chandelas during their decline. Chhatrasal presented this grand fort to his son Shri Jagat Raj in 1731. The Ajaygarh Fort is 36 km from Panna National Park.

Nachna : Nachna was an ancient famous city of the Nagvakataka and Gupta Empire which is stretched across 40 kms from Panna. It is also known for the Chaturmukha Mahadev temple named after the colossal four faced lingam which is still enshrined inside.

Safaris

There are two major entry zones for Panna Tiger Reserve namely Madla and Hinouta which remain open for the tourists between 16th Oct- 30th June, every year.

For the most rewarding safari tour in Panna National Park the jungle authorities present the jeep facilities to get inside the dense ambience of the reserve and encounter the wildest ranges of Panna inhabitants.

An hour long boat ride is also available by the officials to catch the glimpses of aquatic creatures and other animals around the lake. Besides all these availing for Panna Safari, an elephant safari is one of the best admiring facilities for getting the complete visualization of Panna creatures in a natural high definition mode. And the major attraction of the reserve is the night safari being offered at Gangau regions for the most adventurous and challenging approach in Panna.

Travel Information

By Air : The nearest airport is Khajuraho (25 km) which is well connected to the capital city Delhi & the city of Taj Mahal-Agra.

By Bus : Four wheel drive petrol vehicles can be perfect for the wildlife enthusiasts watching and going around the reserve. Rough terrain, un- medaled roads; steep inclines are difficult for other vehicles. Private vehicles can be hired at Khajuraho/ Panna.

By Train : Jhansi (180 km) for those travelling from Mumbai, Delhi and Chennai; Satna (90 km) for those travelling from Delhi, Kolkata and Varanasi; Katni (150 km) for those travelling from Mumbai, Chennai and Nagpur.

Hotels in Panna Tiger Reserve

For a rewarding Panna Jungle tour the visitors can take the added advantages of staying at the impressive resorts and hotels of Panna National Park. The presence of historical and erotic palace-resorts makes the area more appealing. Besides, if anyone is looking for a standard living option in Panna vicinity, different government lodges are also bringing much fascination to their stay during the complete Panna Wildlife Tour.

HOW TO REACH

Reaching Panna National Park is no tough task, there is several ways to get into this place, the conditions of the Roads which connects other major places to this Park, are very good. Here are three common ways to reach Panna National Park :-

By Flight: The nearest airport to Panna National Park is Khajuraho Airport (IATA Code: HJR), which is about 45km (01hrs ride). Khajuraho Airport is a upgraded airport having direct flight connectivity with popular cultural tourist destination Varanasi. Flights from Khajuraho goes to Delhi via Varanasi. Very soon, through air-taxi service, Khajuraho airport will be connected with other important cities of Madhya Pradesh state like Jabalpur, Indore, Bhopal, Gwalior etc. Second best option for reaching Panna Tiger Reserve is Jabalpur Airport which is about 250kms/05:30hrs away. Jabalpur Airport (IATA Code: JLR) has direct flight connectivity with Delhi

By Train: Satna is a nearest railway station from Panna National Park; it has the connectivity from all the major cities of state and country specially connected to many places in central and western India. Daily trains connecting Delhi to Satna include the Mahakoshal Exp. NDLS Rewa Exp. while daily trains from Mumbai are Kamayani Exp., Mahanagari Exp, Rajendra Ngr. Exp, Kolkata Mail, LTT RJPB Exp & Gorakhpur Exp. Other important trains include Sanghamitra Exp. from Bangalore & Varanasi Exp. from Chennai.

By Road: The road network is very good to reach Panna National Park, nearest bus stand is in Panna town which is connected to Khajuraho, Satna and many other places in Madhya Pradesh by a good road network. Madla, at a distance of around 24 km south west of Khajuraho, is a good transport centre. One can get buses and other road transport modes from here to the Panna National Park. To reach by road from Delhi, take the National Highway-2 to Agra, National Highway-3 to Gwalior, National Highway-75 to Panna via Jhansi, Bamitha and Madla. From the months of December to June you will get good road conditions. During monsoon months and later 2 months road conditions becomes poor and damaged which is repaired in later months.

PANNA TAXI SERVICE

For visiting Panna national park, tourists mostly arrives at Satna railway station or Khajuraho airport/railway station. In addition to this, during tour, many tourists reaches Panna national park from Bandhavgarh, Jabalpur, Jhansi, Orchha, Kundalpur, Chitrakoot etc. We offer car rental service for visiting Panna national park. Our taxi service is running in complete Central India. Our Panna car rental service offers taxi transfers from Panna to Khajuraho, Panna to Bandhavgarh, Jhansi to Panna national park, Orchha to Panna, Satna to Panna national park etc.

Jungle Safari

Just like other national parks of state, management of Panna National Park is also under Forest Department of Madhya Pradesh so safari rules are almost same as in Kanha national park & Bandhavgarh. Panna National Park is open for visitors from 01-October to 30-June (dates may get changed by Forest Department). Being less crowded, route system and zone restrictions are not applicable here.

It means while doing Panna jungle safari, tourists can move around any place, inside park without any worry to observe route system. It is possible to enter from one entrance gate and exit from other safari gate like if we enter from Hinauta gate, then we may take exit from Madla safari gate.

Here safari tickets are easily available on online and current basis. Their is no tough fight for getting safari tickets as less number of tourists are reaching this tiger reserve. Here two rounds of Jungle safaris are offered per day, one in morning & second one in late afternoon till evening. On every Wednesday, park remain closed for evening safari round. For doing jungle safari, all the visitors are mandatory to carry their original ID documents. For foreigner tourists, his/her active Passport is the only ID document.

Panna National Park safari booking can be done online as well as from booking counter. Park management issues maximum 63 safari tickets or entrance passes for single round of jungle safari.

It means maximum 63 vehicles can go inside at a particular safari time which is more than enough. Here only one safari zone prevails called "Panna Zone" where we can enter from any one of 02 entrance gates: "Madla" and "Hinnouta".

While doing jungle safari, one can also have a chance to go for boating in Ken river for spotting long snouted gharials (Gavialis gangeticus) and other aquatic species. Jungle safari charges includes Entrance Ticket, Guide Fee & Vehicle Fee. Maximum 06 passengers are allowed to do safari in a single vehicle (excluding guide and driver).

PANNA WILDLIFE

Forest of Panna National Park lies on Vindhya ranges in which Bandhavgarh national park forest area is also covered. Here forest are dense with many scenic waterfalls. But due to consistently remaining in news due to negative reasons Panna National Park wildlife is now underestimated which is not justified. If we leave the tigers one side, then its overall wildlife is no way behind Bandhavgarh. With re-introduction of tigers, Panna tiger reserve in on the track to revive its glory and justification to be called as genuine Tiger Reserve. New generation of Tigers is now flourishing successfully in forest. In addition to forest area, one amazing adventure comes with River Ken which is passes through the Panna National Park; it surrounds along greeneries and bird life also Indian species of crocodiles like mugger and long snout gharial in the Ken River that flows from here toward the north harbors. This river is a lifeline of the park as most of visitors enjoys boat ride along the course of the River, it is a best way to explore some aquatic life while floating over the water in the Park, the chances getting high of spotting Eurasion Eagle Owls who used to nest on river islands, Black Ibises basking, and scary marshy muggers (crocodiles) usually appears at the wet or dry bank of the River, sometimes half submerged. Many varieties of reptiles like pythons, king cobras are also present in the park to have a glance over them. Vultures sighting track record of this park is very good. We can identify almost 06 different species of vultures here. By going through this information, we can confidently say that Panna National Park offer variety in wildlife from mammals, birds to reptiles.

Mammals

While doing the jungle safari in Panna Tiger Reserve, we can identify more than 22 distinguished mammal species. Tiger (Panthera tigris) is the top carnivore in the reserve with its nearest competitor Leopard (Panthera pardus). If we go by the history of Panna, it was under Bundela rulers and was a princely state. Forest was a private hunting reserve where hunting was taken as a sports with permission to kill 9ft. or more long tigers. Killing of breeding females from carnivore & herbivores are prohibited by the order to State. Here popular forest ranges are Madla & Hinouta where animal distribution is good. After translocation, tiger are mainly seen in Hinouta region where under rocky terrains they have good place to take shelter and survive. Here in Panna although tiger sighting is not good but one can enjoy good sighting of Sloth bear, Leopard(Panthera pardus), Chinkara(Gazella gazella), Nilgai (Blue bull), Hyena, Jackal etc. Hilly terrains and rocky surroundings offers good shelter and conditions for sloth beer. If we travel to Bhairon ghat, Sukwaha ghat and few more sites, we will find Rhesus monekey (Macaca multta). Wild Cat sighting is good in Bhadar & Badgadi stretch of Hinouta range and other wooden areas of park. Like Kanha National Park Indian Gaurs & Barasingha are not found in this forest areas. Earlier Black bucks are present in Panna forest but not seen since many years. While one can easily find out Indian deers, Chital and Chowsingha and chances even grow to spot dotted Sambar in wooden areas, Nilgai and Chinkara can be seen in most open areas in the grasslands, especially on the periphery. Here population of Nilgai & Sambhar is very good in compare to any other mammal species.

Birds

In Panna National Park there is more than 200 species of bird reported so far. This is also a host for a number of migratory birds during the winter season. Vulture sighting in Panna National Park is also great. Here one can notify about 06 rare species of vultures: Long Billed Vulture (Gyps indicus), White Backed Vulture (Gyps africanus), Asian King Vulture (Sarcogyps calvus), Himalayan Griffon Vulture (Gyps himalayensis), Egyptian Vulture (Neophron percnopterus), Eurasian Vulture (Aegypius monachus).

Hilly & rocky terrains of Panna forest are more suitable for vultures to make nests. In addition to this, in winters (Nov-Jan) many migratory birds visits Panna forest and spend some times here. Important Panna national park birds are: Paradise Flycatcher, Pond Heron, White-necked Stork, Honey Buzzard, Slaty-headed Parakeet, Night Jar, Peafowls, Spotted Doves, Blossom-headed Parakeet, Bare-headed Goose, Lark, Pipit, Minivets, Partridges, Quails, Crested Serpent Eagle, Peregrine Falcon, Lesser Adjutant, Black drongo, Pied Myna, Bulbul, Indian Baya weaver, Crow Pheasants, Cuckoo, Kingfishers, Indian Roller, Brown Fish Owl etc.

Flora

The climate of the Panna National Park is tropical and in summer it hikes at the most like 41 °C. In union with shallow Vindhyan soils has given rise to dry Teak and dry mixed forest. The dominating vegetation type is miscellaneous dry deciduous forest inter spread with grassland areas. Other major forest types are reveries, open grasslands, open woodlands with tall grasses and thorny woodlands. The characteristic floral species of this area include tree species such as Tectona grandis, Diospyros melanoxylon, Madhuca Indica (Mahua), Buchnania latifolia, Anogeissus latifolia, Anogeissus pendula, Lannea coromandelica, Bosswelia serrata etc.

Tourist Attractions

Panna national park is just close to UNESCO World Heritage site "Khajuraho Temples". Distance is just 35kms thus we can include this site among Panna tourist attractions. In addition to this, their are many other tourist places like Ken Gharial Sanctuary, Raneh Fall, Pandav Fall, Dhubela Museum, Ajaygarh Fort, Kalinjar Fort etc. Panna national park is know for its scenic beauty. It is the only national park in Central India which offers scenic water falls inside the park with varying bird species. Different vulture species, leopard photography and sloth bear photography are the major attraction among tourists doing jungle safari.

Climate & Weather

Park can be visited either in winter or in summer and the remaining time during the rainy season park remains closed due to heavy rain and no accessibility in the park.

If you wish to visit the Park in the winters, which starts from mid of October and lasts till mid of February, it is recommend that winter can be sever during December to January as mercury dips below 5 °C, so getting a mild experience of the weather one should visit the park between mid of October to mid of December and between February to march.

During February to March mercury hang around 32 °C to 35 °C which considered a best temperature time, as there is clear sky, better sighting of wild animals and mild breeze makes you notice it.

If you dare enough to visit Panna National Park in the summers so this can be little unpleasant due to being excessive hot, yet here is more chances to spot wild being and probability goes up to spotting tiger as water sources being dry up and other remaining sources like little ponds, lakes or Ken river attracts tiger, Chital and many other species to vent their thirstiness up.

The mercury remains so flared in the month of May and June with the temperature of around 41 °C to 45 °C.

BEST TIME TO VISIT

Panna National Park is in Panna & Chhatarpur districts at Northern part of Madhya Pradesh state in Central India.

It is just 45kms from World Heritage Site: Khajuraho. In addition to a National Park it is also a Tiger Reserve under Project Tiger India.

Just like other national parks of Madhya Pradesh, it remains open from 16th October to 30th June for visitors.

Here monsoon rain starts from July and lasts till October, during this time river, lakes, small canals show their best flow volume of rainy water and some times over-flow also.

During monsoon season, park remain closed as tracks inside park were not good enough to drive. Being close to evergreen site Khajuraho, it can be visited throughout the season when it is open for visitors.

Best time to visit Panna National Park is from November to April during which climate remain good so that tourists can enjoy the Panna jungle safaris and boating in Ken river. Pandav cave is another attraction for visitors which remain open throughout the year for visitors and can be visited separately from jungle safari. During summers from April to June, rocky surroundings makes the region hot with severe heat waves which poses challenge but evening boating in Ken river makes a healing effect. Jungle safari with boating makes a good combination for tourists visiting Panna National Park. It can also be taken a excursion tour to Khajuraho or while staying in resort at Panna National Park, one can take excursion tour to Khajuraho.

Accommodation

Being located close to World Heritage Site Khajuraho, Panna National Park can be visited even by staying at hotel in Khajuraho. In Khajuraho you can find all category of hotels at good rates. Still their are resorts & safari lodges located in Panna to provide accommodation to park visitors. Here limited resorts are located like Pashan Garh (Taj Safari Lodge), Ken river lodge, Sarai at Toria, Jewel of the Jungle. Panna Tiger Resort, Jungle Camp Madla etc.

Next To Panna National Park

Panna Tiger Reserve is in North East of Madhya Pradesh in Vindhyan range. Some of the tourist attractions that can be visited next to Panna are as follows:

Khajuraho: It is a World Heritage site about 45Kms North-West from Tiger Reserve. Through out the year, it is open for visitors in day time. Here you can find the sand-stone's artistically sculptured Hindu & Jain temples with some erotic sculpture work which is unique and makes it different from other temples of India.

Bandhavgarh: It is a world famous tiger reserve know for it good tiger sighting records. It is about 230Kms South-East of Panna National Park where you can do jungle safari on jeep, elephant ride. In addition to this their is a small fort on hilltop inside park which is a special tourist attraction for tourists.

Orchha: It is a small town on the bank of Betwa river, about 230Kms North-West from Panna National Park. Here you can find Bundela dynasty historical monuments which includes forts, palace, temples, cenotaphs. Tourists can also enjoy river-rafting on betwa river in season time when river have enough water flow to do so. Very scenic place to visit with perfect combination of heritage with green nature.

Chanderi: Chanderi is a another historical tourist destination in Madhya Pradesh about 260kms West from Panna. It is a hidden treasure with large number of historical monuments, mountains, lakes etc. Chanderi lies in border of Malwa & Bundelkhand regions. It is also popular for handloom industry producing Chanderi Sarees, popular all over India.

Chitrakoot: It is a holy town on the border of Madhya Pradesh & Uttar Pradesh states, about 170Kms West of Panna National Park. It is a sacred town for Hindu devotees as its reference comes in famous Hindu epic "Ramayana". It is said that lord Rama with Sita & Laxmana spend long time of their 14 years exile in Chitrakoot. Their are number of tourist spots associated with Lord Rama. Town is on the bank of Mandakini river.

13

Periyar National Park, Kerala

The Periyar National Park, Kerala is the only national park in South India as well as in India that has an artificial lake flowing through the forests. Located on the evergreen hills of the Western Ghats, this wildlife sanctuary is also one of the Tiger Reserve Forests in India.

While boating in the Periyar Lake, visitors can behold the mighty beasts of this park, quenching their thirsts on the lakesides. Elephants, Deer, Nilgiri Tahrs and Langurs are the other attractions of this park.

HISTORY OF PERIYAR NATIONAL PARK

Periyar National Park and Wildlife Sanctuary (PNP) is a protected area in the districts of Idukki and Pathanamthitta in Kerala, India. It is notable as an elephant reserve and a tiger reserve. The protected area covers an area of 925 km^2 (357 sq mi). 350 km^2 (140 sq mi) of the core zone was declared as the Periyar National Park in 1982.

The park is often called the Periyar Wildlife Sanctuary or Thekkady. It is located high in the Cardamom Hills and Pandalam Hillsof the southern Western Ghats along the border with Tamil Nadu. It is 4 km (2.5 mi) from Kumily, approximately 100 km (62 mi) east of Kottayam, 110 km (68 mi) west of Madurai and 120 km (75 mi) southeast of Kochi.

History

The first official action towards the conservation of wildlife and biodiversity in Kerala was taken in 1934 by the Maharaja ofTravancore, Chithira Thirunal Balarama Varma, by declaring the forests around Periyar lake as a private game reserve to stop the encroachment of tea plantations. It was founded as Nellikkampatty Game Reserve. It was consolidated as a wildlife sanctuary in 1950 after the political integration of India.

Geography

The misty mountain ranges of the Periyar region

Periyar National Park lies in the middle of a mountainous area of the Cardamom Hills. In the north and the east it is bounded by mountain ridges of over 1,700 m (5,600 ft) altitude and toward the west it expands into a 1,200 metres (3,900 ft) high plateau.

From this level the altitude drops steeply to the deepest point of the reserve, the 100 metre valley of the Pamba River. The highest peak is the 2,019 m (6,624 ft) high Kottamalai.

The Periyar and Pamba Rivers originate in the forests of the reserve. The sanctuary surrounds Periyar Lake, a reservoir measuring 26 km² (10 sq mi) which was formed when the Mullaperiyar Dam was erected in 1895. The reservoir and the Periyar River meander around the contours of the wooded hills, providing a permanent source of water for the local wildlife.

Climate

The temperature varies depending upon the altitude and it ranges between 15°Celsius in December and January and 31°Celsius in April and May. Annual precipitation is between 2000 and 3000 mm, about two thirds occurring during the southwest monsoon between June to September. Much of the rest occurs during the northeast monsoonbetween October and December.

Flora

Spider flower (Cleome hassleriana) *in the park*

The park is made up of tropical evergreen and moist deciduous forests, grasslands, stands of eucalyptus, and lake and riverecosystems.

There are many hundreds of flowering plant taxa, including about 171 species of grass and 140 species of orchids. The forests contain teak, rosewoods, terminalias, sandalwoods, jacarandas, mangoes, jamun, tamarind, banyans, sacred fig, plumerias,royal poinciana, kino tree, bamboos, and the only South Indian conifer, *Nageia wallichiana.*

The medicinal gloriosa lily grows in the park. The endemic flora includes *Habenaria periyarensis* and *Syzygium periyarensis.*

Submerged trees in Periyar Lake

The park is surrounded by agricultural regions, especially plantations of such crops as tea, cardamom, and coffee.

Fauna

Mammals

Herd of Indian bisons, gaur, at the Periyar Lake.

There are 35 species of mammals recorded in the park, including many threatened species. It is an important tiger and elephant reserve. A total of 24 Bengal tigers were counted across 640 square kilometers of the park in 2008. It is valuable for Indian elephant.

Other mammals include the gaur, sambar, wild pig, Indian giant squirrel, Travancore flying squirrel, jungle cat, sloth bear, Nilgiri tahr, lion-tailed macaque, Nilgiri langur, Salim Ali's fruit bat, stripe-necked mongoose, and Nilgiri marten.

An adult Nilgiri langur in the Periyar National Park and Wildlife Sanctuary

Birds

About 265 species of birds can be seen in the park, including migrants. Endemic birds include the Malabar Grey Hornbill, Nilgiri Wood Pigeon, Blue-winged Parakeet, Nilgiri Flycatcher, Crimson-backed Sunbird, and White-bellied Blue Flycatcher.

Other birds include theBlack Baza, Spot-bellied Eagle-Owl, Nilgiri Thrush, Little Spiderhunter, Rufous-bellied Hawk-Eagle, Brahminy Kite, Great Hornbill, Sri Lanka Frogmouth, Oriental Darter, and Black-necked Stork.

Reptiles

There are 45 species of reptiles: 30 snakes, 13 lizards, and two turtles. Snakes include the king cobra, Malabar pit viper, and striped coral snake.

Bicolored frog (Malabar frog) **Clinotarsus curtipes**

Insects

There are about 160 butterfly taxa, including the lime butterfly, Malabar tree nymph, and Travancore evening brown, and many kinds of moths, such as the Atlas moth.

Mycalesis patnia junonia *in Periyar National Park*

Hemicordulia asiatica *in Periyar National Park*

Fish

The 40 species of fish in the local lakes and rivers include the Periyar trout, Periyar latia, Periyar barb, channa barb, and Travancore loach.

Amphibians

Amphibians in the park include caecilians, frogs, and toads. Species include the Malabar gliding frog, Asian toad, fungoid frog, and bicolored frog.

History

- 1895 - Construction of the Mullaperiyar Dam
- 1899 - Formation of the Periyar Lake Reserve
- 1933 - S.C.H. Robinson made the first game warden
- 1934 - Formation of Nellikkampatty Game Sanctuary
- 1950 - Consolidation of Periyar as a wildlife sanctuary
- 1978 - Declaration of Periyar as a tiger reserve
- 1982 - Preliminary notification of the core area as a national park
- 1991 - Brought under Project Elephant
- 1996 - India Ecodevelopment Project launched
- 2001 - Divided into Periyar East and Periyar West
- 2004 – Formation of Periyar Foundation
- 2007 – 148 km^2 of the Goodrical Range added to the reserve
- 2011 - The management of Periyar Tiger Reserve has been assessed as "very good" by the National Tiger Conservation Authority and the Union Ministry of Environment and Forests.
- 2012 - An additional 148 km^2 of evergreen forest at Ponnambalamedu added to the reserve

Ecosystem valuation

It is estimated that the Periyar Tiger Reserve (PTR) provides flow benefits worth 17.6 billion rupees (1.9 lakh (190,000)/ hectare) annually. Important ecosystem services included gene-pool protection (7.86 billion), water provisioning to districts of Tamil Nadu (4.05 billion), habitat and refugia for wildlife (3.55 billion), employment generation for local communities (25 million), water purification services to nearby towns and districts (483 million) and recreation value (425 million).

DIFFERENT AREAS IN THE PARK

Mangala Devi temple: This is an ancient temple located inside the national park. People are allowed to enter this temple only once in a year during a Hindu festival.

Pullumedu: It is an important spot for pilgrims. This grassland overlooks the auspicious Lord Iyyappan temple of Sabari Mala. During January, many people visit Pullumedu to spot a glittering light in the sky, which is considered as the deity in spiritual form

Periyar Lake: This is a large lake, which is famous for river rafting. It is one of the famous attractions in the park. The bamboo rafting starts by 8 am. A tour stretches for three hours and tourists have to hitchhike at certain areas to spot animals. An armed guard and numerous guides would accompany during rafting. Boat cruise and boat rides are common in this lake. Birdwatching is common in this area.

Hill region: The north and the east borders of the park are covered by mountains. These mountains form a great trekking train. Prior permissions have to be obtained to take up trekking. Hiring a guide is mandatory in this region. Kurisamala to Kumily and, Kumily to Pandikuzhi are some of the famous routes.

Cardamom hills: This is one of the most exotic spots in the park. As the name indicates, it is a hill with cardamom plantation. Guided trips through the hills are available via jeep. Tourists usually take up a trip to this hill from outside the park.

Forest regions: The thick forest regions inside the park are filled with thick tropical evergreen trees, which make sunrays hard to penetrate. These trees make a canopy and creates a great area for forest trekking. Grasses and small shrubs are hard to spot in this region due to lack of sunlight.

Flora of Periyar National Park

The park is covered with moist deciduous forest, tropical evergreen forest and eucalyptus groves. There are more than 171 species of grasses in the park. 140

species of orchids can be found here. Elephant grass covers most of the grasslands in this park. Top flora to spot in this part are teak, mangoes, rosewood, jamun, jacarandas, terminalias, tamarind, royal ponciana, bamboos, Indian conifer, plumerias, sacred fig, sandalwood, medicinal gloriosa lily and others. Many medicinal plants are found in this region. The park also covers agricultural regions, which includes coffee, cardamom and tea plantations.

Fauna of Periyar National Park

There are 35 major mammals in this park. This includes many threatened species like elephants and tigers about 24 Bengal tigers are found here. Top mammals to spot here are white tiger, Indian elephants, flying squirrel, wild pig, sambar, gaur, fruit bat, Nilgiri marten, Nilgiri langur, sloth bear, jungle cat and others.More than 266 species of birds can be spotted in this park. This includes numerous migration birds too. Top birds to spot in the park are Malabar grey hornbill, white bellied blue flycatcher, sunbird, great hornbill, Sri Lanka frogmouth, black necked stork, oriental darter, brahminy kite, little spiderhunter, eagle owl, Nilgiri wood pigeon and others. New bird species like steppe gull, paddyfield warbler, grey-necked bunting and others are recently spotted in this park.

45 species of reptiles are found in the park. This includes turtles, lizards and snakes. Top reptiles to spot are striped coral snake, Malabar pit viper, king cobra and others. Top amphibians to spot in the park are Malabar gliding frog, bicolored frog, Asian toad and others. In the lakes and rivers found in the park, about 40 species of fishes are found. Top fishes are Priyar barb, Periyar trout, channa barb, Travancore loach and others.

More than 160 butterfly species are found here. This includes the largest butterfly of South India, Southern birdwing. Other top butterflies to spot are Malabar tree nymph, lime butterfly and Travancore evening brown. Numerous species of moths are also found here.

Climate of Periyar National Park

The temperature ranges from 15 degree C to 31 degree C. The highest temperature is found during Aril and May and the lowest is experienced in December. June to September is the monsoon season, which provides average rainfall. October to December also gets rainfall due to the northeast monsoon. Heavy to moderately mild rainfall can be experienced during this season.

Summer: The summer season starts in March and ends in May. Though it is easy to spot animals that come to quench the thirst near the lake, the climate will be hot and dehydrating. Evening safari tours are common during summer. The temperature can go as high as 36 degree C and the vegetation would be lean.

Monsoon: Monsoon season is the worst time to visit the park. Water activities might be stopped due to heavy rains. The animals would be hard to spot and many interesting safaris to many regions inside the park would be restricted.

Winter: October to March is the winter season in Thekkady. The water bodies will be rich with water. The vegetation will be lush with recent rains.

The temperature will be mild and showers, if any will be very mild. Many flowering plants will be at bloom during this season. Animals can be spotted with their small ones and, many migration birds are easy to spot. Rafting and boat cruise would be more interesting due to recent rains.

Best Season to Visit Periyar National Park

December to March is the right time due to lack of rain and very mild temperature. The animals, migration birds and butterflies are easier to spot during this season. Photography tours are best when taken during this time.

Wildlife Safari in Periyar National Park

Safari is the best way to scale the national park. Top safaris available in the park are elephant safari, jeep safari and boat cruise on Periyar Lake. The boat cruise is the most opted one by all tourists. It is the best way to spot wild animals like elephants, wild boar and others. Spotting deers near the water body edges is very common. Boat cruise might not be available throughout the year. During heavy rains, the boating might be stopped temporarily.

Elephant safari is common among tourists with children. It is easier to cover trails that are harder to reach. Moreover, elephant safaris provide more interesting experience than jeep or others. Since tigers are afraid to attack elephants, it is a safer option for those who want to spot a few tigers.

Jeep safari is for small groups and for individuals. It suites people who love photography and to spot ferocious animals. Walking tour with guides are also available. The distance to be covers in very long and thus, it is not recommended for old people and children.

Wildlife Safari Timings

Boat cruise stretches for 30 minutes. Timings for boat cruise are 7:25 am, 9:15 am, 11:15 am, 1:30 pm and 4:00 pm.

There are two types of jeep safari. Full day safari starts by early morning and the last trip starts by three in the evening. The night safari starts by 11:00 pm and ends by 3:00 am.

Elephant safari stretches for 30 minutes. The tour starts by early morning 6:00am and the last trip starts by five in the evening.

How to Reach Periyar National Park

By air: Nearest international airports are located in Madurai and Kochi. Madurai airport is located 136 km from Thekkady and Kochi airport is located 190 km from Thekkadi. Madurai and Kochi are connected with all the important airports in the country and major destinations outside the country.

Buses are available from various states to Thekkady. Thekkady is connected with other states and cities via direct buses from Bangalore, Chennai, Salem, Trichy, Hosur, Viluppuram, Krishnagiri and others. Both private and government buses are available throughout the year.

Nearest railway station is located in Kottayam which 114 km away from Thekkady. Trains that run to Trivandrum will halt at Kottayam.

Trains connects almost all major cities with Trivandrum and runs all seven days a week. Cabs and buses can be hired from the railway station to reach Thekkady or the park. Private cabs can be hired from all major cities to reach Thekkady.

Distance between major cities and Periyar National Park
- Kumily to Periyar National Park – 4 km
- Kottayam to Periyar National Park – 100 km
- Madurai to Periyar National Park– 110 km
- Kochi to Periyar National Park – 120 km

Best Places to Stay in Thekkady

Inside Periyar National park, you will find forest guesthouse to stay. Prior booking is required for accommodation. Due to high demand getting accommodation during peak season is rare.
- Wild Corridor resort and spa, Kumily
- Kofiland, Kumily
- The mountain courtyard, Kumily
- Wildernest, Kumily
- Hills and Hues, Kumily
- Springdale Heritage, Kumily
- PoetreeSarovar Portico, Kumily
- Hotel treetop, Kumily
- Green ark resort, Munnai Kumily highway
- Elephant Route resort, Thekkady junction

- Hotel Tigers Roare, KumilyThekkady road
- Greenwoods resort, Kumily
- Periyar Woods, KumilyThekkady road
- Hotel Sandra palace, Thekkady junction
- Hotel Grand Thekkady, Kumily

Thekkady has three 5-star hotels, 15 4-star hotels, 23 3-star hotels and numerous budget hotels. There are hundreds of hotels in Murikkady, Kumily and other surrounding areas. There are a few government hotels and lodges inside the park too.

Conservation History of Bandipur National Park

In 12th century, the Mullaperiyar dam was built and this let to the formation of the Periyar lake reserve. This artificial lake helped the region to bloom into a rich land that attracted numerous species of animals. Maharaja of Travancore declared the area now under the name of Periyar national park as private game reserve. Maharaja Balarama Varma took this measure in 1934 to avoid encroachment of tea plantations in this area. It was named as Nellikkampatty game reserve. After the political integration of the country, this sanctuary was declared as a wildlife reserve area in 1950. In 1978, the park was declared as a tiger reserve and in 1982, it gained the recognition as a national park. In 1991, the park was taken under Project Elephant. In 2007, 148 square kilometers were added to the park. In 2012, another 148 square kilometer area was added to the park. The tiger reserve and the park creates 1.9 lakhs INR per hectare annually.

MEDICINAL PLANTS

More than 350 medicinal plants, including trees, shrubs and herbs, have been identified at the Periyar Tiger Reserve, mainly in the evergreen and moist deciduous forests. Plants belonging to the family of Fabaceae and Euphorbiaceae are the major ones among them. Glory Lily (Gloriosa superba) and Kino Tree (Pterocarpus marsupium) are two plants with medicinal value found here.

Plantations

The Periyar Tiger Reserve is surrounded by tea, cardamom, pepper and coffee plantations. The arresting green of the plantations add considerable charm to the region.

14

Pench National Park, Madhya Pradesh

While visiting the Pench National Park in Madhaya Pradesh, the childhood fantasy of most of the visitors will turns into reality. Rudyard Kipling's 'The Jungle Book' is based on the natural surroundings of this national park; this park is also known as 'Mowgli Land'.

While Tigers are the most dominant species of this park, Leopards, Sloth Bear, Wild Dog, Barking Deer are some of the other attractions. With more than 170 species of birds, this park has also become one of the best places for birdwatchers.

HISTORY OF PENCH NATIONAL PARK

Pench National Park is situated in Seoni and Chhindwara districts of Madhya Pradesh in India. It derives its name from thePench River that flows through the National park from north to south dividing the park into almost equal western and eastern halves- the well forested areas of Seoni and Chhindwara districts respectively. It was declared a sanctuary in 1977 but raised to the status of National park in 1983. Later it was established as Tiger Reserve area in 1992. Park is famous for water rafting, only national park. In year 2011 park won the *Best Management Award*. This Park is accessible from Pauni on National Highway 7. This point is close to Nagpur, Maharashtra and is the most convenient to enter from Nagpur. Park have two famous gates as tourists entry, Turiya and Karmajhiri.

History

The area of the present tiger reserve has a glorious history. A description of its natural wealth and richness occurs in Ain-i-Akbari. Pench Tiger Reserve and its neighbourhood is the original setting of Rudyard Kipling's most famous work, The Jungle Book. Rudyard Kipling's The Jungle Book and its character Mowgli is based on Pench National Park. This park is also famously called as Mowgli Land.

Location

Pench National Park is located at 21° 402 17.763 North, 79° 182 11.883 East. The terrain of Pench is covered with small hills and well-stocked teak mixed forest in the southern reaches of Satpura Ranges. Altitude varies from 425 to 620 metres above msl. The temperature varies from 4 °C in December to 42 °C in May. Average rainfall is 1300 mm.

Pench National Park, comprises 758 km^2, out of which 299 km^2 form a core are (Pench National Park core area and Mowgli Pench Sanctuary). The remaining 464 km^2 form the buffer area.

Vegetation

The forest cover in the park area includes grand Teak *(Tectona grandis)* mixed with other magnificent species like saja *(Terminalia tomentosa)*, bija *(Pterocarpus marsupium)*,lendia *(Lagerstroemia parviflora)*, haldu *(Adina cardifolia)*, dhaora *(Anogeissus latifolia)*, salai *(Boswellia serrata)*, aonla *(Emblica officinalis)*, amaltas *(Cassia fistula)*, etc.

The ground is covered with maze of grasses, plants, bushes and saplings. Bamboo is also found at places. Dazzling white kulu *(Sterculia urens)* trees scattered around stand out conspicuously among the various hues of green.

Wildlife

Tiger is the main cat species of the park present in good numbers but sighted infrequently.

Commonly seen wildlife is chital, sambhar, nilgai, wild boar, and jackal. Other wild animals found are leopard, sloth bear, wild dog, porcupine, monkey, jungle cat, fox, striped hyena, gaur, chowsingha and barking deer.

There are more than 170 species of birds including several migratory ones. Some of them are peafowl, junglefowl, crow pheasant, crimson-breasted barbet, red-vented bulbul, racket-tailed drongo, magpie robin,lesser whistling teal, pintail, shoveler, egret and herons.

The Pench national park has a count of 8 tigers (as in 1998) and 7 panthers (as in 1998).This national park is rich with chitals i.e. axis axis or more commonly spotted deer.

There are 10 villages in the national park - 1 inside the park (Fulzari) and 9 on the periphery.

As per 2011 Tiger Census; There are 25 tigers under this umbrella of the Park. 39 species of mammals, 13 species of reptiles, 3 species of amphibians. Apart from mammals and other land-based wildlife, the park is also rich in bird life.

According to an estimation of the wildlife authorities, the bird population in the park counts to be over 210 species like barbets, bulbul, minivets orioles, wagtails, munias, mynas, waterfowls and blue kingfishers.

Visiting Times & Nearest Station

The best time to visit the park is between February and April. The Park is open to visitors between 6 am to 10:30 am and 3 pm to 6 pm. The park remains closed during the months of July, August and September. It can be accessed by road as well as railway. The nearest Airport, railway station is Nagpur and closest city is Seoni, bus can be taken to the Park.

In Popular Culture

The Pench national park provided the location used by the BBC for the innovative wildlife series *Tiger: Spy in the Jungle*, a three part documentary narrated by Sir David Attenborough which used concealed cameras, placed by elephants, in order to capture intimate tiger behaviour. The programme aired for the first time in April 2008.

WILDLIFE IN PARK

Pench National Park is very rich in fauna and it's an abode to a large number of endangered species. The most dominant predator is Tiger and there are around 25 of them in these prey-rich woodlands. There are some other predators like dhol (Indian Wild Dog), leopard, hyena, wolf, jackal and jungle cat. Some prey species observed in the park are sambhar, chital, gaur, muntjac, langur, wild boar, and rhesus macaques. Commonly seen species are herd of deer.

There are more than 170 species of birds comprising various migratory ones like peafowl, crow pheasant, junglefowl, red-vented bulbul, crimson-breasted barbet, magpie robin, lesser whistling teal, racket-tailed drongo, egret, pintail, shoveler, herons to name a few.

As per the study in the year 1, 25 tigers were found under the umbrella of the park along with 39 mammals, 13 reptiles, and 3 amphibians. Aside from mammals and other land-based flora & fauna, the park is also rich in bird life. As per the evaluation of the wildlife authorities, 210 species of birds was observed in this park like munias, barbets, minivets orioles, bulbul, waterfowls, wagtails, mynas, and blue kingfishers.

Flora in Park

The park is blessed with rich and verdant forests, spread throughout the area of the National Park. Southern dry broadleaf teak forests are there, which blend with tropical mixed deciduous forests.

The flora in Pench includes different kinds of shrubs, climbers and tress. It has some uncommon varieties of herbs with medicinal properties that are mentioned below:

Flora in Pench National Park

- Teak (Tectona Grandis)
- Saja (Terminalia Tomentosa)
- Bija (Pterocarpus Marsupium)
- Lendia (Lagerstroemia Parviflora)

- Haldu (Adina Cardifolia)
- Dhaora (Anogeissus Latifolia)
- Salai (Boswellia Serrata)
- Aonla (Emblica Officinalis)
- Amaltas (Cassia Fistula)

Safari Timings

The Safari timing in Pench National Park is almost similar like other parks of the country. The entry and exit of the park vary as per the season. The best time to visit Pench National Park is between February and April. Due to the shorter duration of daylight in winters, the morning entry time is quite late and evening exit time is early. The National Park remains open for visitors from 16th October to the end of June and closed during the rainy season (July-October) every year. Early morning safari is the most worthwhile to spot tigers and other rare animals.

Winter Safari Timings

Entry:

Morning Safari: 07:30 hrs

Evening Safari: 15:00 hrs

Exit:

Morning Safari: 10:30 hrs

Evening Safari: 17:30 hrs

Summer Safari Timings

Entry:

Morning Safari: 06:30 hrs

Evening Safari: 16:00 hrs

Exit:

Morning Safari: 09:30 hrs

Evening Safari: 18:30 hrs

Activities to Do in Park

Pench National Park is popular for its wildlife and flora & fauna. There are many ways to explore the wildlife of forest. They are:

- Jeep Safaris

- Elephant Ride
- Bird Watching
- Jungle Walk
- Walking Safaris (12 km)

Tourist Attractions in Pench National Park

Sitaghat- This spot is winding path that is close to the bank of river Pench, speckled with rocks and artistic looking trees. During summer season, white flowers and bushes lope all along with bank.

To view these flowers in full blossom, it is must to visit in the early morning hours. The place also appears to be a splendid spot for wildlife sightseeing.

Alikatta- This place is another exciting attraction that has fascinating area of grassland, where animals are also observed. In evening time, there is excellent view of grazing herds comprising of thousands of spotted deer. One can also enjoy elephant rides that begin from this place.

Chhindimatta Road- Journeying over rocky hills, it is considered as place of interest in the huge Pench reservoir. The rocky cliffs make tremendous places for leopards. Other species like Eagles, Buzzards, and hawks are observed looming over their nests.

Bodhanala Range- This area is worth sightseeing for visitors. It starts from slopy hill, bamboo forest to a huge pond close to the border of the park. It is a perfect area for raptors.

Above all, there are some other attractions to explore in Pench like Raiyakassa, Doob Road, and Kalapahad. Travelling to all these places give wonderful opportunity to come across huge herds and king of jungle.

Tourist Places near Pench National Park

There are some main tourist attractions nearby Pench National Park, which add more fun and excitement in trip. They are:

Bandhavgarh National Park- This park is 338.7 Km away (approx.7 hours) from Pench and it gives a wildlife retreat where nature and history meet together. Positioned amidst the Vindhyan hills, the park has a series of ridgelines successively running through it. The major attractions of the area are however in the heart of the Park with its 32 beautiful wooded hills.

Kanha National Park- Just 2 hours drive (136.5 kms) from Pench National Park, there resides Kanha National Park. Situated in the district of Mandia (Madhya Pradesh), the park is a Tiger Reserve that leads over 1945 sq. km of undulating country. It is an abode to over 1000 species of flower plants. It has important population of leopards, royal Bengal tiger, sloth bear, barasingha, Indian wild dog, etc.

Nagzira National Park- The wildlife of this park is sheltered in the arms of nature and festooned with a picturesque landscape and exuberant vegetation. Only 3 hours drive (176.5 km) from Pench National Park, this park is placed in the Bhandara district of Maharashtra. The small reserve is a vital corridor that connects central and southern forested areas such as Kanha Tiger Reserves and Tadoba-Andhari.

Tadoba National Park-Just 256.4 km away from Pench, Tadoba National Park lies in Chandrapur district of the north-eastern part of Maharashtra. Popular as 'The Jewel of Vidharba', this park is placed in the core of a reserved forest. The park is widely popular for its plants life and wildlife. It has tropical dry deciduous forest where teak is the dominant species.

Climate

Pench National Park is situated at 21° 402 17.763 North and 79° 182 11.883 East. The Pench land is surrounded with small hills and well-stocked teak mixed forest in the southern part of Satpura Ranges. The park has a tropical continental climate with distinct monsoons (July-September), winters (November-February) and summers (April-June). The altitude variegates from 425 to 620 meters above msl. The temperature of this region is 4°C in December and 42°C in May & June. Average rainfall is 1300 mm.

During summer, casual summer clothing of natural colors is perfect from March to May while from November to February, carrying warm apparels for chilly mornings and hazy evening is very important.

15

Manas National Park, Assam

Considered as one of the youngest names in the list of National Parks in India, the Manas National Park or Manas Wildlife Sanctuary, Assam has a large number of rare and endangered species. Assam Roofed Turtle, Hispid Hare, Golden Langur and Pygmy Hod are some of the most endangered species of this park. Witness the best wildlife experience n your next Assam holiday.

This park boasts of its 55 species of mammals, 380 species of birds and a substantial number of reptiles and amphibians. Asian Elephant, Indian Rhinoceros, Water Buffaloes, Leopard and Assamese Macaques are the other dwellers of this park. It is also one of the popular destinations for river rafting.

MANAS NATIONAL PARK

Manas National Park or Manas Wildlife Sanctuary is a national park, UNESCO Natural World Heritage site, a Project Tiger reserve, an elephant reserve and a biosphere reserve in Assam, India. Located in the Himalayan foothills, it is contiguous with the Royal Manas National Park in Bhutan. The park is known for its rare and endangered endemic wildlife such as the Assam roofed turtle, hispid hare, golden langur and pygmy hog. Manas is famous for its population of the wild water buffalo.

Origin of the name

The name of the park is originated from the Manas River, which is named after the serpent goddess Manasa. The Manas river is a major tributary of Brahmaputra River, which passes through the heart of the national park.

History

The Manas National Park was declared a sanctuary on 1 October 1928 with an area of 360 km². Manas bioreserve was created in 1973. Prior to the declaration of the sanctuary it was a reserved forest called Manas R.F. and North Kamrup R.F. It was used by the Cooch Behar royal family and Raja of Gauripur as a hunting reserve. In 1951 and 1955 the area was increased to 391 km². It was declared a World Heritage site in December 1985 by UNESCO. Kahitama R.F. the Kokilabari R.F. and the Panbari R.F. were added in the year 1990 to form the Manas National Park. In 1992, UNESCO declared it as a world heritage site in danger due to heavy poaching and terrorist activities. On 25 February 2008 the area was increased to 950 km². On 21 June 2011, it was removed from the List of World Heritage in Danger and was commended for its efforts in preservation.

Human history

There is only one forest village, Agrang, in the core of the national park. Apart from this village 56 more villages surround the park. Many more fringe villages are directly or indirectly dependent on the park.

Geography

Political Geography: The park area falls in two districts: Chirang and Baksa in the state of Assam in India.

The park is divided into three ranges. The western range is based at Panbari, the central at Bansbari near Barpeta Road, and the eastern at Bhuiyapara near Pathsala.

The ranges are not well connected; while two major rivers need to be forded in going from the centre to the Panbari, there is a rough trail (the *daimAri road*) connecting the central to the eastern range. Most visitors come to Bansbari and then spend some time inside the forest at Mathanguri on the Manas river at the Bhutan border.

A view of mountains from the park

Physical Geography: Manas is located in the foothills of the Eastern Himalaya and is densely forested. The Manas river flows through the west of the park and is the main river within it. It is a major tributary of Brahmaputra river and splits into two separate rivers, the Bwrsi and Bholkaduba as it reaches the plains. Five other smaller rivers also flow through the national park which lies on a wide, low-lying alluvial terrace spreading out below the foothills of the outer Himalaya.

The Manas river also serves as an international border dividing India and Bhutan. The bedrock of the savanna area in the north of the park is made up of limestone and sandstone, whereas the grasslands in the south of the park stand on deep deposits of fine alluvium.

The combination of Sub-Himalayan Bhabar Terai formation along with the riverine succession continuing up to Sub-Himalayan mountain forest make it one of the richest areas of biodiversity in the world.

The park is 950 km². in area and is situated at a height of 61m to 110m above mean sea level.

Climate: The minimum temperature is around 15 degrees C and maximum temperature is around 37 degrees C. Heavy rainfall occurs between May and September. The annual average rainfall is around 333 cm.

Natural history

Flora

Vegetation: The monsoon forests of Manas lie in the Brahmaputra Valley semi-evergreen forests ecoregion. The combination of Sub-Himalayan Bhabar Terai formation with riverine succession leading up to the Himalayan subtropical broadleaf forests makes it one of the richest biodiversity areas in the world.

The main vegetation types are:

- Sub-Himalayan Light Alluvial Semi-Evergreen forests in the northern parts.
- East Himalayan mixed Moist and Dry Deciduous forests (the most common type).
- Low Alluvial Savanna Woodland, and
- Assam Valley Semi-Evergreen Alluvial Grasslands which cover almost 50% of the park.

Jungle owl in manas

Much of the riverine dry deciduous forest is at an early successional stage. It is replaced by moist deciduous forest away from water courses, which is succeeded by semi-evergreen climax forest in the northern part of the park.

A total of 543 plants species have been recorded from the core zone. Of these, 374 species are dicotyledons (including 89 trees), 139 species monocotyledons and 30 are Pteridophytes and Gymnosperms.

The park's common trees include *Aphanamixis polystachya, Anthocephalus chinensis, Syzygium cumini, Syzygium formosum, Syzygium oblatum, Bauhinia purpurea, Mallotus philippensis, Cinnamomum tamala, Actinodaphne obvata, Bombax ceiba, Sterculia villosa, Dillenia indica, Dillenia pentagyna, Careya arborea, Lagerstroemia parviflora, Lagerstroemia speciosa, Terminalia bellirica, Terminalia chebula, Trewia polycarpa, Gmelina arborea, Oroxylum indicum* and *Bridelia* spp.

The grasslands are dominated by *Imperata cylindrica, Saccharum naranga,*

Phragmites karka, Arundo donax, Dillenia pentagyna, Phyllanthus emblica, Bombax ceiba, and species of *Clerodendrum, Leea, Grewia, Premna* and *Mussaenda.*

Fauna

A capped langur in Manas

The sanctuary has recorded 55 species of mammals, 380 species of birds, 50 of reptiles, and 3 species of amphibians. Out of these wildlife, 21 mammals are India's Schedule I mammals and 31 of them are threatened.

The fauna of the sanctuary include Indian elephants, Indian rhinoceros, gaurs, Asian water buffaloes, barasingha, Indian tigers, Indian leopards, clouded leopards, Asian golden cats, dholes, capped langurs, golden langurs, Assamese macaques, slow loris, hoolock gibbons, smooth-coated otters, sloth bears, barking deers, hog deers, black panthers, sambar deers and chitals. The park is well known for species of rare and endangered wildlife that are not found anywhere else in the world like the Assam roofed turtle, hispid hare, golden langur and pygmy hog. The Manas hosts more than 450 species of birds. It has the largest population of the endangered Bengal florican to be found anywhere. Other major bird species include great hornbills, jungle fowls, bulbuls, brahminy ducks, kalij pheasants, egrets, pelicans, fishing eagles, crested serpent-eagles, falcons, scarlet minivets, bee-eaters, magpie robins, pied hornbills, grey hornbills, mergansers, harriers, Indian Peafowl, ospreys and herons.

Biomes

There are two major biomes present in Manas:

- The grassland biomes : pygmy hog, Indian rhinoceros (re-introduced in 2007 after extinction due to heavy poaching during the Bodo uprising), bengal florican, wild Asian buffalo, etc.
- The forest biomes : slow loris, capped langur, wild pig, sambar, great hornbill, Malayan giant squirrel or black giant squirrel, Chinese pangolin etc.

Tephrodornis gularis

HOW TO REACH

By Air- Nagpur Airport (88 Km) is the nearest one to reach the park. Other option is Jabalpur Airport, which is 200 km away from the park.

By Rail- The nearest railway station is Nagpur (90 km), well connected to all the cities of India.

By Road- Nagpur is 88 km away from Pench through Seoni (NH No. 7).

Permits & Entry Fee: To enter into the park, you require permits which you will obtain from the Field's Director Office on Barpeta Road. You can also hire private jeeps from here since the forest department does not provide any jeep or guides. You can take your own four-wheeler inside the park too. The entry fee for the park is paid at Bansbari Range Office.

16

Ranthambore National Park, Rajasthan

The Ranthambore National Park, Rajasthan, is one of the royal national parks in India. It is ranked as one of the top 10 wildlife sanctuaries in India.

The majestic Tigers are the pride of this national park. Surrounded by the Banas and Chambal River, this park serves as an ideal habitat for the predators and other animals of this park. Leopard, Nilgai, Wild Boar, Sambar and Hyena are some of the major animals found in this park. Tiger Safaris are immensely popular among the visitors of Ranthambore National Park.

HISTORY OF RANTHAMBORE NATIONAL PARK

Ranthambore National Park or Ranthambhore is one of the largest national parks in northernIndia, covering an area of 392 km². It is situated in the Sawai Madhopur district of southeastern Rajasthan, about 110 km northeast of Kota and 160 km southeast of Jaipur, which is also the nearest airport.

The nearest town and railway station is at Sawai Madhopur, about 11 km away. The park is also close to the Kota train station. RIDCOR operates a mega-highway between Kota and Ranthambhore.

The park lies at the edge of a plateau and is bounded to the north by the Banas River and to the south by the Chambal River. It is named for the historic Ranthambhore fortress, which lies within the park.

Ranthambhore was established as the *Sawai Madhopur Game Sanctuary* in 1955 by the Government of India and was declared one of the Project Tiger reserves in 1973.

Ranthambore became a national park in 1980. In 1984, the adjacent forests were declared the *Sawai Man Singh Sanctuary and Keladevi Sanctuary*, and in 1991 the tiger reserve was enlarged to include the Sawai Man Singh and Keladevi sanctuaries.

Ranthambore wildlife sanctuary is known for its tigers and is one of the best places in India to see these animals in their naturaljungle habitat.

Tigers can even be easily spotted in the daytime. The best time for tiger sightings at Ranthambore National Park is in November and May.

The park's deciduous forests are characteristic examples of the type of jungle found in Central India. Other major wild animals include leopard, nilgai, wild boar, sambar, hyena, sloth bear and chital. It is home to wide variety oftrees, plants, birds and reptiles, as well as one of the largest banyan trees in India.

TIGERS

T-24, considered to be the largest tiger in the park

FEATURES

A panoramic view of Ranthambhore NP from Ranthambhore Fort.

General information

Aravali Range inside Ranthambhore, Rajasthan.

- National Park area: 275 km² core area. 392 km² including buffer zone
- Tiger Reserve area: 334 km². Today it covers an area of 1334 km.
- Altitude: 215 to 505 meters above sea level.
- Kota Station is a stop for all trains for 10 minutes and connects Sawai Madhopur with almost 50 trains.
- Closest airport is Jaipur, 160 km away.
- Terrain: Dense tropical dry forest, open bushland and rocky terrain interspersed with lakes and streams.
- Ecoregion: Kathiawar-Gir dry deciduous forests.
- Best Season: From November to March.
- Closed: Monsoon season (July - September).

Ecosystem Valuation

An economic valuation of the tiger reserve estimated that its flow benefits are worth 8.3 billion rupees (0.56 lakh / hectare) annually. Gene-pool protection services (7.11 billion), provisioning of water to the neighbouring region (115 million) and provisioning of habitat and refugia for wildlife (182 million) were some of the important services that emanated from the tiger reserve. Other services included nutrient cycling (34 million) and sequestration of carbon (69 million).

WILDLIFE

Ranthambore is best known for its large tiger population. As park tourism and the population of neighbouring villages increased, there were more frequent fatal human-tiger interactions and poaching. The Indian government started Project Tigerin 1973 and allotted an area of 60 mi^2 of the Park as Tiger sanctuary.This area later expanded to become what is now the Ranthambore National Park.

In 2005, there were 26 tigers living in Ranthambore. This was significantly lower than the recorded tiger population of the reserve in 1982, which stood at 44. According to non-government sources there were 34 adult tigers in the Ranthambore National Park in 2008, and more than 14 cubs.

This increase was largely attributed to sustained efforts of forest officials to curb poaching. Villagers in the region were being given incentives to stay out of the park and surveillance cameras were also fitted across the reserve. The Indian government committed US$153 million for the efforts.

These efforts were successful enough to make Ranthambore eligible to participate in the Sariska Tiger Reservere location efforts. The first aerial relocation of the male tiger (Dara) from Ranthambore to Sariska was done using a Mi-17 helicopter on 28 Jun 2008 by Wing Commander Vimal Raj. Unfortunately, this translocated tiger died on 15 November 2010 due to poisoning.

Tigers

During the past few years, there has been a decline in tiger population in Ranthambore due to poaching and other reasons.

A tigress known as "Lady of the Lakes" was, at a very young age, separated from her parents because of poaching. The young tigress was names Machli after the mark on her body that resembles a fish. She gave birth to three female cubs, one being dubbed 'Machli - The Junior'. The father of Machli Jr. died early from an unknown disease, as confirmed by forest officer Fateh Singh Rathore. Machli Jr. mated with male tiger Bumburam, and gave birth to two cubs: Slant Ear and Broken Tail. Baccha is believed to be her grandson. At 17 years old, Machli Sr. is the world's oldest tigress. Machli recently went missing, raising concern among forest officials as hunting is difficult at her age. After twenty-six days Machli was spotted and located by forest officials. Machli's daughter T19 is the current queen tigress of Ranthambore. She recently gave birth to four cubs, with three surviving.

Another popular tigress from Ranthambore is tigress T39, also known as Mala or Noor. Her name comes from the decorative bead like stripes alongside her body. She was born to tigress T-13 and were fathered by T-12. In March and April of 2014, she was seen with her second litter of three cubs. Noor is 6 years old and her son, T72, or Sultan, is from her first litter and is approximately three years old.

Broken Tail was made international headway in a film made about his life. He left the park area and traveled from Ranthambore to Darra where he was killed by a train while crossing the railway tracks.

The documentary film called *Broken Tail* features his last journey and has been shown worldwide on many TV channels including the BBC, PBS, CBC, RTÉ among others, and won the top awards at two of the world's most prestigious wildlife film festivals.

As per the 2014 census of tigers, there were 61 tigers in the Ranthambore national park. The number of tigers in 2013 was 48 and 25 in 2005. Due to recent increase in the number of tigers, the park is planning to transfer a few to other parks, such as Sariska and others.

Features

Forests: The Park terrain alternates between dry deciduous forests and open grassy meadow. The flora of the park is represented by 539 species of flowering plants.

Tigers: Ranthambore is one of the best national parks in the country to spot a tiger. The majestic predator can be spotted ambling or basking under the sun.

Safari Rides: Rides are carried out at 6:30 and 14:30. Each ride lasts for about three hours. There are two options of vehicles for the safari: 20 seater open top canter or 6 seater open top gypsy.

Each ride costs around Rs700-800 per person. The core park area has been divided into several zones and the safari vehicles go on one of those zones. Visitors often take multiple tours, as tiger spotting is rare. There many resorts to reside in on the way from Sawai Madhopur to the national park.

Ranthambore Fort: The majestic fort, built in 10th-century, towers over the entire park area. It stands 700 feet above the surrounding plain. Inside the fort, there are three red Karauli stone temples devoted to Ganesh, Shiva and Ramlalaji. There is a Digamber Jain temple of Lord Sumatinath (5th Jain Tirthankar) and Lord Sambhavanath. The temples were constructed in 12th and 13th centuries.

Padam Talao: This is the largest of the many lakes located in the park. A red sandstone Jogi Mahal can be found at the edge of the lake. A gigantic banyan tree, considered to be India's second largest, is also near the lake.

Transportation

Air: Jaipur at 160 km away, is the nearest airport from Ranthambore wildlife sanctuary.

Rail: Ranthambore National Park is around 11 km from Sawai Madhopur Railway Station, that lies on the Delhi to Mumbai trunk route. The city is a stop for many trains, including Jaipur - Indore Super Fast, Dayodaya Express (Ajmer - Jabalpur Express), Jodhpur - Indore Intercity, Hazrat Nizamuddin - Indore Express, Marusagar Express (Ajmer - Ernakulam Express / Ernakulam Express), Jaipur - Mysore Express, Jaipur - Chennai Express, Jaipur - Coimbatore Express, Jodhpur - Puri Express, Jodhpur - Bhopal Express, Jodhpur - Indore Intercity, and the Mumbai Rajdhani Express.

The Jaipur - Indore Super Fast connects Sawai Madhopur to major city of Madhya Pradesh, Indore Junction. There is also a Kota Jan Shatabdi Express train, from Kota to national capital Delhi via Sawai MAdhopur. The other includes Kota - Hanumangarh Express, Sawai Madhopur-Mathura Passenger, Jaipur-Kota Passenger. Kota - Patna Express connects Sawai Madhopur and Patna cities via Agra, Kanpur, Lucknow and Varanasi.

Luxury trains The Palace on Wheels, The Royal Rajasthan on Wheels, Maharajas' Express, The Indian Maharaja make a scheduled stop at Sawai Madhopur on their eight-day round trip of tourist destinations.

Roads : A network of buses connect Sawai Madhopur, the nearest town, to all the major cities within the state of Rajasthan. The frequency of direct services though is not very great. A car or taxi must be hired from Kota to Ranthambhore. Kota - Ranthambore is a mega highway and can be covered in 1.5 hours.

REASONS TO VISIT RANTHAMBORE TIGER RESERVE IN RAJASTHAN

Tiger Sighting in India is a common activity with tourists from around the world. Year round wildlife lovers hop from one wildlife reserve to another to get the glimpse of the majestic and ferocious tigers. Ranthambore National Park is one such national parks to visit in India with an area of 1,334 sq km that is famous for its Royal Bengal Tigers.

This wildlife reserve is certainly a dream destination for wildlife photography enthusiasts that will transit you to a surreal place away from the city, isolated in the land of dust and stone. There are many wildlife reserves all around India but what makes Ranthambore one and only is its exotic site, the destination is even more fascinating with dry barren lands, colorful atmosphere, gravel roads and historical forts. And if you still need more reasons to visit this tiger reserve in India, this blog here can be of help.

Dedicated to the Wild

Unlike most visited national parks in India there is Ranthambore which offers rich biodiversity and a unique ecosystem. At Ranthambore one has the convenience not only to see the magnificent Tigers but many exotic animals that includes Leopard, Jackals, Indian Flying Fox, Black Bucks, Sloth Bears, Desert Cats, Mongoose, Rattles and Five-stripped Palm Squirrels. The list does not end here-the park also has a large collection of Reptiles like the Snub Nosed Marsh Crocodile, Pythons, Cobras, Desert Monitor Lizard and the list goes on and the visit will be an ongoing gala for wildlife lovers.

Enthralling Ranthambore Forest Safari

Wildlife safari is an opportunity to see and photograph the major highlights of the park, it is an overland journey into the thick forest. In Ranthambore National Park you have options to either take a Canter consisting of twenty seats or a Jeep filled with six seats, the prices may vary with your pick. Get lost as you enter the animal kingdom to watch the wild run free in their natural habitat. It is a different experience playing hide and seek with the animals and your heart will definitely skip a beat when you spot one.

Ideal Bird Watching Site

If you like something less walking or impelling then lift your feet off the ground and look in the grassland and discover some of India's enchanting birds. Bird watching is perhaps only for people with staying-power. For bird watching experience calmness and patience is crucial and of course good set of binoculars to set one's eyes on the feathered creature. The chase is an endless event trying to name many rare and elegant birds.

Ranthambore habitat is enclosed with varied terrains and water bodies which results excellent element for unique birds and animals. With 272 species documented so far some of the exotic birds are: Flamingos, Gray Hornbills, Flycatchers, and Nightjars for instance.

An Ancient Banyan Tree and the Rich Vegetation

With animals and birds meandering in the wild wood, the vegetation plays its part simultaneously. The dry grassland accommodates large section of flora and fauna consisting over 300 species that will captivate you. Ranthambore National Park is famous for its Banyan Tree; the large leathery leaves cover a vast area making it a perfect shade. The forest of Ranthambore has a lot of contrasting vegetation, plants and unique solitary flowers.

A Fort Amidst the Thick Woods

Ranthambore is also cited as a heritage site because of the descriptive ruins of the fort within the park. Some of the authentic forts and lakes around the national park are standing majestically inside the wildlife reserve overlooking the entire park. The Ranthambore fort is built about 700ft high and is situated about 5 km inside the park. The fort is recognized and is a part of UNESCO World Heritage Site under the title "Hill Forts of Rajasthan".

FLORA AND FAUNA

Flora in Ranthambhore : Ranthambore National Park is also rich in flora. There is a plenty of water available to support a variety of flora and fauna. According to estimates, there are around 300 plant species in the Ranthambore National Park. Due to its proximity to the Thar, the region receives very scanty rainfalls and so the vegetation in the park mainly comprises of the dry deciduous type. The Reserve comprises of shallow perennial lakes, steep hills, gentle slopes, plateaus, narrow valleys, etc. and as such a variety of plant communities or associations are found.

The most noticeable tree in the Ranthambore National Park is the 'Dhok' (Anogeissus pendula). It is dominant species and constitutes about 80% of the vegetation cover and found on hill slopes and valleys and maintains luxuriant growth due to better soil formation and water holding capacity. The leaves of the Dhok trees form a favorite diet for the Deer, Nilgai and Antelope. Its height is approximately 10-15 meters. The growth of Anogeissus pendula is generally stunted on plateaus where the residual soil is poor and shallow.

Other most prominent trees in the park are the Banyan (Ficus bengalensis) and Pipal (Ficus religiosa) It is worshipped and also has medicinal uses. The largest Banyan tree of India stands just behind the Jogi Mahal, the hunting lodge in Ranthambore national Park. The Neem (Azadirachta indiaca) tree, which is universally known for its medicinal properties, grows abundantly in the Ranthambore National Park.

Among the fruit trees found in the Ranthambore, the most prominent include the Mango(Magnifera indica), Jamun (Syzygium cumini) also known as the Indian blackberry, Ber (Zizyphus mauritania), and Tamarind (Tamarindicus indica-popularly called Imli) known for its pulpy fruit used in the preparation of pickles. In addition, there are many trees such as Chhila (Butea monosperma, the flame of the forest), which sets the forest alights with the bright orange red color, offering a spectacular sight to park's visitors.

Other important flora in the Ranthambore include the Babul (Accasia nilotica), Gurjan (Lannea coromandelica), Gum (Sterculia urens), Kadam (Authocephalus cadamba), Khajur (Phoenix sylvestris), Khair (Accacia catechu) This is one of the most common trees in Ranthambore and is regarded across north India as a very valuable tree, since extracts from its bark are the mixture that make the paste katha for paans. The bark is frequently chewed by porcupines who seem to have an addiction to this tree in Ranthambore., Kakera (Flacourtia indica), Karel (Capparis decidua), Khimi (Manilkara hexandra), Kikar (Acacia nilotica), Mahua (Madhuca indica), Kulu (Sterculia urens), Ronj (Acacia leucophloea), Salar (Boswellia serrata) and Tendu (Diospyrous melanoxylon) The leaves of this tree are much in demand for making bidis (hand rolled cigarettes), the timber is also valuable. Tendu trees are found in large numbers near Sultanpur-ki-kui and beyond. A favorite fruit of sloth bears. Khus grass (Vetivaria zizznioides) The roots of this grass yield an aromatic oil known as vetiveria oil , a large quantity of which is exported from India . The roots are woven into curtains , and when moistened they cool and scent the air at the same time. The edges of the lakes in Ranthambore are full of Khus grass. This is the grass that is used to make boxes and containers that are available in the old part of Sawai Madhopur town. The aquatic flora in the Ranthambore National Park includes a variety of lovely flowers such as lotus and water lilies.

Fauna in Ranthambhore : Ranthambhore's unique climatic and vegetation features have given rise to forests that are dry and open with little and stunted ground cover. This makes wildlife viewing relatively easier on the safari. Ranthambhore is virtually an island rich in fauna. Tiger, at the apex of the food chain, lord of the kingdom in a subtle way. Solitary by nature, it operates in the stealth. Therefore tiger sightings, frequent as they are, are always a matter of chance. However even evidences of tiger's activities are very exciting. Other kinds of cats found in Ranthambore are Leopard, Caracal, Leopard cat, Fishing cat and Jungle cat. The other large predators include Sloth Bear, Striped Hyena, Jackal, Desert fox, Palm civet, common mongoose, crocodile, python etc. There are two species of antlers the spotted deer (chital), and Sambhar deer and two kinds of antelopes namely the Indian Gazelle (chinkara) and the Bluebull (Nilgai).

Besides tiger, there are many other animals to observe, understand and enjoy. Elegant and graceful spotted deer, huge sambhar deer, crocodiles basking around the lakes, vultures soaring in the sky, Serpent eagles scanning the ground from its perch or the kaleidoscope of waterfowl at the pools are all the interest for a visitor with sensitivity. Ranthmbhore is a great experience in totality and Jungle safari will enhance your experience in wildlife. Ranthambore is also rich in bird life with around 300 species of birds. Infact for a keen bird watcher Ranthambore and the surrounding area is a paradise. Some interesting resident species of birds are large Cormorant, Painted Spurfowl, Sarus Crane, Bronzed winged Jacana, Sandpiper, Kingfisher, Nightjar, Painted Sandgrouse, Great horned owl and many more regular winter migrants which come from their nesting ground north of Himalayas to Ranthambore and surrounding areas.

WILD ANIMALS

Ranthambore National park contains a huge variety of animals, birds and reptiles within it. Primarlily the population consists of...

Animals: Tigers, Leopards, Striped Hyenas, Sambar deer, Chital, Nilgai, Common or Hanuman langurs, Macaques, Jackals, Jungle cats, Caracals, Sloth bears, Black bucks, Rufoustailed Hare, Indian Wild Boar, Chinkara, Common Palm Civets or Toddy cat, Coomon Yellow Bats, Desert Cats, Fivestriped Palm Squirels, Indian False Vampires, Indian Flying Foxes, Indian Foxes, Indian Gerbilles, Indian Mole Rats, Indian Porcupines, Longeared Hedgehogs, Ratels, Small Indian Mongoose, Small Indian Civets and Common mongoose.

The amphibian species only consist of the Common India Toad and the Common Frog.

The park is most famous for it's diurnal tigers.

The park also has a large number of marsh crocs Reptiles: Snub Nosed Marsh Crocodiles, Desert Monitor Lizards, Tortoise, Banded Kraits, Cobras, Common Kraits, Ganga Soft Shelled Turtles, Indian Pythons, North Indian Flap Shelled Turtles, Rat Snakes, Russel's Vipers, Saw-scaled Vipers and the Indian Chamaeleon.

THE TIGRESS RESORT RANTHAMBORE

The Tigress Resort Ranthambore National Park is one of the most beautiful resort located at Sawai Madhopur in Rajasthan. The majestic view of the Aravalli hills is very awe inspiring and the sightseeing of the beautiful forest or national park where one can see the majestic tiger gives you some moment of ecstasy. The services of the resort is one of the best place to stay for all those people who want to get a peaceful stay in wilderness. The nearby areas to visit are Bakaula, Kachida Valley, Lakarda and Anantpura. The Raj Bagh Ruins is another majestic place to visit which reminds of the erstwhile supremacy of the Rajputana rulers.

The entire Ranthambore was earlier the hunting field of the Rajputana Rulers but now it has been turned into a wildlife sanctuary. The resort has all the facilities from restaurant along with internet access and provides nature walk in the forest trail. In case you face any medical emergency then you will get doctor on call. The services of the resort are one of the best and it helps you to enjoy a refreshing day by having a dip in the swimming pool. Also, for foreign tourist they can get foreign exchange through the help desk at the resort. You get a fitness centre in the form of Gymkhana which helps you to stay fit. The spa facility helps you to rejuvenate and relax in the most majestic settings. When it comes to the dining facility nothing can match the unbeatable experience of the royal treat which you get here. The expert chefs help you to get the most amazing dining experience where you get the delicious food. So, if you are looking for one of the best accommodation in the wilderness and if you are getting the call of the wild then be here.

Accommodation

The accommodation resort offers Royal Luxury Suites and Royal Luxury Villas which are tastefully designed with modern amenities ensuring that your stay is memorable along with comfortability.

The room amenities are one of the best which includes central air conditioning and spacious living area along with Mini Bar, 32" LED Television along with personal sit out area.

You also get unlimited free Wi-Fi internet and conveniences along with courteous room service. Our services are one of the finest in terms of spa and if you are getting to go along the tiger trail then you will be provided with the vehicle so that you can do jungle safaris.

Dinning

Enjoy the royal ambience and traditional flavors of Indian and International cuisine which you can get it at "The Tigress Resort". The overall experience will get you mesmerized and you will certainly soak in the atmosphere of the great food with authentic flavors. There are restaurants which will pull you with the aroma of the food and all those food connoisseurs who love to taste the great food will certainly get the gastronomic delight. The resorts have unique which match with the kind of ambience and the food it serves:

- Royal Flavours Restaurant - When it comes to living the splendour of the bygone era of the erstwhile Rajas and Maharajas then you can get that at this restaurant which serves authentic Indian and International cuisine. The ingredients used are of the finest quality and gives you a memorable fine dining experience.

- Royal Panama Roof Top Barbecue - The rooftop restaurant gives a panoramic view of the city and one can gaze the stars in the sky. The restaurant will help you to choose the kind of food ingredients which are brought to table side and you select your own foods giving you a personalized experience giving you to relish the foods.

- Royal Beans Coffee shop - The Royal Beans Coffee Shop is located at the ground floor and is surrounded by lush Green Surroundings. The coffee shop will help you to not only get the coffee but one can also relish the authentic Indian food including breakfast, lunch and dinner.

- Solar shack Pool Bar - One can enjoy the poolside romance by sipping your favorite drink and soak up the sun while enjoying refreshing drinks. The refreshing drinks can be enjoyed while having a dip in the pool because the drinks will be served right at the poolside.

- Royal Fusion Bar - The beautiful moments which you can cherish at the Royal Fusion Bar will help you to relax and unwind. It will help you to enjoy the best of the drinks and give you enjoyment and pleasure which will be an affair to remember.

The other facilities and services offered here are Spa along with the tours to the forest.

Spa: The Spa is by the name of Shanti which means peace so you can get the ultimate peace of mind and relaxation which includes sauna and steam bath after an aromatic massage.

A chilled shower cleans the skin and contracts the skin back to normal which leaves a smooth clean skin and refreshing feeling.

Tiger trail: The Tiger trail is one of the most mesmerizing experience and it will help you to get the view of the royal tiger which will be a memorable experience for you.

So, if you are looking for one of the best kind of experience which will be a remembrance for a lifetime then you can get the best of the experience here.

So, your trip to Ranthambore will certainly get more memorable if you spend some time at The Tigress Resort, Ranthambore National Park. You will be certainly amazed by the experience and it will be a life time experience for you.

HOW TO REACH RANTHAMBORE

One of the most celebrated tiger reserve forests in India, The Ranthambore national park is situated in the Sawai Madhopur district of Rajasthan state in India. The park is well connected through the rail and road with the all major cities of India. Jaipur, the capital of Rajasthan, is around 160 km from the park and is also the nearest airport. Reaching at the Ranthambore Park is easy for tourists from any corner of the world. Here is detailed information on how to reach the Ranthambore National Park-

By Air

The Jaipur International Airport, which is located in the Sanganer, a suburb in Jaipur, is the nearest airport from the Ranthambore Park. The distance between the Airport and the park is 160 km which can be traveled either by the road or by the train.

There are regular flights to Jaipur from all the major cities of India. The airport in Jaipur is an International airport so the city is also well connected through the flight with various overseas cities. The direct bus and taxi services are available from the airport itself to reach the Sawai Madhopur where the Ranthambore Park is located.

By Rail

The easiest way to reach the Ranthambore is the train route. The Sawai Madhopur railway station is the nearest railway station from the Ranthambore Park. The station is located at the distance of about 11 km from the park and the tourist can catch the local bus, taxi or cab to reach the Ranthambore Park from the Sawai Madhopur station. There are direct trains to Sawai Madhopur station from the major cities of India like Jaipur, Delhi, Mumbai and others. The station is a heritage railway station and awarded for the best tourist friendly station in India. Many luxury trains such as Palace on Wheels, Royal Rajasthan on Wheels, Maharaja Express and The Indian Maharaja are scheduled to make a stop here.

By Road

The Ranthambore Park is directly connected through the road with all the major cities and town of India. By availing the state bus service or hiring the private buses and taxis, tourists can easily reach the Ranthambore Park from the cities like Jaipur, Jodhpur, Kota, Delhi, Agra, Mumbai, Ahmedabad, Ajmer, etc.

Road Distance between Ranthambore and other cities-

- Jaipur to Ranthambore - 160 Km
- Udaipur to Ranthambore - 388 Km
- Jodhpur to Ranthambore - 456 Km
- Delhi to Ranthambore - 381 Km
- Agra to Ranthambore - 239 Km
- Mumbai to Ranthambore - 1031 Km

17

Sariska National Park, Rajasthan

Sariska National Park is located in the Alwar district of Rajasthan. Though it was declared as a Wildlife Reserve in 1955, due to the large number of Tigers within this park, it was later declared as one of the Tiger Reserve Forests in 1978.

Sariska National Park was the first national park in the world, which was successfully adapted by the majestic Royal Bengal Tigers as their natural habitat. Leopard, Jungle Cat, Stripped Hyena and Golden Jackal are also found in this national park.

HISTORY OF SARISKA TIGER RESERVE

The Sariska Tiger Reserve is an Indian national park and Wildlife Sanctuary located in the Alwar district of the state ofRajasthan. The topography of Sariska supports scrub-thorn arid forests, rocky landscapes, dry deciduous forests, rocks, grasses and hilly cliffs. This area was a hunting preserve of the Alwar state and it was declared a wildlife reserve in 1955. In 1978, it was given the status of a tiger reserve making it a part of India's Project Tiger. The present area of the park is 866 km². The park is situated 107 km from Jaipur and 200 km from Delhi.

The area of Sariska, being a part of the Aravalli Range, is rich in mineral resources, such as copper. In spite of the Supreme Court's 1991 ban on mining in the area, marble mining continues to threaten the environment.

The most attractive feature of this Reserve has always been its Bengal Tigers. It is the first Tiger reserve in the world to have successfully relocated tigers.

Apart from the Bengal Tiger, the reserve includes many species of wild life, such as the leopard, jungle cat, caracal, striped hyena, golden jackal, chital, sambhar, nilgai, chinkara, four-horned antelope, wild boar, hare, hanuman langur, Rhesus monkeys. Sasrika is also ethereal for bird watchers with some of the rarest feathered species like Grey Partridge, White-throated kingfisher, Indian peafowl, Bush Quail, Sandgrouse, Treepie, Golden-backed Woodpecker, Crested serpent eagle and the Indian eagle-owl.

Historical places

The reserve is also the location of several sites of historical importance such as the 16th-century Kankwadi fort, originally built by Jai Singh II, is located near the centre of the park. The Mughal Emperor Aurangzeb briefly imprisoned his brother Dara Shikoh in the struggle to become king. Pandupol in the hills in the centre of the reserve is believed to be one of the retreats of Pandava. Hanuman temple in Pandupol is a pilgrimage site which causes problems for the wildlife, due to the heavy traffic. The area also has buildings associated with the kings of Alwar such as the Sariska Palace, which was used as a royal hunting lodge of Maharaja

Tiger population

In 2004, there were strong and persistent reports that no tigers were being sighted in the reserve. It was not only that tigers were not being seen but also and more alarmingly, there was no indirect evidence of the tigers' presence (such as pugmarks, scratch marks on trees, etc.). The Rajasthan Forest Department took the stand that "the tigers had temporarily migrated outside the reserve and would be back after monsoon season". Project Tiger, now National Tiger Conservation Authority (NTCA), backed this assumption. There were 16 tigers in the previous year. In January 2005, journalist Jay Mazoomdaar broke the news that there were no tigers left in Sariska. Soon the Rajasthan Forest Department and the Project Tiger Director declared an "emergency tiger census" in Sariska and the Central Bureau of Investigation, India's intelligence agency, conducted a probe. After a two month investigation they finally declared that Sariska did not have any tigers left. Poaching was blamed for the disappearance of tigers. In order to repopulate Sariska with Tigers 3 Tigers were relocated to the reserve and authorities planned to relocate two more tigers by the end of the following year. Recently, two tiger cubs and their mother were spotted in the reserve bringing the total number of tigers to seven with five adults. In July 2014, 2 more tiger cubs were spotted taking the total of tigers in the reserve to 11 with 9 adults. Two cubs were further sighted in August 2014, making the total of tigers in Sariska to 13, with 7 females, 2 males and 4 cubs. This significant increase in tigers' population has given a wide smile to wildlife enthusiasts and therefore the footfall has been increased by a huge amount.

Relocation efforts

In 2005, the Government of Rajasthan, in cooperation with the Government of India and Wildlife Institute of India (WII), planned the re-introduction of tigers to Sariska and also the relocation of villages. plans to construct a bypass were also discussed.

Tiger in the Sariska Tiger Reserve. The collar around its neck is used to track and monitor it.

It was decided to import one male and two females from Ranthambore National Park The Wildlife Institute of India (WII) along with the Government of Rajasthan started tracking the relocated tigers with the help of ISRO'sreconnaissance satellites. The first aerial translocation of the male tiger (Dara) from Ranthambhore to Sariska was done on 28 June 2008 by Wing Commander Vimal Raj of the Indian Air Force using a Mi-17 Helicopter.

Only two of the four villages' experts had said needed to be relocated were actually moved, though the second, Kankwari, was shifted long after the tigers were re-introduced. However, Kankwari fort has been renovated by the state tourism department, which can possibly violate wildlife protection norms. The first relocated village was Bhagani. Also, the diversion of roads crossing the reserve, an issue critical to the survival of its wildlife, continues to be a problem.

One more tigress was shifted to Sariska from Ranthambhore in February 2009. On 28 July 2010, another tigress was brought from Ranthambhore National Park. Totaling five tigers — two males and three females — were living in the reserve until November 2010 when the first relocated tiger died due to poisoning.

Unfortunately, the first three of the relocated tigers came from one father. Moreover, the first two tigresses have the same mother. The breeding of close relatives leads to inbreeding.

General information

Water body within the Sariska Reserve, Rajasthan.

- Area: 866 km^2
- Altitude: between 300 m and 722 m MSL
- Rainfall: average 650 mm (per year)
- Forest types: tropical, dry, deciduous, and tropical thorn

Flora and fauna

Apart from the Bengal tiger, the reserve includes many species of wildlife, such as the Indian leopard, jungle cat, caracal, striped hyena, Indian jackal, chital, sambhar, nilgai, chinkara, four-horned antelope, wild boar, hare, hanuman langur, rhesus monkeys.

Sariska is also ethereal for bird watchers with some of the rarest feathered species like grey partridge, white-throated kingfisher, Indian peafowl, bush quail, sandgrouse, treepie, golden-backed woodpecker, crested serpent eagle and the Indian eagle-owl.

The dominant tree in the forests is dhok (*Anogeissus pendula*). Other trees include the salar (*Boswellia serrata*), kadaya (Sterculia urens), dhak (*Butea monosperma*), gol (*Lannea coromandelica*), ber (*Ziziphus mauritiana*) and khair (*Acacia catechu*). Bargad (*Ficus benghalensis*), arjun (*Terminalia arjuna*), gugal (*Commiphora wightii*) or bamboo. Shrubs are numerous, such as kair (*Capparis decidua*), adusta (*Adhatoda vesica*) and jhar ber (*Ziziphus nummularia*).

Places of interest

- Ruins of Bhangarh
- Kankwadi Fort - A 16th century fort, originally built by Jai Singh II, located near the centre of the park.
- Temple of Neelkanth
- Pandupol Hanumanji Temple - Located in the hills in the centre of the reserve is believed to be one of the retreats of the Pandava. This pilgrimage site causes problems for the wildlife, due to heavy traffic.
- Sariska Palace - Was used as a royal hunting lodge of Maharaja, was associated with the kings of Alwar.

FLORA IN SARISKA WILDLIFE SANCTUARY

The Flora in Sariska Wildlife Sanctuary is indeed very interesting. Firstly the Sariska Wildlife Sanctuary can be regarded as the sole forest patch in the whole of the western Aravali hills. Greenery can rarely be traced in the vast stretches of desert that are to be found in the state of Rajasthan and the Sariska Wildlife Reserve is a welcome exception.

The topography of Sariska Wildlife Sanctuary comprises of small hills and narrow valleys.

All in all it is a rocky terrain. This kind of landscape and the lack of adequate rainfall lead to the growth of dense vegetation consisting of stunted trees and bushes.

Thorny shrubs and grasses are to be found in plenty. The Flora in Sariska Wildlife Sanctuary consists of arid forests.

The dry deciduous forest that is found in the Sariska Wildlife Sanctuary comprises of different kinds of trees including Goria, Surwal, Ber, Tendu, and Khair. Dhok is however the most prominent tree in the Sariska Wildlife Sanctuary. It makes up a major part of the vegetation.

In the summers, the forest displays an arid landscape. However the look of the forest changes drastically after the monsoons. Receiving rainfall, all the trees seem to get a fresh lease of life and the lush foliage impresses you highly. The Flora in the Sariska Wildlife Sanctuary is seen at its best after the monsoons.

It is indeed a matter of great concern that the indiscriminate felling of trees has resulted in shrinkage of the forest cover. Steps should be taken to see to it that the Flora of the Sariska Wildlife Sanctuary is not lost because of the ignorance of people. They should be enlightened on the disastrous consequences of cutting of trees so that the Flora of Sariska Wildlife Sanctuary is well preserved.

MEDICINAL PLANTS OF SARISKA TIGER RESERVE (RAJASTHAN) INDIA

Abstract: Sariska Tiger Reserve, one of the 42 Tiger Reserves of India, is located in the undulating plateau lands and wide valleys of the hill ranges of Aravalli system, near the civil district of Alwar in Rajasthan. The forest of Sariska Tiger Reserve especially undulating plateaus, lands and wide velleys of the hill ranges of Aravalli hills. Rajasthan have great diversity of flora. This paper gives an account of 99 medicinal plants found in Sariska Tiger Reserve Rajasthan state, India along with their local name, family, habit and medicinal uses.

HOW TO REACH SARISKA NATIONAL PARK

By Air

The Jaipur Sanganer Airport is the nearest airport from Sariska and is located in Sanganer, approximately 110 kilometers from the National Park. Sanganer airport is well connected by road and rail network to Sariska National Park.

By Train

The nearest railway station is Alwar, which is about 35 km from Sariska. Alwar railway station is well connected by road to Sariska National Park.

By Road

Sariska National Park is well connected to Major Cities and Places by road network. There are a number of government and privately operated vehicles that go to Sariska National Park at frequent intervals.

Sariska National Park is located off the Delhi-Alwar-Jaipur Road. Bus service available from all major Cities.

18

Tadoba Andhari Tiger Reserve, Maharashtra

There is a great history behind the name of Tadoba National Park. Tadoba or Taru was the name of god of tribal people who reside in the dense Tadoba region of the forest.

It is believed that Taru was a chief of village, who was killed in a legendary encounter with a tiger. After this, a shrine was made dedicated to the God Taru that exists under a huge tree and on the bank of Tadoba Lake. Likewise, 'Andhari' name was given due to Andhari River that wanders through the forest.

Earlier, the kings of Gond ruled this forest in the vicinage of the Chimur hills. During 1935, hunting was totally restricted, but later in the year 1955; the area of 116.54 sq. km (45.00 sq mi) was acknowledged as The National Park. Andhari Wildlife Sanctuary was made on the next forests in 1986 and later in the year 1995, the park & the sanctuary were combined together to form the present India's 41 "Project Tiger"-Tiger Reserves.

Tadoba Andhari Tiger Project, a Tiger Reserve in Chandrapur district of Maharashtra is the oldest and the largest National Park in Maharashtra.

Bengal Tigers, Leopards, Stripped Hyena and Jungle Cats are some of the commonly found carnivores of this park. Sloth Bears, Gaur, Nilgai and Spotted Deer are the herbivores.

Forests of this park always bear the green colour due to the geographical topography of the park's location. Axle-wood, a fire-resistant species of trees can be commonly found in this park. Among the other species, Black Plum, Arjun and Palas are dominant.

HISTORY OF TADOBA ANDHARI TIGER PROJECT

Tadoba Andhari Tiger Reserve is a Tiger reserves in Chandrapur district of Maharashtra state in central India. It is notable as Maharashtra's oldest and largest National Park. It is one of India's 43 "Project Tiger" - Tiger reserves.

Etymology

The name 'Tadoba' is the name of the God "Tadoba" or "Taru", praised by the tribal people who live in the dense forests of the Tadoba and Andhari region, while the Andhari River that meanders through the forest. gives the 'Andhari' name.

History

Legend holds that Taru was a village chief who was killed in a mythological encounter with a tiger. A shrine dedicated to the God Taru now exists beneath a huge tree, on the banks of the Tadoba Lake. The temple is frequented by adivasis, especially during the fair held every year in the Hindu month of Pausha, between December and January.

The Gond kings once ruled these forests in the vicinity of the Chimur hills. Hunting was completely banned in 1935. Two decades later, in 1955, 116.54 km^2 (45.00 sq mi) was declared a National Park. Andhari Wildlife Sanctuary was created on the adjacent forests in 1986, and in 1995, both the park and the sanctuary were merged to establish the present Tiger Reserve.

Topography

Tadoba Andhari Reserve is the largest national park in Maharashtra. Total area of the Reserve is 1727 km². This includes Tadoba National Park, created in 1955.

Etymology

The name +(9)9'Tadoba' is the name of the God "Tadoba" or "Taru", praised by the tribal people who live in the dense forests of the Tadoba and Andhari region, while the Andhari River that meanders through the forest. gives the 'Andhari' name.

Legend holds that Taru was a village chief who was killed in a mythological encounter with a tiger. A shrine dedicated to the God Taru now exists beneath a huge tree, on the banks of the Tadoba Lake. The temple is frequented by adivasis, especially during the fair held every year in the Hindu month of Pausha, between December and January. The Gond kings once ruled these forests in the vicinity of the Chimur hills. Hunting was completely banned in 1935. Two decades later, in 1955, 116.54 km2 (45.00 sq mi) was declared a National Park. Andhari Wildlife Sanctuary was created on the adjacent forests in 1986, and in 1995, both the park and the sanctuary were merged to establish the present Tiger Reserve.

TIGERS AT TADOBA

There are about 43 Tigers (2010 National Census on Tigers) in the reserve, one of the highest in India.

Tadoba Andhari Reserve

Tadoba Andhari Reserve is the largest national park in Maharashtra. Total area of the Reserve is 625.4 square kilometres (241.5 sq mi). This includes Tadoba National Park, created in 1955 with an area of 116.55 square kilometres (45.00 sq mi) and Andhari Wildlife Sanctuary created in 1986 with an area of 508.85 square kilometres (196.47 sq mi). The Reserve also includes 32.51 square kilometres (12.55 sq mi) Protected Forest and 14.93 square kilometres (5.76 sq mi) 'Other areas'.

Densely forested hills form the northern and western boundary of the Tiger Reserve. The elevation of the hills ranges from 200 m (660 ft) to350 m (1,150 ft). To the southwest is the 120 ha (300 acres) Tadoba lake which acts as a buffer between the park's forest and the extensive farmland which extends up to Irai water reservoir.

This lake is a perennial water source which offers good habitat for Muggar crocodiles to thrive. Other wetland areas within the reserve include the Kolsa lake and Andhari river. Tadoba reserve covers the Chimur Hills, and the Andhari sanctuary covers Moharli and Kolsa ranges. It's bounded on the northern and the western side by densely forested hills. Thick forests are relieved by smooth meadows and deep valleys as the terrain slopes from north to south.

Cliffs, talus and caves provide refuge for several animals. The two forested rectangles are formed of Tadoba and Andhari range. The south part of the park is less hilly. Tadoba reserve is a predominantly Southern tropical Dry Deciduous Forest with dense woodlands comprising about 87 per cent of the protected area. Teakis the prdominant tree species. Other deciduous trees include Ain (crocodile bark), Bija, Dhauda, Haldu, Salai, Semal and Tendu. beheda, hirda, karaya gum, mahua Madhuca (Crepe myrtle) and Lannea coramandelica (Wodier Tree) are other common species. Axlewood Anogeissus latifolia is a fire-resistant species growing here. Palas or Flame of the Forest Butea monosperma adds vibrant colour to the forest. Black plum trees grow in the riparian habitat around the lake. At the waterhole at Panchadhara, huge arjun trees are seen. Patches of grasses are found throughout the reserve. Bamboo thickets grow throughout the reserve. The climber Kach Kujali (velvet bean) found here is a medicinal plant used to treat Parkinson's disease. The leaves of bheria are used as an insect repellant and bija is a medicinal gum. Beheda is also an important medicine found here. Aside from around 65 of the keystone species Bengal tiger, Tadoba Tiger Reserve is home to other mammals, including: Indian leopards, sloth bears, gaur, nilgai, dhole, striped hyena, small Indian Civet, jungle cats, sambar, spotted deer, barking deer, chital, and chausingha.

Threats

There are 41,644 people living in and around the reserve in 59 villages of which 5 are inside the core zone, These villages in the core zone still do farming activity inside the core area. The process of rehabilitation is going on but the Indian bureaucracy has been at its slowest in the forest department.Recently the Navegaon village was rehabilitated and a grassland is expected on the place where the village existed.

There are 41,820 cattle with the villagers in the core and buffer zone. While cattle grazing is not allowed in the core zone, regulated grazing in the buffer zone is allowed to cattle of the village inhabitants. However, cattle of peripheral villages sometimes sneak into the reserve and cause additional damage to the habitat. Forest fires are a constant problem in the dry season, consistently burning between

2% and 16% of the park each year.With killing of domestic livestock by tigers and leopards as a frequent phenomenon in the areas neighboring villages.

This has an adverse impact on the economic condition of the local people and results into antagonism towards the management. In the year 2013 so far there have been up to 4 people and 30-50 cattle heads killed by leopards, tigers or Sloth Bears. Densely forested hills form the northern and western boundary of the Tiger Reserve. The elevation of the hills ranges from 200 m (660 ft) to350 m (1,150 ft). To the southwest is the 120 ha (300 acres) Tadoba lake which acts as a buffer between the park's forest and the extensive farmland which extends up to Irai water reservoir. This lake is a perennial water source which offers good habitat for Muggar crocodiles to thrive. Other wetland areas within the reserve include the Kolsa lake and Andhari river.

Tadoba reserve covers the Chimur Hills, and the Andhari sanctuary covers Moharli and Kolsa ranges. It's bounded on the northern and the western side by densely forested hills. Thick forests are relieved by smooth meadows and deep valleys as the terrain slopes from north to south. Cliffs, talus and caves provide refuge for several animals. The two forested rectangles are formed of Tadoba and Andhari range. The south part of the park is less hilly.

FLORA

Tadoba reserve is a predominantly Southern tropical Dry Deciduous Forest with dense woodlands comprising about 87 per cent of the protected area. Teakis the prdominant tree species. Other deciduous trees include Ain (crocodile bark), Bija, Dhauda, Hald, Salai, Semal and Tendu. beheda, hirda, karaya gum, mahua Madhuca (Crepe myrtle) andLannea coramandelica (Wodier Tree) are other common species.

Axlewood Anogeissus latifolia is a fire-resistant species growing here. Palas or Flame of the Forest Butea monosperma adds vibrant colour to the forest. Black plum trees grow in the riparian habitat around the lake. At the waterhole at Panchadhara, huge arjun trees are seen.

Patches of grasses are found throughout the reserve. Bamboo thickets grow throughout the reserve. The climber Kach Kujali (velvet bean) found here is a medicinal plant used to treat Parkinson's disease. The leaves of bheria are used as an insect repellant and bija is a medicinal gum. Beheda is also an important medicine found here.

Flora in Tadoba Tiger Reserve

The most popular species of trees is Teak and bamboo in this forest. Other common trees include:

- Ain (Crocodile Bark)
- Bija
- Dhaudab
- Hald
- Salai
- Semal
- Shisham
- Sisoo
- Shivan
- Surya
- Sirus
- Tendu
- Beheda
- Bel
- Chichwa
- Dhawada
- Kusum
- Hirda
- Karaya Gum
- Mahua Madhuca (Crepe Myrtle)
- Lannea Coramandelica (Wodier Tree)

In addition, Axlewood Anogeissus Latifolia is also found here that is fire-resistant species, while on the other side, Butea monosperma adds vivacious color to this forest. Arjun trees are also found at Panchadhara.

FAUNA

Aside from around 65 of the keystone species Bengal tiger, Tadoba Tiger Reserve is home to other mammals, including: Indian leopards, sloth bears, gaur, nilgai, dhole, striped hyena, small Indian civet, jungle cats, sambar, spotted deer, barking deer, chital, and chausingha. Tadoba lake sustains the marsh crocodile, which were once common all over Maharashtra.

Reptiles here include the endangered Indian python and the common Indian monitor. Terrapins, Indian star tortoise, Indian cobra and Russel's viper also live in Tadoba. The lake is an ornithologist's paradise with a wide diversity of water birds, and raptors. 195 species of birds have been recorded, including three endangered species. The grey-headed fish eagle, the crested serpent eagle, and the changeable hawk-eagle are some of the raptors.

Other interesting species include the orange-headed thrush, Indian pitta, crested treeswift, stone curlew, crested honey buzzard,paradise flycatcher, bronze-winged jacana and lesser goldenbacked woodpecker. Warblers and the black-naped blue flycatcher exist here and the call of the peacock may often be heard.

74 species of butterflies have been recorded including the pansies, monarch, Mormons and swordtails.

Insect species include the endangered danaid egg-fly and great eggfly. Dragonflies, stick insects, jewel beetles and the praying mantis are other insects located in the reserve.

The signature spider, giant wood spider and red wood spiders are often seen during the monsoon and soon after. Some hunting spiders like the wolf spiders, crab spiders andlynx spiders are also common.

Fauna in Tadoba

Tadoba National Park is a popular tiger reserve that's affably known as 'The Land of Tigers' as large number of tigers (approx.43) are found here.

Apart from the species of Bengal Tiger, this park is home to other mammals like Sloth Bear, Leopard, Rusty Spotted Cat, Gaur (Indian Bison), Indian Mouse Deer, Ratel, Sambar, Wild Pig, Spotted Deer, Flying Squirrel, Four Horned Antelope, to name a few.

As soon the night falls, the Small Indian Civet, the Palm Civet, the Ratel, and the Flying squirrel make their presence felt.

Some of the major wild animals that are always found in this park include:

- Hyenas
- Spotted Deer
- Wild Boars
- Barking deer
- Gaurs
- Four horned Antelopes
- Blue bulls
- Indian Pangolins
- Common Langoors
- Porcupines

Above all, there are approx 195 species of birds that include honey buzzard, crested serpent eagle, the shy jungle fowl, grey-headed fishing eagle, paradise flycatcher, etc.

Species of reptiles are also found in this park like endangered Indian python, terrapins, star tortoise, cobra, etc.

Apart from this, giant wood spider, the signature spider, and red wood spiders are also found during monsoon season.

In and Around Tourist Attractions of Tadoba

Tadoba National Park is enclosed by some beautiful places and temples like Tadoba Lake, Sankatmochan Hanuman Mandir, Shiv Mandir, and Urjanagar Lake.

Visit the oldest national park of Madhya Pradesh and get an opportunity to view the striped creature at Tadoba National Park.

Apart from this, there are some popular tourist attractions that are in close proximity from the national park like St. Michael Church, Durga Maa Temple and Ayyappa Temple. Other than this, Nagpur is very close from the park that is also known as 'Tiger Capital of India' as it is linked with many tiger reserves in India.

Best Time to Visit Tadoba

This park gives a large visual treat of wildlife, especially while getting a chance to spot tigers. To view the real wildlife, the best time to visit is from February to May. During this time, Gaurs, tigers, herd of deer and other animals are easily seen in large numbers. Exploring these animals give thrilling experience and big treat to a trip.

Safari Activities & Timings

Gypsy and Jeep Safaris are always available in Tadoba National Park that help in exploring the wildlife of the forest.

Safari Timings are:
- Morning Jeep: 6.00 A.M to 10.00 A.M. (entry allowed until 8.00 a.m.)
- Afternoon Jeep: 3.00 P.M. until 6.00 P.M (entry allowed until 4.30 p.m.)

Accommodation in Tadoba Tiger Reserve

Accommodation in Tadoba offers luxury stay amidst the forest. Some of the major hotels for comfortable stay include:
- Svasara Jungle Lodge
- Serai Tiger Camp

- Irai Safari Retreat
- Tiger Trails Jungle Eco Lodge

For budget options, Maharastra Tourism Development Corporation hotel (Mohrali) and the Forest Development Corporation of Maharashtra guesthouse and dormitory room are also perfect for comfy accommodation. Apart from this, Eco huts provided by the Forest Development Corporation of Maharashtra are also good for those who are looking for budget lodging in Tadoba National Park.

How to Reach

By Air-Nagpur (140 Km) is the nearest airport from where it takes 3 hour taxi rides to reach the park.

By Rail-Chandrapur (49 kms) and Nagpur (151kms) are nearest railheads.

By Road-Nearest bus stop is Chandrapur and Chimur (32 km), but bus or cabs are also available from Chandrapur to Mohrali Village.

19

National Parks and Wildlife Sanctuary

CORBETT NATIONAL PARK

The first wildlife reserve of India, Corbett National Park was established in 1936, as the Hailey National Park. Later it changed to Ramganga and finally Corbett National Park in the honour of legendary hunter-turned- conservationist, best known for hunting man-eating tigers and leopards in The Kumaon and lower Garhwal.

Corbett National Park is known for its varied wildlife, and as the site for the launching of Project Tiger. Corbett National Park was one of the nine tiger reserves created at the launch of the Project Tiger in 1973. The area of the Corbett National Park is 520.84 sq. km. In 1991, an area of 797.72 sq km was added as buffer area of the Corbett Tiger Reserve. Wildlife found in the Corbett National Park include the tiger, elephant, chital, sambar, nilgai, gharial, King Cobra, wild boar, hedgehog, common musk shrew, flying fox, Indian Pangolin, and nearly 600 species of birds. A variety of facilities are available to house tourists within and outside the park.

When to visit: The Park remains open from 15th Nov- 31st March and reopen from 1st Feb to 15th June.

How To Reach Corbett National Park:

By Air: Pantnagar at a distance of 50 km is the nearest airport. Delhi at a distance of 300 km is the nearest international airport. By Rail: Ramnagar is on the broad gauge track from where the road transport options have to be availed to reach the Park.

The main reception centre is located in Ramnagar where where permits are issued for the three tourism zone of the National Park.

By Road: Dhikala is 300 km from Delhi, 403 km from Lucknow and 51 km from

Ramnagar. The route from Delhi spans Hapur-Murababad-Ramnagar. The turn off is some 7 km beyond Muradabad to the left, marked by a small board. The route from Lucknow spans Bareilly. Kichha. Rudrapur. Doraha. Kashipur.

Where to stay

Accomadation is avaible in the several Forest Rest Houses maintained by the Forest Department. Permission for staying in the Forest Rest Houses inside the park needs to be taken in advance from the office of the Director. However there are several hotels and resorts outside the Park offering varied accomadation. Garwal Mandal Vikas Nigan too has a TRC in Ramnagar.

FLORA IN KEOLADEO NATIONAL PARK

As the Keoladeo Ghana National Park has a high density of vegetation, hence the term 'Ghana' or thick forest. Bharatpur Bird Sanctuary contains a wide variety of flora representing 64 families, 181 genera and 227 subspecies. Flora in Bharatpur consists of different vegetation types. The principal vegetation types are tropical dry deciduous forest dominated by Acacia nilotica intermixed with dry grassland. Besides the artificially managed marshes, much of the area is covered by medium-sized trees and shrubs.

The forests are dominated by kadam (Mitragyna parvifolia), babul (Acacia nilotica) and jamun (Syzygium cuminii). The open woodland is mostly babul, with a small amount of kandi (Prosopis spicigera) and ber (Zizyphus mauritiana).

The scrublands are dominated by ber and kair (Capparis decidua). Khus grass (Vetiveria zizanoides) is the ruling graminae of the reserve.

Aquatic vegetation consists of water lilies (Nymphea nouchatia), N.stellata and N.cristata, the lotus (Nilumbium sp.), duckweeds (Lemna sp.) and water fern (Azola sp.). Sedges (Cyperus sp.), reedmace (Typhea angustata) and (Ipomia sp.) dominate in some areas. Submerged plants include Vallesneria sp., Hydrilla sp., Naga sp. and Chara sp.. Paspalum distichum, a perennial amphibious grass constitutes a major portion of the biomass.

The 'Kadam' trees, the most commonly seen flora in Bharatpur, indicate that this region was once part of extensive floodplains and that this was the site of confluence of the Rivers Gambhir and Banganga.

BHARATPUR BIRD SANCTUARY

Some address it Keoladeo National Park and some define as Ghana National Park; the Bharatpur Bird Sanctuary, a World Heritage Site, is the perfect home to almost thousands of birds all across the world. Located in Bharatpur, Rajasthan, it's a famous Avifauna Sanctuary that hosts almost thousands of birds especially in winter season to find the migratory species. Amazingly, at least 230 species of birds have made this sanctuary their favorite home and is the most favorable and protected zone for them. Nesting indigenous water birds and migratory water birds specifically the Siberian Crane, the Bharatpur Sanctuary also boasts with many species of Sambar, Chital, Nilgai and Boar. It is the major tourist spot for most of the ornithologists today during hibernal season.

History of Bharatpur Sanctuary

Bharatpur Sanctuary is one of the oldest wild reserves in India and was created 250 years ago when it was named after the Keoladeo (Shiva) temple within its boundaries. Earlier, the park was a traditional hunting spot for the Maharajas of Bharatpur in the year 1850.

It was a tradition to shoot many ducks in the lake of the reserve in the honor of the British viceroys. In 1938, over 4273 birds including mallards and teals were killed by Lord Linlithgrow, the then Governor General of India. After independence, the royal beings were allowed to shoot here but in the year 1982, every such activity was completely banned and resultedin the clashes between the local farmers & Gujjar communities and the Government. It was considered as the world heritage site in December 1985.

The park is also referred as Ghana National Park since 'Ghana' means dense referring to the thick forest that covers the whole Bharatpur area.

Wildlife in Bharatpur Bird Sanctuary

The numerous counts of the bird species are the major attractions for the tourists in Bharatpur. These species fly through distant places like Siberia and Central Asia specifically in winters. Migratory birds at Bharatpur Bird Sanctuary include several species of Cranes, Pelicans, Geese, Ducks, Eagles, Hawks, Shanks, Stints, Wagtails, Warblers, Wheatears, Flycatchers, Buntings, Larks and Pipits, etc.

Along with that some major counts of Sambal, Chital, Nilgai and Boar can also be found at the sanctuary.

Flora

The forest in Bahratpur is semi-arid biotype with significant vegetation and that is why the sanctuary is termed as 'Ghana'-thicket. Principally it is a dry deciduous forest type, intermixed with dry grassland in the area where the forest has been degraded. Along with that the forest is also being covered with medium sized trees and shrubs.

The north-east region of the forest is being ruled by kalam or kadam (Mitragyna parvifolia), Jamun (Syzygium cumini) and Babul (Acacia nilotica). The open woodland is mostly babul with a small amount of Kandi (Prosopis cineraria) and Ber (Zizyphus).

The open woodland is coveredwith babul with a small amount of kandi and ber. Scrublands are dominated by ber and kair (Capparis decidua). Piloo (Salvadora oleoides and Salvadora persica) are virtually the only woody plants found in areas of saline soil. The aquatic vegetation is rich and provides a valuable food source for waterfowl.

The scrublands are filled with Ber and Kair and the soils are greatly alluvial with some of the clays being formed as a result of periodic torrents. The annual precipitation at Bharatpur zone is 662mm, with rain falling on an average of 36 days per year.

Fauna

In Bharatpur, mostly the macro invertebrates like worms, insects and mollusks can be found in abundance which are mostly can be found n aquatic marine. These insects are the common foods of the birds and the fishes of the marine world and bring a major link in the food chain with a good control in the ecosystem. . Land insects are in abundance and have a positive effect on the breeding of land birds.

Basically a bird paradise, the Bharatpur Sanctuary boasts almost 370 bird species. This sanctuary is an ideal host for so many bird species because of its strategic location to attract migratory waterfowl in the Indian subcontinent before dispersing to various regions. In addition, the wetland is a wintering area for massive congregations of waterfowl. It is the only regular wintering area in India for the Critically Endangered Siberian Crane.

ANCIENT PALACES & MONUMENTS & NEAR BHARATPUR SANCTUARY

Bharatpur Palace

A perfect blend of Mughal and Rajputana style of architecture, the Baharatpur Palace was built in different phases by different kings. The palace is entrancingly decorated with amazing interiors and designs with patterned floor tiles. The museum at the center displays the 2nd century art and skills of the state and the region.

Lohagarh Fort

The "Iron Fort" is specially conceived and designed so that it may last longer;and amazingly justified by its name the Lohagarh Fort stood strongly against many attacks by the British. This fort is quite different from other forts in the state in terms of construction and appearance. Although not quite attractive but the fort radiates an aura of strength and magnificence. It is surrounded by a moat which was once filled with water to prevent the enemy attack.

There are many attractive monuments inside the fort built by Raja Suraj Mal to commemorate victories over the Mughals and the Britishers. These monuments are Kishori Mahal, Mahal Khas, Moti Mahal, Kothi Khas, Jawahar Burj and Fateh Burj. The amazing Ashtadhatu (eight-metal) gateway has paintings of huge elephants.

Bharatpur Government Museum

Within the Lohagarh Fort, the building- Kamra Khas has been converted into a museum that displays a rich collection of antiquities, exquisite sculptures and some ancient inscription. These sculptures reflect the art and culture of that era and the inscriptions are of immense value as they trace the royal lineage and local life.

Deeg Palace

The Deeg Palace is an amazing fort built by Raja Suraj Mal that stands majestically over a slightly elevated point and is surrounded by impressive moats, ramparts and gateways. One can find the interiors in the ruined position but the watch tower still exists in the vigil position keeping an eye over the city and the palace. Many canons and guns of ancient periods of different rulers can be found at this palace to remember as a victory over the neighboring palaces.

The whole Bharatpur Sanctuary is being spread with well defined forest trails and can easily be covered on foot or on a cycle. Motor vehicles are not allowed inside the vicinity but you can hire a rickshaw available there. You can also enjoy an early morning or late evening boating trip to add more excitement to the birding tour.

Bharatpur Sanctuary at a Glance

- Location- Bharatpur, Rajasthan
- Established- 10 March 1982
- Nearest Access- Bharatpur, Jaipur, Agra, Delhi
- Main Wildlife Found- Sambal, Chital, Nilgai, Boar, Migratory Birds
- Coverage Areas- 29 sq kms, 2873 hectares
- Types- Natural (Dry Deciduous with dry grassland)

Best Time to Visit Bharatpur Sanctuary

Although remain opened throughout the year, still the ideal months to make a visit are:

- For resident breeding birds- during Aug-Nov
- For migrant birds-from Oct-Feb

RAJAJI NATIONAL PARK

Rajaji National Park is situated along the hills and foothills of Shivalik ranges in the Himalayan foothills and represents the Shivalik eco-system. Spread over an area of 820.42 sq km, Rajaji is a magnificent ecosystem nestled in the Shivalik ranges and the beginning of the vast Indo–Gangetic plains, thus representing vegetation of several distinct zones and forest types like sal forests, riverine forests, board–leaved mixed forests, scrubland and grassy.

On the map it is located between Haridwar and Dehradun and Chillawali. Three sancturies in the Uttarakhand Shivaliks - Rajaji, Motichur and Chila were amalgamated into a large protected area and named Rajaji National Park in the year 1983 after the famous freedom fighter Late Sri C. Rajgopalachari; popularly known as "Rajaji".

It possesses as many as 23 species of mammals and 315 bird species. The abundance of nature's bounties heaped in and around this park, attracts a large number of wildlife conversationalists, nature lovers to visit this most breathtaking wilderness area.

The uniqueness of the Parks stands in that it is the northern most limits of the Tiger, Asian elephants, King Cobra and certain bird species.

When to visit: The Park remains open from 15th Nov- 31st March and reopens from 1st Feb to 15th June.

Where to Stay the Park has excellent lodging facility with 10 Forest Rest Houses maintained by the Park authorities in the four tourism zones. Catering facilities are not available in some of the FRH, but visitors are allowed to cook their own food. Permission needs to be obtained in advance from the Director of the Park who has his office in Dehradun.

NANDA DEVI NATIONAL PARKS & WILDLIFE SANCTUARIES

Nanda Devi National Park offers an unparallel experience. The Nanda Devi National Park (NDNP) is one of the very few wilderness area in India that has remained naturally protected. The Nanda Devi basin was declared as Nanda Devi Sanctuary in 1939. An area of 630 sq. Km. was added as Nanda Devi National Park in the year 1982 which is now a part and core zone of Nanda Devi Biosphere Reserve. The Park became a world heritage site in the year 1988. Some of the important peaks encircling the National Park are Dunagiri (7066mt), Changband

(6864mt), Kalnka (6931mt) Rishi pahar (6992 mt) Mangraon (6765mt), Nanda Khat (6631 mt), Maiktoli (6803 mt), Mrigthuni (6655mt), Trishul-1 (7120mt), Trishul-II (6319mt), Bethartoli Himal (6352mt) and Nandadevi East (7434 mt.).

Nanda Devi National Park is an outstanding mountain wilderness with few if any parallels elsewhere in the Himalayas on account of its concentration of high peaks and glaciers lying within a range of near – pristine habitats. It lies within a bio geographical transition zone between the Western and Eastern Himalayas and supports a variety of threatened and uncommon species of large mammals.

The Nanda Devi National Park the world heritage site has unique topography, climate, and soil and it supports diverse habitat, species, communities and ecosystems. The area is reputed as one of the most spectacular wilderness in the Himalaya and is dominated by "Nanda Devi Peak" which is a natural monument and India's second highest peak.

Trek for the park negotiates a steep assent at high altitude zones within 13km route from 2000 mt. at village Lata to 4250mt.to Dharasi – the topmost point. Get a thorough medical check up done before taking this arduous trek.

THE VALLEY OF FLOWERS NATIONAL PARK

The Valley of Flowers National Park is the second core zone of the Nanda Devi Biosphere Reserve. The credit for the discovery of the Valley of Flowers goes to the British mountaineers Franks S. Smythe and R.L. Holdsworth who incidentally reached this valley after a successful expedition of Mount Kamet in 1931. Fascinated by its beauty and grandeur Frank S. Smythe revisited this area in 1937 and published a book named "Valley of Flowers" (1938). However, there is no doubt that Frank s. Smythe's writing made this valley world famous. The valley of flowers lies in the main valley of Alaknanda and Laxman Ganga in the Garhwal Himalayas in Chamoli district of Uttarakhand. Pushpawati river flows through this valley which has it's source in the Tipra Glacier which extends upto Ghori Parbat Peak. It is a flat valley 5km. long and 2km. wide. Its altitudinal range varies from 3200 to 6675m.

The Park is surrounded by Gauri Parbat (6590m) and Rataban (6126m) in the east, Kunthal (4430m) in the west, in the west, Saptsring (5030m) in the south and Nilgiri Parvat (6479m) in the north.

Valley of flowers is a trek of about 16km from Govindghat which is 25km from Joshimath. From Govindghat one has to trek of 13km to reach Ghangaria. After crossing the Alaknanda river at Govindghat, an ascending bridle path along Bhyundar Ganga leads to Ghangharia. From here the valley is situated at a distance of 3km.

Almost 300 species of wild flowers bloom here in natural way. Wherein some of the species are Anemone, Geranium, March marigold. Primula, Potentilla, Geum. Asters Lilium, Himalayam Blue poppy, Aconitum, Delphinium, Ranunculus, Rhododendrons and numerous other. Most of the flowers have medicinal values too. The abundance of Asmanda fern in this valley is a rare sight than in other Himalayan valleys.

Apart from the flowers some species of Butterfly, Musk deer. Blue sheep (Bharal), Himalayan birds & Snow leopard are also found in the park.

One fully equipped interpretation centre at Ghangaria is available. At this interpretation centre regular slide shows on Valley of Flowers and wildlife is held in the evening hours through out the season.

The Valley of Flowers National park remains open for visitors from 1st June to 31st October.

CHIEF WILDLIFE WARDEN, UTTARAKHAND

Gangotri National Park The Park is situated in Uttarkashi District over a vast area of 2390.02sq.km.. Gangotri, after which the park is named, is one of the four *dhamas* (pilgrim sites) of Uttarakhand. The park located within the upper catchment area of the Bhagirathi river offers a panoramic view of several waterfalls. It also forms a vital link in the green corridor that extends between the Govind National Park and Kedarnath Wildlife Sanctuary.

It provides majestic beauty of coniferous forests and grandeur of glacial world combined with lush green meadows. The forests are Himalayan moist temperate type. Vegetation consists of chirpine deodar, fir, spruce, oak and rhododendrons. The fauna includes snow leopard, brown bear, black bear, Himalayan thar, serow, musk deer, cheer pheasants, partridges, monal, Himalayan snow cock etc.

How to Reach: The airport and rail head is Dehradun. The nearest town is Harsil 30 km away from Gangotri. The ideal season for visiting the park is summer (April to October).

Accomodation is available at the Forest Rest Houses at Harsil, Bhaironghati, and Gangotri. Garhwal Mandal Vikas Nigam to has TRC at Uttarkashi, Bhaironghati, Lanka, Gangotri and Bhojwasa.

Kedarnath Musk Deer Sanctuary

The Kedarnath Musk Deer Sanctuary is the most blissful chime of Nature's bounty and magnanimity. It is spread over an area of 97517.80ha. (25293.70ha. in Chamoli district, and 72224.10ha. in Rudraprayag district.)

And was established in the year 1972. Named after the famous shrine of God Kedarnath, located just outside the Sanctuary, it sprawls across the districts of Chamoli & Rudraprayag in the state of Uttarakhand.The pristine forests and bugyals, in their captivating wilderness, along with their keenly preserved and managed rich floral and faunal biodiversity transcend one to a different world of truly idyllic existence. The call of the wild is mesmerizing and captures Garhwal in its true spirit.

The globally dwindling population of the endangered Himalayan Musk Deer (*Moschus Chrysogaster*) is the cynosure, the flagship species of the sanctuary. It was formed with a primary goal of conserving the globally significant and endangered Himalayan musk deer. However, the rich mixed forests and beautiful terrain of the Garhwal Himalayas, coupled with the presence of the famous Kedarnath temple, has made the area just as famous for its biodiversity and cultural heritage. The sanctuary has some of the richest mixed forests of the Western Himalayas. Sub-tropical, temperate, sub-alpine and alpine forests are all found on the slopes of the innumerable mountains and valleys of the sanctuary, stretching across altitudes from 1160m to 7068m above sea level.

There are as many as 23 mammal species in the Sanctuary, 11 of which are threatened. The high number of endangered animals, including the Snow leopard, Himalayan musk deer, Himalayan thar, Serow, Himalayan black bears, Himalayan brown bears, and Pheasants, make the Kedarnath Sanctuary an area of immense significance.

Over 230 species of birds are found in the sanctuary. A Musk Deer Breeding Centre was established in 1982, at Kanchulakharak within the sanctuary, where Musk deer are bred in captivity and then released into the wild.

The surrounding areas of the sanctuary are popularly called Kedar Khand, and are home to the temples of Triyginarayan, Guptkashi, Ukhimath, Kalimath, and Gopeshwar. Access to the temples and the Sanctuary is possible through the Rudraprayag-Gaurikund road, which passes through the western sector, and the Chamoli-Kund road that runs approximately along the south-western boundary of the sanctuary from Mandal to Tala.

Best time to Visit: April & June & September to November.

Nearest Railway Station: Rishikesh, Dist. Dehradun.

Nearest Airport: Jollygrant Airport, District. Dehradun (17km. from Rishikesh)

How to reach:

The two main approaches leading to the sanctuary area are – from Gopeshwar (about 20km. away) and from Guptkashi (about 15km. away)

GOVIND WILDLIFE SANCTUARY AND NATIONAL PARK

The Park is spread over an area of 472sq.km. and sanctuary in 485.89sq km. in Uttarkashi District. The forest of the park consists of Chirpine, scrub tropical Euphorbia scrub and oak species.

Govind National Park, also known as Govind Pashu Vihar, was established to save the increasingly endangered species. The park is located in the Purola Tehsil of Uttarakashi district in Uttarakhand. Naitwar is the entrance and starting point of the sanctuary.

The Govind wild life Sanctuary and National Park is located in a remote area in the district Uttarkashi also known as Govind Pashu Vihar. The wonderfully remote Har ki Dun (3510m) is a botanical paradise criss-crossed by glacial streams and surrounded by pristine forests and snowy peaks spread over an area of 957.969 sq. kms with a varying altitude of 1,300 m to 6,323 m. River Tons enriches the entire area with its sediments and helps the vegetation in the sanctuary to grow uninhibited. This area is extremely rich in medicinal plants and is a treasure trove for those versed in Ayurveda

There are about 15 species of mammals and 150 species of birds that call Govind Wildlife Sanctuary their home. The most notable of these animals are the Snow leopard, Himalayan Black bear, Brown bear, Musk deer, Bharal, Himalayan Tahr, Serow and Common leopard.

The endangered birds found in this region are Monal Pheasant, Koklas Pheasant, Bearded Vulture Himalayan Snow fowl, Golden Eagle, Western Tragopan, Steppe Eagle and Black Eagle. Other varieties of birds include Owls, Pigeons, Minivets, Thrush, Warblers, Bulbul, Cuckoo and Finches.

In the Eighth Five-year plan, the Government of India set up the "Snow Leopard Project" to ensure the long-term conservation of the elusive and endangered Snow Leopard. In 1990, a team of experts chose the Govind Wildlife Sanctuary as one of the implementation sites of the project and, subsequently, 472 sq. km within the upper reaches of the sanctuary (the Snow leopard's preferred habitat) were notified as the Govind National Park. It lies between Longitude: 78.05°E and Latitude: 31.00 to 31.25°N.

The wild life species found in the park are snow leopard, leopard cat, the brown and the black Himalayan bear, fishing cat, musk deer, serow, thar, goral, sambar, wild boar, etc. The birds found are monal, snow pigeon, green pigeon. The best period for visiting the best park is from May to October. Accomadation is available in Forest Rest Houses. The altitude within the park ranges from 1400m to 6323m above sea level and magnificent, jaggered snow-capped peaks mesmerize all visitors.

Within the park, the emerald greenery of the Har-ki-dun valley is a paradise for trekkers, while the Ruinsiyara high altitude lake is popular amongst nature lovers. Tourists also frequent the Har-ki-dun Forest Rest House, known for its location amidst a valley of wild flowers. The forest rest houses of Naitwar, Taluka and Osla are en-route to Hari-ki-dun and are worthy attractions in their own right.

Nearest town from the park is Dharkadhi 17km from the Park. The nearest airport is Dehradun at a distance of 190 km. The rail head is also Dehradun.

ASKOT WILDLIFE SANCTUARY

Askot sanctuary is situated in Pithoragrah district of state Utarankhand surrounded by the mountain and forest is often called a "Miniature Kashmir" due to its stunning beauty and the presence of several high Himalayan peaks. The sanctuary is a house of many wild animals such leopard, deer, beers, kakars and a great variety of birds. Lying in the lap of Kumaon Himalayas at a height of 5412 ft., the sanctuary is visited by many Indian and foreign scientists for the research projects.

The Askot Wildlife Sanctuary is a 600 sq km area established primarily for the conservation of the Himalayan Musk deer in the Himalayan moist temperate zone. It is thus characterized by sub-alpine forest, alpine moist pastures and alpine moist scrub. Three species of Oak and Conifers such as Chirpine, Blue Pine Deodar, Fir and Spruce are found in the sanctuary. The forests are fed by the Gauri Ganga and Dhauli Ganga rivers, both of which drain into the Kali Nadi.

The area is populated by the Himalayan thar, Himalayan water shrew, Assamese macaque Stone / beach martin, Himalayan musk deer, Leopard, Leopard cat, Serow, Himalayan bear, and the Fulvous fruit Bat. Also found here are the endangered Snow leopard and the Goral with the Bengal fox and the Red fox, both of which are threatened species.

Best Time To Visit: April to September. How to Reach:

By Air Nearest airport is Naina Sani in Pithoragrah, At a Distance of less than 60 km. By Rail:Nearest railway station is Tanakpur,Distance 204 km. By Road: From Pithoragarh at a distance of 55 km. From Almora at a distance of 150(approx.) km.

BINOG WILDLIFE SANCTUARY

The Binog Widlife Sanctuary lies on the outer most ridge of the Himalayas, 2150m to 2800m above sea level in Mussoorie. Set up in 1993, Known as much for the Kempty falls as for its widlife, the sanctuary lies within the catchments of the Aglar River, a tributary of the Yamuna.

The sanctuary was set up primarily with the objective of protecting the area's dwindling bird population and diversity, especially the Himalayan pheasant and the Monal (the state bird of Uttarakhand) which are becoming rare. The white crested Kaleej Pheasant, Snow partridge, Bush quail, Blue rock pigeon, Fire tailed sun bird, and the Whistling thrush are some of the other birds found here, and the now extinct Mountain Quail was last sighted in the Binog forests back in 1986. The sanctuary also has a vast floral diversity, consisting of mosses, ferns, flowers, and orchids. The mountainsides are covered with a dense forest of Banj and Oak interspersed with Deodar and Kail patches. Under the Banj, a light undergrowth of shrubs and grasses cover the forest floor. Leopards, lagurs, Ghoral, Kakar, Lepoard cat, Flying Squirrel etc. are found here. A trek to find the source of the Kempty falls takes you through the dense forests of the area, and is well worth the effort. Several cliffs and the undulating terrain make the area ideal for trekking, though the slippery surfaces makes winter trekking hazardous. For the culturally curious adventurous, there is an observatory set up by George Everest on the periphery, as well as an old temple of Jwala Mata which hosts an annual fair in the month of November.

BINSAR WILDLIFE SANCTUARY

Binsar is a beautiful, quite and wild Himalayan destination with rich natural surroundings among dense forest. Binsar is perched on top of the Jhandi Dhar hills. This place is situated 30 km north of the Almora town in the Uttarakhand. Binsar was the ancient summer capital of the Chand Kings who ruled in the 7th and 8th centuries AD. This area is a small Wildlife Sanctuary for the conservation and protection of the broad leaf oak (Quercus) forests. Binsar Wildlife Sanctuary was established in 1988. From Binsar one can see the panoramic view of the Himalayan peaks like Kedarnath Peak, Shivling, Trisul and majestic Nanda Devi from a place called 'Zero Point'. Binsar Wildlife Sanctuary inhabits 200 bird species. Binsar Wildlife Sanctuary is spread over 45.59km^2 and situated at an altitude varying 900 to 2500 metres with an average height of 2412 mts. Binsar is rich in its flora and fauna.

Fauna These includes Leopard (Panthera Pardus), Nemorhaedus goral (goral), Chital (Axis axis) Musk deer, Serow (Capricornis sumatiensis), Jungle Cat (Felis chaus), Sus scrofa, Black Bear, red fox, pine marten,Fox (Vulpes vulpes), Langur (Presbytis entellus), monkey (Macaca mulatta), Porcupine, amongst others. It has been declared an Important Bird Area by BirdLife International with over 200 species including Tits, Forktail, Nuthatches, Blackbirds, Flying Squirrel (Petaurista petaurista), Parakeets, Laughingthrush, Magpies, Kalij Pheasant (Lophura leucomelana), Eagles, Monal, Koklas, Barking Deer (Muntiacus muntjak),

Woodpeckers and a range of others. Binsar is also home to many reptiles and innumerable invertebrates including a wide range of Butterflies. The place has Pine forest at the lower level and Oak and Rhododendron at the higher altitude. This place is abundant in alpine flora, Bryophytes, Pteridophytes, hanging mosses and many other species of wild flowers. Other main plants of this sanctuary are Kaphal (Myrica esculenta), Pinus roxburghii, Engelhardtia spiicata, Macaranga pustulata, Quercus gloca, Quercus incana, Quercus leucotricophora(Banjh), Quercus semicarpifolia, Quercus dilatata, Cedrus deodara, Alnus napalensis, Aesculus indica, Pinus wallichiana, Quercus lanuginosa and Quercus floribunda, etc.

SONANADI WILDLIFE SANCTUARY

The Sonanadi Wildlife Sanctuary, home to the migratory Asiatic Elephant, was established in 1987 in the Kotdwar *tehsi* within Pauri Garhwal district. It covers an area of 301.76 sq. km. at the north end of the Ramganga river.

The region has FRHs in both the Sonanadi Wildlife Sanctuary and the Domunda Tourism Zone of the Corbett Tiger Reserve. Halduparao, the only FRH in the Sonanadi Sanctuary and can be accessed from the Vatanvasa gate. The FRH at Kanda is in Corbett National Park. The FRHs of Morghatti and Pakhro are on the periphery of the Sonanadi Sanctuary and can be approached from Kalagarh and Kotdwar. The FRHs of Lohachaur, Rathuawadhab and Mundiyapani are in the Domunda Tourism Zone of CTR accessed from the. Durgadevi gate ahead of Ramnagar, The FRH of Kalagarh can be approached short of Ramnagar while that of Mohaan is 3okm ahead of Ramnagar. Sonanadi Sanctuary is spread over 301.18 sqkm of prime forests of the Shiwalik Terai biotic province. Sonanadi literally means the river of gold. Gold panning used to be carried out in the river before the area became a sanctuary. The Palain and the Mandal are the perennial streams of the sanctuary. Historically, it was carved out of Kalagarh Forest Division. It was brought under the umbrella of Project Tiger and became a part of the Corbett Tiger Reserve in 1991 and also a part of Project Elephant. There are no villages inside the sanctuary. The forests of Sonanadi are remarkable for dense sal and rich bamboo clusters besides other species and is teeming with wildlife. Sonanadi range is located in Sonanadi Wildlife Sanctuary which is a part of Corbett National Park. Developed as a natural habitat of wildlife animals and birds, Sonanadi range is blessed with amazing beauty of flora and fauna. Situated in the north of Sonanadi river, this zone is favorite place for Asiatic Elephant along with tiger, cheetal, sambhar, leopard and reptiles. Visitors can also enjoy over 550 of birds in their natural habitat.

Lohachaur, Rithuadhab and Halduparao are some Forest Rest Houses in

Sonanadi range available for night stay. Safari options like Jeep and elephant are available to enjoy wildlife at Sonanadi Range. Tourists are advised to pre-book entry ticket for a Safari in Sonanadi Zone. One can pre-book entry tickets from Ramnagar office. Sonanadi Zone is open for visitors from 15 October to 15 June and closed for monsoon. There are several safaris operated during a day in Sonanadi zone.

Sonanadi zone falls on Sonanadi Wildlife Sanctuary which is a part of Corbett Tiger Reserve. This is the only zone in Jim Corbett where tourists can walk on foot but richly housed by non-venomous snakes of different kinds. Popular mammals in the region are tiger, leopards and elephants. Tourists can take wildlife safari on jeep around Sonanadi zone observing the wild beings at proximity and enjoying the enchanting beauty of greenery and nature.

In the rainy season, the sanctuary is the favorite haunt of the Asiatic Elephant, who migrates along a corridor connecting the Sharda and Yamuna rivers. The creation of the Sonanadi Sanctuary helps safeguard this corridor by creating a protected area between the Corbett National Park and the Rajaji National Park, a link that is now threatened by the Kalagarh Dam. The construction of the dam has submerged 82 sq. km. of forest land separating the Corbett National Park and the Sonanadi Sanctuary, significantly obstructing the movement of elephants. Wildlife in the Sanctuary includes tigers, leopards, sambars, cheetal, gorals, kakars, bears, magars, ghariyals, otters, pythons and the King Cobra. The area's healthy tiger population has also led to its inclusion in the Corbett Tiger Reserve. Additionally, there are about 550 species and sub-species of bird life in this sanctuary. The Pied hornbill, Palash Fishing eagle, Hawk eagle, Black necked stork, Kaleej pheasant, and the collared falconets are just a few examples of the local avifaunal diversity.

The sanctuary's forests are full of Sal, Shisam, Khair, Asna trees and Bamboo. In the buffer zone of the sanctuary - from Marchula to Doumunda – 'angling' is permitted with a permit issued by the forest department. The fresh water fish, Mahasheer, is found in abundance here.

20

Indian National Parks

National Park is a suitable place for biodiversity conservation. National Park declared by the Central Government such animal or any article, trophy, uncured trophy or meat [derived from such animal or any vehicle, vessel, weapon, trap, or tool used in such hunting, 3] shall be the property of Central Government.

National park is an area which is strictly reserved for the betterment of the wildlife & biodiversity, and where activities like developmental, forestry, poaching, hunting and grazing on cultivation are not permitted. In these parks, even private ownership rights are not allowed. Their boundaries are well marked and circumscribed. They are usually small reserves spreading in an area of 100 sq. km. to 500 sq. km. In national parks, the emphasis is on the preservation of a single floral or faunal species. "National Park" means an area declared, whether under sec.35. or sec.38 or deemed, under sub-section (3) of sec.66. to be declared, as a National Park.

Every specified plant or part or derivative thereof, in respect of which any offence against this Act or any rule or order made there under has been committed, shall be the property of the State Government, and, where such plant or part or derivative thereof has been collected or acquired from a sanctuary or National Park declared by the Central Government, such plant or part or derivative thereof shall be the property of the Central Government.

NATIONAL PARKS (ACCORDING TO WILDLIFE PROTECTION ACT 1972)

Declaration of National Parks – (1) Whenever it appears to the State Government that an area, whether within a sanctuary or not, is, by reason of its ecological, faunal, floral, Geo-morphological, or zoological association or importance, needed to be constituted as a National Park for the purpose of protection & propagating or developing wildlife therein or its environment, it may, by notification, declare its intention to constitute such area as a National Park.

[11(1) Provided that where any part of the territorial waters is proposed to be included in such National Park, the provisions of Sec.26A shall, as far as may be, apply in relation to the declaration of a National Park as they apply in relation to the declaration of a sanctuary.]

The notification referred to in sub-section (1) shall define the limits of the area which is intended to be declared as a National Park.

Where any area is intended to be declared as a National Park, the provisions of Sec. [1219 to 26-A (both inclusive except clause (c) of sub-section (2) of section 24)] shall, as far as may be, apply to the investigation and determination of claims and extinguishment of rights, in relation to any land in such area as they apply to the said matters in relation to any land in a sanctuary.

When the following events have occurred, namely the period for preferring claims has elapsed, and all claims, if any, made in relation to any land in an area intended to be declared as a National Park, have been disposed of by the State Government, and all rights in respect of lands proposed to be included in the National Park have become vested in the State Government the State Government shall publish a notification specifying the limits of the area which shall be comprised within the National Park and declare that the said area shall be a National Park on and from such date as may be specified in the notification.

No alteration of the boundaries of a National Park shall be made except on a resolution passed by the Legislature of the State.

No person shall, destroy, exploit, or remove any wildlife from a National Park or destroy or damage the habitat or any wild animal or deprive any wild animal or its habitat within such National Park except under and in accordance with a permit granted by the Chief Wildlife Warden and no such permit shall be granted unless the State Government, being satisfied that such destruction, exploitation, or removal of wildlife from the National Park is necessary for the improvement and better management of wildlife therein, authorizes the issue of such permit.

No grazing of any [livestock13] shall be permitted in a National Park and no livestock shall be allowed to enter except where such [livestock] is used as a vehicle by a person authorized to enter such National Park.

The provisions of secs. 27 and 28, secs.30 to 32 (both inclusive), and CIS, (a), (b) and (c) of [Sec.33, 33A14] and sec.34 shall, as far as may be, apply in relation to a National Park as they apply in relation to a sanctuary.

KANGER GHATI NATIONAL PARK

Located amidst the 34 km long and scenic Kanger Valley, a Biosphere Reserve, Kanger Valley National Park is one of the most beautiful and picturesque national parks of India. The beautiful park is located on the banks of Kholaba River at a distance of about 27 km from Jagdalpur (headquarter of Bastar). Spread over an area of approximately 200 sq km comprising mainly of hilly terrain, the Park derives its name from the Kanger River, which flows throughout its length.

Known for its scenic beauty and the unique and rich biodiversity, Kanger Valley attained the status of a National Park in 1982. Besides wildlife and plants, there are many tourist attractions inside the park such as the Kutamsar Caves, Kailash Caves, Dandak Caves and Tiratgarh Waterfalls.

Kanger Dhara and Bhaimsa Dhara (a Crocodile Park) are the two beautiful and exotic picnic resorts in the Park. The Park also has a sizable tribal population and can be an ideal destination for wildlife enthusiasts, nature lovers, researchers, anthropologists and for anyone who wants to discover the very best of Chhattisgarh wildlife and unique tribes of the region.

Flora and Fauna - Kanger Valley National Park

The flora in the park chiefly comprises of mixed moist deciduous type of forests with predominance of Sal, Teak and Bamboo trees. In fact, the Kanger Valley is the only region in the Peninsular India where one of the last pockets of virgin and untouched forests still left. Major Wildlife of the Kanger Valley National Park are the Tigers, Leopards, Mouse Deer, Wild Cat, Chital, Sambar, Barking Deer, Jackals, Langurs, Rhesus Macaque, Sloth Bear, Flying Squirrel, Wild Boar, Striped Hyena, Rabbits, Pythons, Cobra, Crocodiles, Monitor Lizards and Snakes to name a few. The avian fauna at the Park includes Hill Myna, Spotted Owlet, Red Jungle Fowls, Racket-tailed Drongos, Peacocks, Parrots, Steppe Eagles, Red Spur Fall, Phakta, Bhura Teeter, Tree Pie and Heron among many others.

Best Season to Visit - Kanger Valley National Park

The best season to visit the Kanger Valley is November - June

How to Reach - Kanger Valley National Park

Kanger Valley is well approachable from Jagdalpur, district head quarter of Bastar. It is at a distance of about 27 km from Jagdalpur on the Jagdalpur - Konta road. You can also approach the park via Jagdalpur - Sargipal - Jatam - Nianar - Bodal road. Raipur (330 km) is the nearest airport and Jagdalpur (27 km) is the nearest railhead and bus stand from the Kanger Valley National Park

NATIONAL PARKS IN INDIA, A HOME FOR THE WILD

India not only nestles diversity in religion, culture, traditions and its people but it also is a home to a unique wildlife. It is known to provide shelter to numerous birds and animals that have made this country their home. National Parks in India are the world famous breeding grounds of the unique wildlife that this country bears and are also considered to be one of the most popular tourist's hot spots in the country. The rich and diverse wildlife of India is simply worth exploring.

RAJAJI NATIONAL PARK

The National Park very famous for the presence of elephants, tigers and leopards, it is an ultimate place for animal and bird lovers. Rajaji National Park is known to have the largest population of elephants and rest of the wildlife habitat present here include the Bengal tiger, barking deer, monitor lizard, rhesus macaque. If one talks about the birds, this place serves as a home to many native and migratory birds such as great piped hornbill, fire tailed sunbird and a variety of Himalayan & sub continental birds. This National Park is the most suitable place for the ones who are in love with the wild.

RANTHAMBORE NATIONAL PARK

Located in the western state of Rajasthan Ranthambore National Park is not only famous for its wildlife but also for its association with the history. The park is famous for Tigers and unlike other national parks; one can easily witness the presence of these wild cats here as they can be easily spotted out hunting Samabr near the lakes. The visitors can also enjoy the presence of an array of animals and birds namely, jungle cats, desert cats, black bucks, jackals, yellow bats, grey hornbills, Asian palm swift, flinches, egrets, sparrows and many other species of birds and animals as well. Ranthambore is well known as the largest park to conserve tigers.

SILENT VALLEY NATIONAL PARK, KERALA

Silent Valley National Park is perhaps the best kept secret when it comes to wildlife in India. It is located in the Nilgiri Hills, Palakkad district in Kerala and is a part of Western Ghats World Heritage Site as inscribed by UNESCO.

This national park is home to over 20 endangered species of birds as well as the threatened lion-tailed macaque. Over 34 species of mammals reside in this last undisturbed tract of natural rainforest in India.

The chances of sudden rain are always there when you visit this park, but for a nature enthusiast any day is a good day for a walk in the wilderness and silence of Silent Valley surrounded by evergreen forest.

If you are planning a visit advance reservation is necessary as there are not many accommodation options available nearby except for the Inspection Bunglow. Food is only available at local hotels in Mukkali, the nearest town to this park. Which are some endangered species in India and where to find them?

One of the endangered species that is found in India is the Great Single Horned Rhinoceros. 2/3rd of the world's single horned rhino population lives in Kaziranga National Park in Assam.

Yet another endangered animal species found in India is the Asiatic Lion. Gir National Park in Gujarat is the only habitat in the entire world where these big cats are found.

Then there are the rare and elusive Snow Leopard which could be seen prowling - if you are lucky - in Great Himalayan National Park in Himachal or the Hemis National Park in Ladakh.

Is there any National Park in India where I could go during Monsoon?

Yes! Periyar National Park in Kerala is the only wildlife sanctuary in India which is open to visitors even during monsoon. It has substantial population of tigers, elephants and numerous bird species.

Alternate ways to explore Wildlife Sanctuaries and National Parks in India

Apart from tailor made wildlife itineraries and pre-packaged tour, there are other ways — and definitely more luxurious — to explore the Indian wild.

SUNDERBANS NATIONAL PARK

Sunderbans National Park is one of the largest and oldest in India. Located in the deltaic region of India, this park also shares its boundaries with Bangladesh. Covered with mangrove forests, Sundarbans is the original abode of the stunning Royal Bengal Tigers.

It has the highest number of Bengal Tigers than any other parks in the world. Salt-Water Crocodile can also be found in this park. Sundarbans is extremely rich in avifauna, aqua fauna and reptiles. Some of the other endangered species in this park are Gangetic Dolphin, River Terrapin, Hawks Bill Turtle and Mangrove Horseshoe Crab.

History of Sundarbans National Park

The Sundarban National Park is a National Park, Tiger Reserve, and a Biosphere Reserve in West Bengal, India. It is part of the Sundarbans on the Ganges Delta, and adjacent to the Sundarbans Reserve Forest in Bangladesh. The delta is densely covered by mangrove forests, and is one of the largest reserves for the Bengal tiger.

It is also home to a variety of bird, reptile and invertebrate species, including the salt-water crocodile. The present Sundarbans National Park was declared as the core area of Sundarbans Tiger Reserve in 1973 and a wildlife sanctuary in 1977. On 4 May 1984 it was declared a National Park.

Administration

The Directorate of Forest is responsible for the administration and management of Sundarbans. The Principal Chief Conservator of Forests (PCCF), Wildlife & Bio-Diversity & ex-officio Chief Wildlife Warden, West Bengal is the senior most executive officer looking over the administration of the park. The Chief Conservator of Forests (South) & Director, Sundarban Biosphere Reserve is the administrative head of the park at the local level and is assisted by a Deputy Field Director and an Assistant Field Director. The park area is divided into two ranges, overseen by range forest officers. Each range is further sub-divided into beats. The park also has floating watch stations and camps to protect the property from poachers.

The park receives financial aid from the State Government as well as the Ministry of Environment and Forests under various Plan and Non-Plan Budgets. Additional funding is received under the Project Tiger from the Central Government. In 2001, a grant of US$20,000 was received as a preparatory assistance for promotion between India and Bangladesh from the World Heritage Fund.

Geography

Sundarbans National Park is located in between 21° 32' – 21° 55' N latitude and between 88° 42' – 89° 04' E longitude. The average altitude of the park is 7.5 m above sea level. The park is made up of 54 small islands and is crisscrossed by several tributaries of the Ganges.

Climate

The average minimum and maximum temperature is 20 °C and 48 °C respectively. Rainfall is heavy with humidity as high as 80% as it is close to the Bay of Bengal. The monsoon lasts from mid-June to mid-September. Prevailing wind is from the north and northeast from October to mid-March and south west westerlies prevails from mid-March to September. Storms which sometimes develop into cyclones are common during the months of May and October.

Eco-geography, rivers and watercourses

There are seven main rivers and innumerable watercourses forming a network of channels at this estuarine delta. All the rivers have a southward course towards the sea. The eco-geography of this area is totally dependent on the tidal effect of two flow tides and two ebb tides occurring within 24 hours with a tidal range of 3–5 m and up to 8 m in normal spring tide, inundating the whole of Sunderbans in varying depths. The tidal action deposits silts back on the channels and raising the bed, it forms new islands and creeks contributing to uncertain geomorphology. There is a great natural depression called "Swatch of No Ground" in the Bay of Bengal between 21°00' to 21°22' latitude where, the depth of water changes suddenly from 20 m to 500 m. This mysterious depression pushes back the silts towards south and/or further east to form new islands.

Mudflats

The Sunderbans mudflats are found at the estuary and on the deltaic islands where low velocity of river and tidal current occurs. The flats are exposed in low tides and submerged in high tides, thus being changed morphologically even in one tidal cycle. The interior parts of the mudflats are the right environment for mangroves.

There are a number of mudflats outside the Sundarbans National Park is a mudflat that have the potential to be tourist spots in the Sundarbans. One can visit them and enjoy the beauty of the place during low tide. If one is lucky, one can see Sea Anemones, Horseshoe crab (Nearing extinction)and small octopus.

Flora and fauna

The coastal active delta of Sunderbans at the mouth of Bay of Bengal in Bangladesh, having a complex geomorphologic and hydrological character with climatic hazards, has a vast area of mangrove forests with a variety of flora and diverse fauna in a unique ecosystem. The natural environment and coastal ecosystem of this Biosphere Reserve and World Heritage Site is under threat of physical disaster due to unscientific and excessive human interferences. Conservation and environmental management plan for safeguarding this unique coastal ecology and ecosystem is urgently required.

Sunderbans has achieved its name from the Sundari Trees. It is the most exquisite variety of tree that are found in this area, a special kind of Mangrove tree. The main feature of this tree is that it produces spikes that grow above from the ground and help in the respiration of the tree. During the rainy season when the entire forest is water logged, the spikes rising from the ground has their peak in the air and helps in the respiration process.

Fauna

The Sundarbans forest is home to more than 400 tigers. The Royal Bengal Tigers have developed a unique characteristic of swimming in the saline waters, and are famous for their man-eating tendencies. Tigers can be seen on the river banks sunbathing between November and February.

Apart from the Royal Bengal Tiger; Fishing Cats, Leopard Cats, Macaques, Wild Boar, Indian Grey Mongoose, Fox, Jungle Cat, Flying Fox, Pangolin, Chital, are also found in abundance in the Sundarbans.

Avifauna

Some of the birds commonly found in this region are openbill storks, black-capped kingfishers, black-headed ibis, Water Hens, Coots,Pheasant-tailed Jacanas, Pariah Kites, Brahminy Kite, Marsh Harriers, Swamp Partridges, Red Junglefowls, Spotted Doves, Common Mynahs, Jungle Crows, Jungle Babblers, Cotton Teals, Herring Gulls, Caspian Terns, Gray Herons, Common Snipes, Wood Sandpipers, Green pigeons, Rose Ringed Parakeets, paradise-flycatchers, cormorants, Grey-headed Fish Eagles, White-bellied Sea Eagles, Seagulls, Common Kingfishers, Peregrine falcons, Woodpeckers, Whimbrels, Black-tailed Godwits, Little Stints, Eastern Knots, Curlews,Golden Plovers, Northern Pintails, White-eyed Pochards and Whistling teals.

Aqua fauna

Some of the fish and amphibians found in the park are Sawfish, Butter Fish, Electric rays, Silver carp, Star Fish, Common Carp, King crabs, Prawn, Shrimps, Gangetic Dolphins, Skipping Frogs, Common Toads and Tree Frogs.

Reptiles

The Sundarbans National Park houses a large number of reptiles as well, including estuarine crocodiles, chameleons, monitor lizards, turtles, including Olive Ridley, hawksbill, and green turtles; and snakes including pythons, King Cobras, rat snakes, Russell's vipers, Dog Faced Water Snakes, Chequered Killbacks, and Common Kraits.

Endangered species

The endangered species that lives within the Sundarbans are Royal Bengal Tiger, Saltwater Crocodile, River Terrapin, Olive Ridley Turtle, Gangetic dolphin, Ground Turtle, Hawks Bill Turtle and Mangrove horseshoe crab.

Marine mammals

The proposed *Sundarbans Cetacean Diversity Protected Area*, includes the coastal waters off Sundarbans that host critical habitats for endangered cetaceans; resident groups of Bryde's Whales, a newly rediscovered critical population of Irrawaddy

Dolphins, Ganges River Dolphins, and Humpback Dolphins. Finless Porpoises, Indo-Pacific Bottlenose Dolphins, Spinner Dolphins, and Pantropical Spotted Dolphins are also found in this area.

Management and special projects

Bengal tiger is the commonly found species in this national park.The park has had protection since its creation. The core area is free from all human disturbances like collection of wood, honey, fishing and other forest produces. However, in the buffer area fishing, honey collection and wood cutting are permitted in limited form. Protection of the park from poaching and theft of forest products is done by well armed forest staff who patrol in motorboats and launches. Forest offices and camps are located at several important parts of the park. Anti-poaching camps are manned by two to three knowledgeable labourers under supervision of concerned beat guard/ Forester/Range officer.

Habitat of wildlife is maintained through eco-conservation, eco-development, training, education and research. Ten Forest Protection Committees and 14 Eco-development Committees have been formed in the fringe of Sundarbans Tiger Reserve to help in this regard. Seminars, workshops and awareness camps are organised in the vicinity of park to educate the people on eco-conservation, eco-development and such other issues. Mangrove and other plants are planted in the fringe area to meet the local need of fuel wood for about 1000 villages and to conserve the buffer area. Conservation of soil is done to maintain the ecological balance. Several sweet water ponds have been dug up inside the park to provide drinking water for the wild animals.

Controlling man-eating tigers is another major activity. The number of casualties has been reduced from 40 to 10 per year. The reduction in number of casualties is a result of strict control over the movement of the people inside the tiger reserve, alternative income generation and awareness building among people. It is also believed that due to use of human masks and electric human dummies the tigers will stay away from the people. Straying of tigers into nearby villages is prevented through measures such as nylon net fencing and solar illumination of villages. The youths of the villages are given training in controlling the straying of tigers into the villages.

The Mangrove Interpretation Centre is established at Sajnekhali to make the local people and tourists aware of the importance of conservation of nature in general and specially the mangrove ecosystems.

□□□

Bibliography

Butler, Richard W.: *Tourism and Recreation in Rural Areas*, Chichester, U.K., 1998.

Dang, Himraj: *Sariska National Park*. Indus Publishing Company, New Delhi.2005.

Douglas C.: *Heritage Tourism is in the Future of Many Alabama Communities*, Auburn Univ., Auburn, 1991.

Durga Charan Kala: *Jim Corbett of Kumaon*. Ravi Dayal Publishers, 1979.

Edward, M.: *In International Tourism: Identity and Change*, London, Sage, 1995.

Fowler, Peter: *Heritage and Tourism*, New York, Routledge, 1993.

Garfield, Donald: *Partners in Tourism: Culture and Commerce*, Washington, DC, American Association of Museums, 1997.

Gimblett, Barbara: *Destination Culture: Tourism, Museums, and Heritage*, California, University of California, 1998.

Gupta, Reeta Dutta: *Jim Corbett : The Hunter Conservationist*. Rupa & Company. 2006.

Howard Green: *Tourism and the Environment: A Sustainable Relationship*, New York, Routledge, 1995.

Inskeep, E.: *Training for Tourism in Developing Countries*, Chichester, England, 1994.

Jenkins, M.: *Tourism and Recreation in Rural Areas*, Wiley, UK, 1998.

John Sem: *A Training Guide for Rural Tourism Development*, Minnesota: Rural Tourism Center, 1995.

Johnsingh, A. J. T.: *On Jim Corbett's Trail and Other Tales from Tree-tops*. Orient Blackswan. 2004.

Khati, A. S.: *Jim Corbett of India: Life & Legend of a Messiah*. Pelican Creations International. 2003.

Knox, J.: *Tourism Research Priorities in Hawaii and the Pacific*, Honolulu, University of Hawaii, 1979.

Martin Booth: *Carpet Sahib: A Life of Jim Corbett*. Constable. 1986.

Martinus J.: *Tourism by Train: Its Role in Alternative Tourism*, Philadelphia, University of Pennsylvania Press, 1992.

McConnell II, D. W.: *Nature-Based Tourism and Rural Coastal Development: Observations, Options, and Trends*, South Carolina, Clemson University, 1990.

McCool, Stephen F.: *Linking Tourism, the Environment, and Sustainability*, Ogden, Utah, 1995.

Middleton, Victor T. C.: *Sustainable Tourism: A Marketing Perspective*, Woburn, Massachusetts: Butterworth-Heinemann, 1998.

Miriam Davidson: *Convictions of the Heart: Jim Corbett and the Sanctuary Movement*. University of Arizona Press. 1988.

Purcell, Douglas C.: *Heritage Tourism is in the Future of Many Alabama Communities*, Auburn Univ., Auburn, 1991.

Rangarajan, M.: *India's Wildlife History: an Introduction*. Orient Longman. 2005.

Riley, Laura; William Riley : *Nature's Strongholds: The World's Great Wildlife Reserves*. Princeton University Press. 2005.

Sharma, Sunayan: *Sariska: The Tiger Reserve Roars Again*. Niyogi Books, New Delhi. 2015.

Sharpley, Richard: *Rural Tourism: An Introduction,* London, International Thomson Business Press, 1997.

Stabler, Michael J.: *Tourism and Sustainability: Principles to Practice*, New York, CAB International, 1997.

Stephen, C.: *Tourism in the Navajo Country: Resources and Planning*, Winslow Rock, Navajo Tribe, 1967.

Tiwari, P. C.; Joshi, Bhagwati: *Wildlife in the Himalayan Foothills: Conservation and Management*. Indus Publishing Company. 1997

Werling, T.: *Jim Corbett: Master of the Jungle*. Safari Press, 1998.

Ziddi, Suraj: *A guide to the wildlife parks of Rajasthan*. Photo Eye Publications, Jaipur, 1998.